Frommer's

Bangkok day BY day

2nd Edition

by Mick Shippen

Contents

Published by:

FrommerMedia LLC

ISBN: 978-1-62887-238-5 (print); 978-1-62887-239-2 (ebk)

Editorial Director: Pauline Frommer
Editor: Pauline Frommer
Production Editor: Lindsay Conner
Photo Editor: Meghan Lamb
Cartographer: Liz Puhl
Front cover photos, left to right: Floating Market © anekoho; Wat Arun Temple illuminated at twilight © Sarawut Chamsaeng; Novices at Ayutthaya Historical Park © SantiPhotoSS
Back cover photo: Grand Palace Bangkok © image focus

For information on our other products and services, please go to Frommers.com/contactus.

Frommer's also publishes its books in a variety of electronic formats. Some content that appears in print may not be available in electronic formats.

Manufactured in China

5 4 3 2 1

About This Guide

Organizing your time. That's what this guide is all about.

Other guides give you long lists of things to see and do and then expect you to fit the pieces together. The Day by Day guides are different. These guides tell you the best of everything, and then they show you how to see it in the smartest, most time-efficient way. Our authors have designed detailed itineraries organized by time, neighborhood, or special interest. And each tour comes with a bulleted map that takes you from stop to stop.

Hoping to visit Bangkok's awe-inspiring temples and learn about Thai culture? Planning to jostle with the locals at the markets, or scream around Bangkok's backstreets in a tuk-tuk? Not only do we take you to the top attractions, hotels and restaurants, but we also help you access those special moments that locals get to experience—those 'finds' that turn tourists into travellers.

The Day by Days are also your top choice if you're looking for one complete guide for all your travel needs. The best hotels and restaurants for every budget, the greatest shopping values, the wildest nightlife—it's all here.

Why should you trust our judgment? Because our authors personally visit each place they write about. They're an independent lot who say what they think and would never include places they wouldn't recommend to their best friends. They're also open to suggestions from readers. If you'd like to contact them, please send your comments our way at feedback@frommers.com, and we'll pass them on.

Enjoy your Day by Day guide—the most helpful travel companion you can buy. And have the trip of a lifetime.

About the Author

Mick Shippen, a British national, is an award-winning travel photographer and writer. He lived in Thailand from 1997 to 2014 before relocating to Vientiane in Lao PDR. He returns frequently to Bangkok, and did so for the writing of this guide. He is the author of *The Traditional Ceramics of South East Asia*, a beautifully illustrated book documenting the life and work of craftsmen in Thailand, Malaysia, Cambodia, Laos, and Myanmar. He also wrote the photo-rich *Presenting Cambodia* and seven titles in the *Enchanting Asia* series, as well as contributing words and images to numerous books and magazines.

His photography has appeared in *Vanity Fair, NatGeo Traveller*, the UK's *Sunday Times Magazine*, and many more. A keen biker, he spends his spare time motorcycling and has toured extensively on and off-road in Cambodia, Laos, northern Thailand and Sri Lanka.

An Additional Note

Please be advised that travel information is subject to change at any time—and this is especially true of prices. We therefore suggest that you write or call ahead for confirmation when making your travel plans. The authors, editors, and publisher cannot be held responsible for the experiences of readers while traveling. Your safety is important to us, however, so we encourage you to stay alert and be aware of your surroundings.

Star Ratings, Icons & Abbreviations

Every hotel, restaurant, and attraction listing in this guide has been ranked for quality, value, service, amenities, and special features using a **star-rating system.** Hotels, restaurants, attractions, shopping, and nightlife are rated on a scale of zero stars (recommended) to three stars (exceptional). In addition to the star-rating system, we also use a **kids** icon to point out the best bets for families. Within each tour, we recommend cafes, bars, or restaurants where you can take a break. Each of these stops appears in a shaded box marked with a coffee-cup-shaped bullet.

The following **abbreviations** are used for credit cards:

AE	American Express	DISC	Discover	V	Visa
DC	Diners Club	MC	MasterCard		

Frommers.com

Frommer's travel resources don't end with this guide. Frommer's website, **www.frommers.com,** has travel information on more than 4,000 destinations. We update features regularly, giving you access to the most current trip-planning information and the best airfare, lodging, and car-rental bargains. You can also listen to podcasts, connect with other Frommers.com members through our active-reader forums, share your travel photos, read blogs from guidebook editors and fellow travelers, and much more.

A Note on Prices

In the "Take a Break" and "Best Bets" sections of this book, we have used a system of dollar signs to show a range of costs for 1 night in a hotel (the price of a double-occupancy room) or the cost of an entree at a restaurant. Use the following table to decipher the dollar signs:

Cost	Hotels	Restaurants
$	under $130	under $15
$$	$130–$200	$15–$30
$$$	$200–$300	$30–$40
$$$$	$300–$395	$40–$50
$$$$$	over $395	over $50

How to Contact Us

In researching this book, we discovered many wonderful places—hotels, restaurants, shops, and more. We're sure you'll find others. Please tell us about them, so we can share the information with your fellow travelers in upcoming editions. If you were disappointed with a recommendation, we'd love to know that, too. Please write to: Support@FrommerMedia.com

17 Favorite Moments

17 Favorite **Moments**

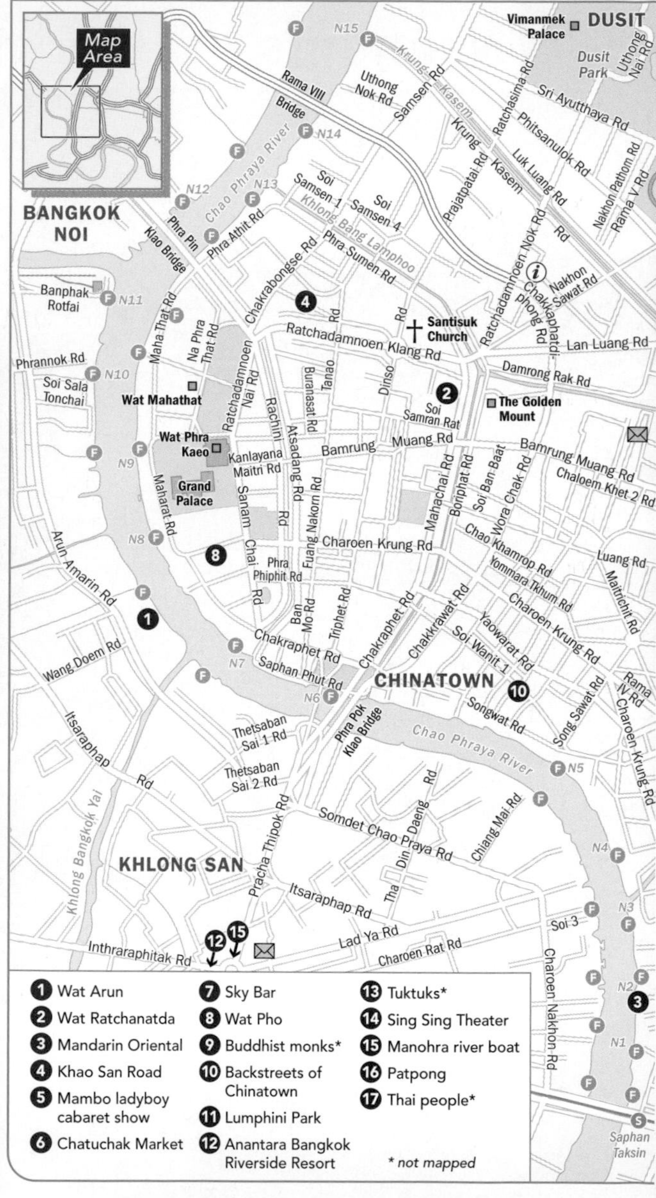

Previous Page: An ornate guard ship on the river in front of the Grand Palace.

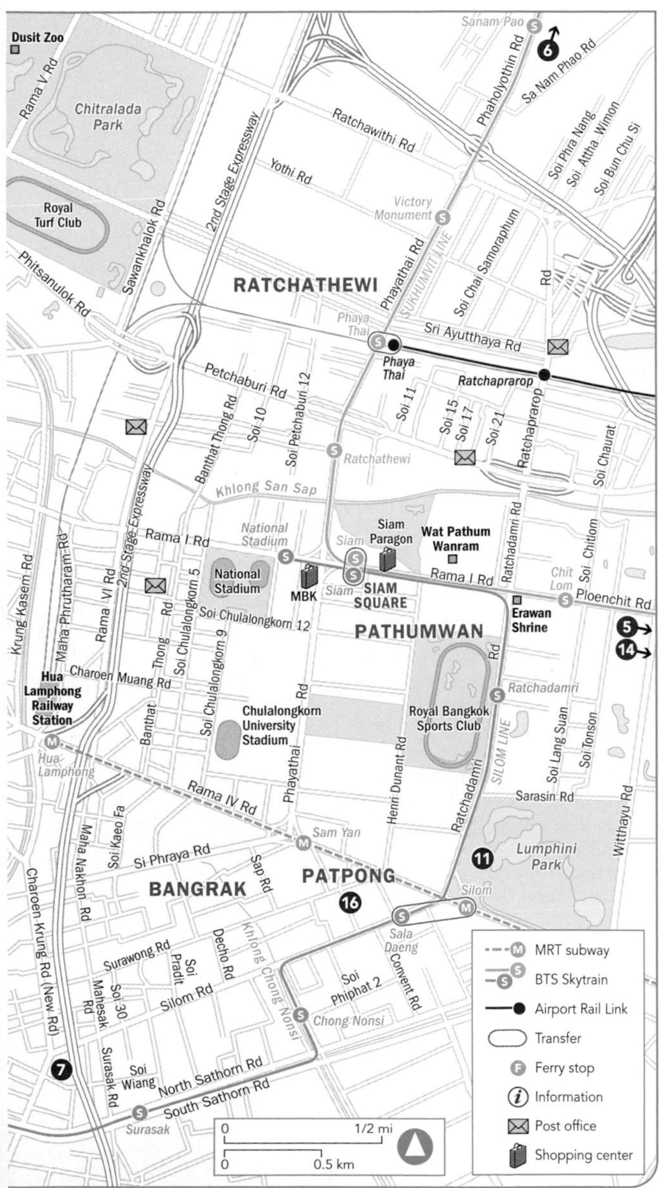

Dusit Zoo
Chitralada Park
Royal Turf Club
Rama V Rd
Sawankhalok Rd
2nd Stage Expressway
Phitsanulok Rd
Ratchawithi Rd
Yothi Rd
Sanam Pao
Phaholyothin Rd
Sa Nam Phao Rd
Soi Phra Nang
Soi Attha Wimon
Soi Bun Chu Si
Victory Monument
SUKHUMVIT LINE
Phayathai Rd
Soi Chai Samoraphum
RATCHATHEWI
Phaya Thai
Sri Ayutthaya Rd
Petchaburi Rd
Soi Petchaburi 12
Soi 10
Banthat Thong Rd
Soi 11
Soi 15
Soi 17
Soi 21
Ratchaprarop
Ratchathewi
Soi Chaurat
Khlong San Sap
National Stadium
Siam
Siam Paragon
Wat Pathum Wanram
Rama I Rd
Ratchadamri Rd
Soi Chitlom
Chit Lom
Ploenchit Rd
MBK
SIAM SQUARE
Erawan Shrine
PATHUMWAN
Soi Chulalongkorn 5
Soi Chulalongkorn 12
Soi Chulalongkorn 9
Krung Kasem Rd
Maha Phrutharam Rd
Rama VI Rd
Hua Lamphong Railway Station
Charoen Muang Rd
Chulalongkorn University Stadium
Royal Bangkok Sports Club
Ratchadamri
SILOM LINE
Soi Lang Suan
Soi Tonson
Hua Lamphong
Rama IV Rd
Henri Dunant Rd
Sarasin Rd
Witthayu Rd
Soi Kaeo Fa
Maha Nakhon Rd
Si Phraya Rd
Sap Rd
Sam Yan
Lumphini Park
PATPONG
BANGRAK
Silom
Charoen Krung Rd (New Rd)
Sala Daeng
Surawong Rd
Soi Pradit
Decho Rd
Khlong Chong Nonsi
Convent Rd
Soi Phiphat 2
Mahesak Rd
Soi 30
Silom Rd
Chong Nonsi
Surasak Rd
Soi Wiang
North Sathorn Rd
South Sathorn Rd
Surasak
0 1/2 mi
0 0.5 km
MRT subway
BTS Skytrain
Airport Rail Link
Transfer
Ferry stop
Information
Post office
Shopping center

Known in Thailand as the 'City of Angels', Bangkok has a rather devilish reputation. In recent years it has become one of the most popular destinations in the world. But what is it that this hot and crowded sprawling Asian city offers that great metropolises such as Paris, Rome, London and New York lack? Of course Bangkok has a deep culture, hundreds of sights to see, great restaurants and a pulsating nightlife, but there's something extra about Thailand's capital that makes people tingle. Even just the name 'Bangkok' conjures images of the exotic—a tropical paradise with an edgy reputation, perhaps a hint of danger and excitement. It's a city with a twist at every corner, a picture postcard of unexpected sights and superlative experiences. Everything you've heard about Bangkok is true . . . and there's more. For whatever Bangkok does, it does with passion. Here are some of my favorite Bangkok experiences.

❶ **Gazing across the river at Wat Arun (the Temple of Dawn) as day is breaking.** Watch the Buddhist monks in their bright saffron robes silently going about their morning chores. See the sun dancing on the millions of pieces of glass and ceramic on the stone walls of the temple, making it change color and sparkle as if alive. *See p 15.*

❷ **Feeling the mystic serenity of a Buddhist temple.** My favorite is Wat Ratchanatda, where monks sweep leaves in the courtyard while others fetch water from a well or meditate in the temple. In a 24/7 city of more than 10 million people where the noise and heat are often exhausting, the sea of calm that washes over me as soon as I enter a temple never fails to impress. *See p 37.*

❸ **Lounging around the Mandarin Oriental hotel on the lookout for celebrities.** It is the most famous hotel in the world, after all! Perhaps if I wear a Panama hat and sip tea in the lobby, someone will wonder if I'm a famous star or the reincarnation of Joseph Conrad, Oscar Wilde, or W Somerset Maugham. Keep dreaming. . . . *See p 57.*

❹ **Listening to travellers' tales at a cafe on Khao San Road.** Bangkok is a magnet for travellers visiting from every corner of the world. Swap stories of journeys through the jungle, bus rides from hell, snakes and scorpions under mattresses, and the myriad other adventures that always happen when you are traveling in exotic lands. *See p 54.*

❺ **Seeing the Best Ladyboy Show on the planet:** Calypso Cabaret is a hugely popular attraction. It

A river view of Wat Arun.

features a cast of ladyboys in an exotic transvestite cabaret with stunning sets and choreography. *See p 130.*

6 Getting lost among the chaos at Chatuchak Weekend Market—known simply as JJ. It's easy to do for hours on end—without finding a postcard to send home to grandma. You'd better leave a trail of breadcrumbs as you wander the maze of shops and stalls at the biggest market in the world, because you'll never find your way out! Still, you're sure to find other treats—from parakeets to copper pots, DVDs to Buddhist antiques, and silk scarves to moonshine snake whisky . . . but I've never seen any postcards. *See p 77.*

7 Watching the sunset while sipping martinis at Sky Bar. The view from the 63rd floor is spectacular, but no matter how many times I've met friends for cocktails at Sky Bar, my heart still leaps into my throat when I look over the edge. I don't know any other city that would even allow a bar such as this to exist. *See p 117.*

8 Getting a hot herbal massage at Wat Pho, then falling asleep and awakening to find your body has turned to jelly. I'm not sure how I survived before I came to Bangkok and started the simple weekly ritual of getting all the tension and knots wrung from my body. Perhaps the most physically and mentally relaxing activity a person can do, massage is cheap, it's good for you, and feels great. What more can you ask for? *See p 48.*

9 Getting up at dawn to watch Buddhist monks collecting alms from local Bangkokians. Rich and poor alike line the roadsides with freshly cooked pots of rice and curry to offer the monks in exchange for a prayer. The parade

A vendor at Chatuchak Market.

of robed monks walking the streets barefoot and single file each morning is one of the most photogenic scenes in Asia.

10 Taking in the aromas of food and spices down the backstreets of Chinatown. You'll find woks full of sizzling chillis, boiling pots of coconut soup, skewered fish barbecuing on grills, and row upon row of cardamom, coriander, ginger, ginseng, colorful fruit, and exotic herbs. *See p 33.*

11 Practicing Tai Chi with nimble octogenarians in Lumphini Park at dawn. I just join in at the back and follow the slow and controlled movements of the class as it flows to the rhythm of an old Chinese soundtrack. Various groups gather in the park every day for a 1-hour session of this graceful martial art. Afterwards, they sit and chat and laugh and drink green tea. I'm sure this is the secret to living over 100. *See p 10.*

12 Lazing in the Jacuzzi at the Anantara Bangkok Riverside Resort & Spa on a sunny day. Sunbathing in Bangkok is usually a no-go: with the humidity, it's more like poaching yourself. The Marriott

Zoom through Bangkok in a tuk-tuk.

Anantara is just far enough from the city center that the air is a bit fresher and a breeze comes off the river. With a day pass you can lie by the tropical pool and bask in the outdoor Jacuzzi. *See p 137.*

⓭ **Screaming down the backstreets in a tuk-tuk, zigzagging through the traffic, mounting the kerbs, and squeezing down alleys.** No trip to Bangkok is complete without a heart-stopping ride around the city's streets with a hysterical tuk-tuk driver (for more thrills, try a motorbike taxi!). *See p 166.*

⓮ **Being seen at Sing Sing Theater**. This visually dramatic night venue is inspired by1930s Shanghai. With oriental lanterns, red lighting, small balconies, speakeasy style private rooms, DJs, and a dancefloor, it's a unique club that attracts Bangkok's trendy set. *See p 121.*

⓯ **Wining and dining on a Manohra dinner cruise under the moonlight.** When romance beckons, an evening dinner on a small cruise boat is the perfect option. It's intimate and exotic and the food is delicious. The Chao Phraya River is glorious at night, and what better way to see it than over an intimate dinner for two? *See p 102.*

⓰ **Haggling for souvenirs at Patpong.** Notorious Patpong comes alive at night in more ways than one. Stalls hug the pavements and spill over down the alleys. Vendors will lure you into a haggling match over little elephant statues, silk ties, the latest DVDs, Buddha paintings, Samurai swords, and copies of high-end fashion, watches, and more. *See p 78.*

⓱ **Smiling back at Thais—the friendliest people in the world.** Thailand is not known as the "Land of Smiles" for nothing. A big beaming smile is as much part of a traditional greeting as a *wai*—the pressing of palms and little bow that Buddhists use to say 'hello'. Even if a Thai slips and falls and bangs his head, he will smile, maybe even laugh, and brush it off with the phrase *"mai pen rai,"* meaning 'it doesn't matter'.

1 The Best **Full-Day Tours**

The Best in 1 Day

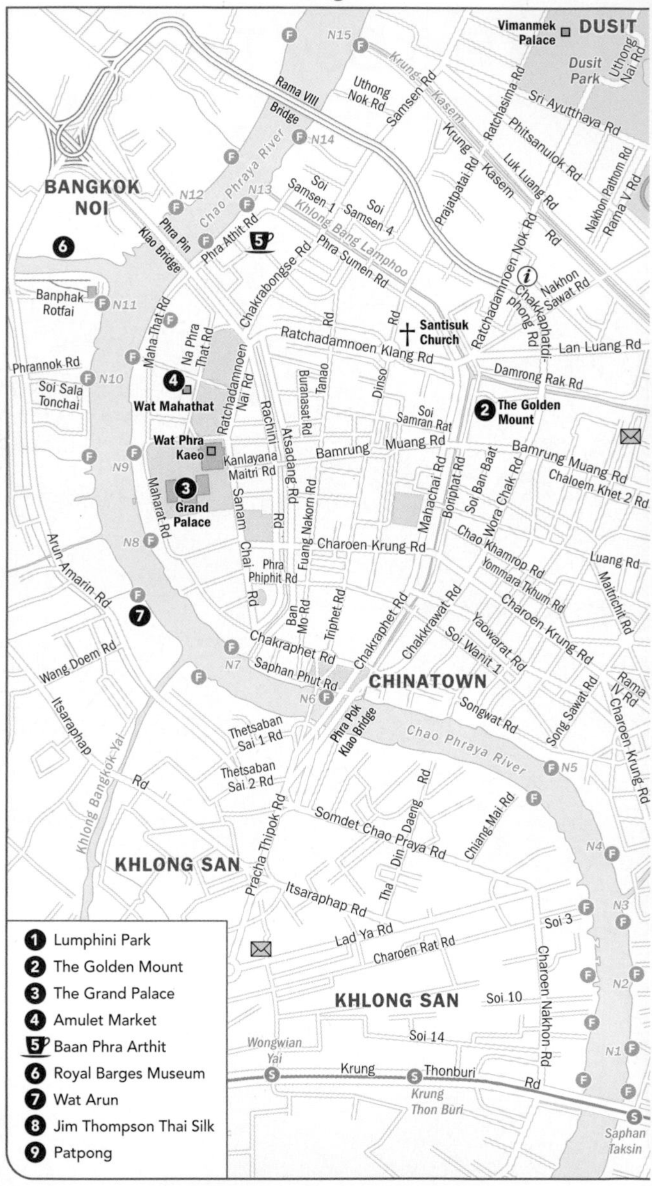

Previous page: Demon Guardian Wat Phra Kaew, Grand Palace Bangkok.

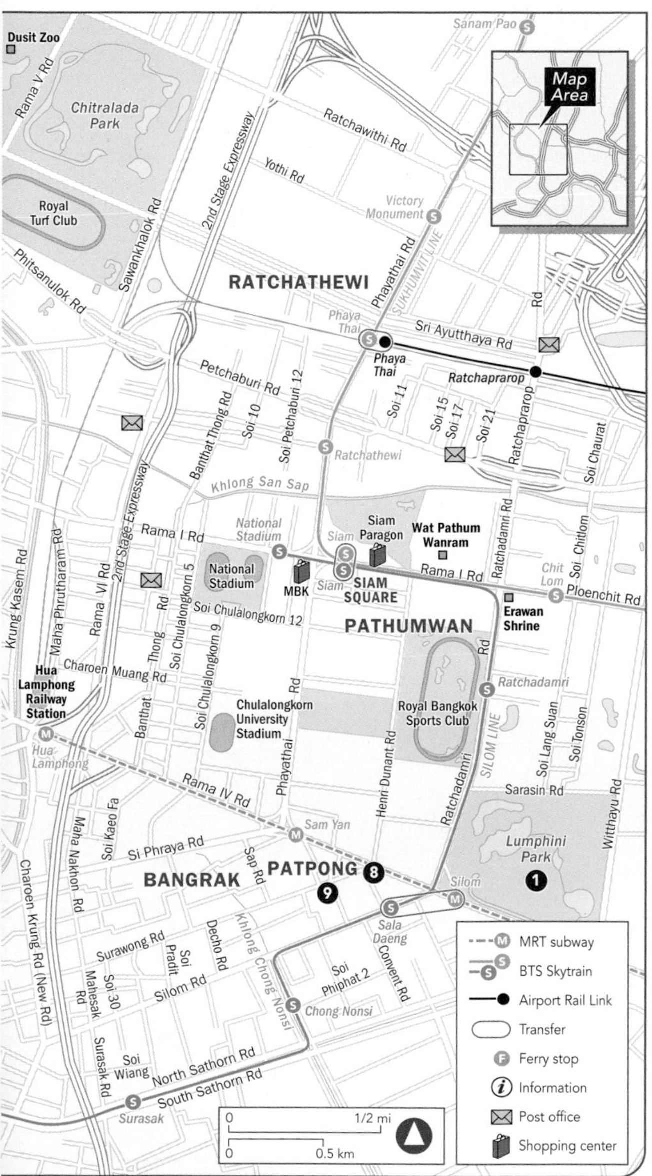
Dusit Zoo
Chitralada Park
Rama V Rd
Royal Turf Club
Sawankhalok Rd
2nd Stage Expressway
Ratchawithi Rd
Yothi Rd
Victory Monument
Sanam Pao
Map Area
Phitsanulok Rd
RATCHATHEWI
Phayathai Rd
SUKHUMVIT LINE
Phaya Thai
Sri Ayutthaya Rd
Ratchaprarop
Petchaburi Rd
Banthat Thong Rd
Soi 10
Soi Petchaburi 12
Soi 11
Soi 15
Soi 17
Soi 21
Ratchaprarop
Soi Chaurat
Ratchathewi
Khlong San Sap
Rama I Rd
National Stadium
Siam
Siam Paragon
Wat Pathum Wanram
Ratchadamri Rd
Soi Chitlom
Chit Lom
Ploenchit Rd
Krung Kasem Rd
Maha Phrutharam Rd
Rama VI Rd
MBK
SIAM SQUARE
Erawan Shrine
Soi Chulalongkorn 5
Soi Chulalongkorn 12
PATHUMWAN
Soi Chulalongkorn 9
Hua Lamphong Railway Station
Charoen Muang Rd
Ratchadamri
Chulalongkorn University Stadium
Royal Bangkok Sports Club
Soi Lang Suan
Soi Tonson
Hua Lamphong
Rama IV Rd
Henri-Dunant Rd
SILOM LINE
Sarasin Rd
Witthayu Rd
Soi Kaeo Fa
Sam Yan
Lumphini Park
Maha Nakhon Rd
Si Phraya Rd
Sap Rd
PATPONG
BANGRAK
Silom
Charoen Krung Rd (New Rd)
Sala Daeng
Surawong Rd
Soi Pradit
Decho Rd
Khlong Chong Nonsi
Soi Phiphat 2
Convent Rd
Mahesak Rd
Soi 30
Silom Rd
Chong Nonsi
Surasak Rd
Soi Wiang
North Sathorn Rd
South Sathorn Rd
Surasak
0
1/2 mi
0.5 km
MRT subway
BTS Skytrain
Airport Rail Link
Transfer
Ferry stop
Information
Post office
Shopping center

Sawatdee khrap! Welcome to Bangkok! With just 1 day to explore this mesmerizing city, get up early and prepare for an exhilarating day full of eye-opening experiences. We're about to immerse ourselves in a 1-day crash course in Thai and Buddhist culture. The one sight you can't miss is, of course, the Grand Palace, and I recommend you allow a couple of hours to take it in. You won't regret it! Dress light but be sure to wear long sleeves and no shorts or short skirts or you will not be allowed inside the Grand Palace or Buddhist temples. Wear comfortable shoes for walking, too. **START: Silom MRT or Sala Daeng BTS stations.**

❶ ★★ Tai Chi at Lumphini Park. For those who can manage it, there's no better way to watch Bangkok wake upthan by catching the locals at their early-morning exercises. From first light at dawn in Lumpini Park (see p 83, bullet ❷), you can join in or watch people doing aerobics or karate, jogging, cycling, and many other forms of sport. But the highlight for me is Tai Chi—especially popular around 6am. A crowd gathers and practices in silence for 1 hour. The gentle movement will invigorate your body and set you up for an energetic day. *1 hr. Rama IV Rd (cnr Ratchadamri & Silom rds). Admission free. Daily 4am–8pm. BTS SkyTrain: Sala Daeng or MRT subway: Silom.*

❷ ★★ The Golden Mount (Phu Khao Tong). The hill was built from waste dredged from the canal in the 19th century, and the spire of the Golden Mount was for a long time the highest point in Bangkok at 78m. But don't worry—the walk isn't too strenuous. A stairway winds its way around the mount, passing small Buddhist shrines and gravestones along the way. There's

Begin your day with Tai Chi in Lumpini Park.

Breezes gently ring these golden bells, donated by the lay community, that are set outside the chedi holding relics of the Buddha at the Golden Mount.

even a small waterfall, and if it's a cool morning you may catch the scent of the frangipani that lines the path. You might even find a mystic fortune-teller waiting for you at the top! A relic of the Buddha is said to be enshrined inside the *chedi*. While you catch your breath, you can take in the view of the Old City to the west. The Golden Mount is within the compound of Wat Saket (see p 36, bullet ❶), which used to be the city crematorium. Best on a weekday as early as possible. *🕓 1:15 hr. 344 Chakkraphatdiphong Rd (off Boriphat Rd). ☎ 02 621 0576. Admission free. Daily 7:30am–5:30pm. No BTS SkyTrain or MRT subway stations.*

❸ ★★★ The Grand Palace. Built by King Rama I as the royal residence of the new capital in 1782, the Grand Palace and its dazzling Buddhist temple, Wat Phra Kaeo, is Thailand's most revered and celebrated site. Nowhere else can you see Thai art, architecture, and history brought together in such outstanding harmony. The royal family no longer lives here and the complex is essentially a tourist attraction nowadays, except on coronations and events of regal significance. It's best to think of Wat Phra Kaeo as a Buddhist complex within the royal complex (the Grand Palace). Thailand's holiest Buddhist site features glittering shrines and stupas, guarded by mythical creatures such as *nagas* (serpents), *singhas* (lions) and *garudas* (half-man, half-bird). Unlike other Buddhist temples, no monks live here. Go as early as you can to avoid tour groups (and the heat!). *🕓 2 hr. Na Phra Lan Rd, Rattanakosin. ☎ 02 623 5500. www.palaces.thai.net. Admission 500 baht. Daily 8:30am–3:30pm. Ferry: Tha Chang (N9). No BTS SkyTrain or MRT subway stations.*

Detail of a spire at the Grand Palace.

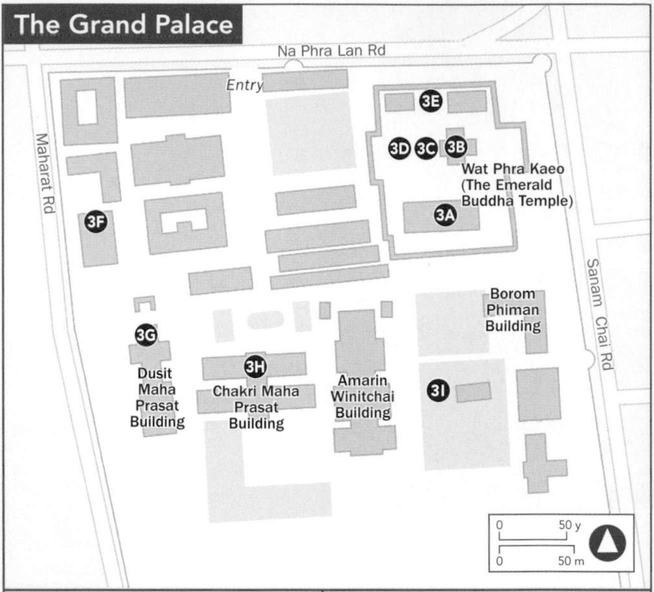

The Grand Palace

Na Phra Lan Rd
Entry
Maharat Rd
Sanam Chai Rd
3E
3D 3C 3B
Wat Phra Kaeo (The Emerald Buddha Temple)
3A
3F
Borom Phiman Building
3G
Dusit Maha Prasat Building
3H
Chakri Maha Prasat Building
Amarin Winitchai Building
3I
0 50 y
0 50 m

3A Emerald Buddha. The centerpiece of the temple is the Emerald Buddha, a 66cm-high statue, which is actually made of jade and is believed to have come from Sri Lanka. It sits above a dazzling gold altar inside the *bot* (main temple). Remember to be quiet and respectful inside the *bot* and do not point your feet towards the Buddha. **3B Royal Pantheon.** Standing in the middle of the temple complex, the pantheon houses life-sized statues of the past kings of the current Chakri dynasty. **3C Phra Mondop.** Easily recognizable by its high spire, green mosaic and gold Buddha on the exterior is this *chedi* that acts as a repository for sacred Buddhist scriptures. **3D Phra Si Rattana Chedi.** This gold-tiled stupa was built by King Mongkut (played by Yul Brynner in the movie *The King and I*). **3E *Ramakien* Gallery.** If you are familiar with the ancient Hindu epic *Ramayana*, then follow the intricate mural clockwise around the cloisters of the compound. The Thai version, *Ramakien*, is told in lively detail.

Mural at the Wat Phra Kaew Museum.

3F Wat Phra Kaew Museum. There's a small cafe for much-needed respite next to the air-conditioned museum. The museum doesn't really feature much (robes of the Emerald Buddha and some white elephant bones), but it's usually a good resting spot. You can get soft drinks, coffee and snacks at the adjoining cafe. *Admission 50 baht.* **3G Dusit Throne Hall.** Built in 1784, this is a replica of a temple in the former capital, Ayutthaya. The tiers and awnings of this magnificent building are stepped up in layers and a golden spire reaches into the heavens as a triumphant testimony to Buddhist symmetry. Beautiful bonsai trees around the lawn in the foreground make this the most photogenic stop of your morning. Inside you'll find the original teak throne of King Rama I.

3H Chakri Maha Prasat. Also known as the Chakri Throne Hall and designed by a British architect in a fusion of Thai and European neoclassical styles, this glitzy and lavish building acts as a reception hall for distinguished foreign guests and houses the ashes of former Chakri dynasty rulers.

3I Siwalai Gardens. The king used these splendid manicured gardens in days of yore for entertaining his guests and ambassadors, as well as a recreation area for royal women and children. If you are tired from walking you'll appreciate the tranquility of this shaded area. King Rama IV's personal chapel is here, laid out in cool marble with blue-and-white glass mosaics.

Tourists gather at the Grand Palace.

Watch the Dress Code!

You must wear long-sleeved shirts and trousers, and skirts and dresses must come below the knee—anyone entering the Grand Palace who is deemed inappropriately dressed will be asked to hire cotton shirts and trousers. It's also wise to carry a parasol and wear a hat and sunglasses to protect you from the bright, hot sun. Keep your ticket to get free entry to **Vimanmek Palace** (see p 87, bullet 3). Once inside, you can hire an audio guide—or a real one—to explain the historical, religious, and royal significance of each site. I recommend either option.

A Buddhist Nature

Visitors to the "Land of Smiles" never fail to remark on the peaceful nature of the Thai people. After just a weekend in Bangkok, they come away with Thai expressions such as *sabai-sabai* (everything's good), *jai yen-yen* (keep cool) and *mai pen rai* (don't worry).

Some 94 per cent of Thai people are Buddhists and they will tell you that these expressions reflect a deeper spiritual concept—the practice of tolerance, humility and patience that is at the heart of Buddhism.

Followers of Buddha do not consider him a god. Instead, they believe in his ancient wisdom and seek to emulate his teachings. In many ways, Buddhism is more a philosophy than a religion. It teaches that we should follow a middle path; that we should concentrate on the here and now; that we should forsake our cravings and instant pleasures; that by simply meditating we can achieve great knowledge; and that life and time are cyclic, and that all creatures are reincarnated according to their past actions, or karma.

The Buddha himself was Siddhartha Gautama, an Indian prince born in the 6th century B.C. He gave up his luxuries for an ascetic life—much as Buddhist monks do nowadays. It is said he attained enlightenment while meditating under a Bodhi tree and reached the state of nirvana.

❹ ★★★ **Amulet Market.** Running along the northern wall of Wat Mahathat, the shaded boulevard of Phra Chan Road is Bangkok's best-known area to buy Buddhist amulets and lucky charms. Vendors line the street with miniature Buddhas, astrological icons, pendants, ivory, gems, and other assorted paraphernalia for the religious, the superstitious and the curious. Buyers study antique amulets through magnifying glasses while housewives haggle over marble pieces for their mantelpieces. There are even amulet magazines for devotees to scan. You too might like to buy a few souvenirs or an amulet to bring you health, wealth, protection from danger, or even a new baby in the family! ⏲ *30 min. Phra Chan Rd. Daily 6am–8pm. No BTS SkyTrain or MRT subway stations.*

5 **Baan Phra Arthit.** Your feet will undoubtedly be feeling the pinch by now. Time to find a little air-conditioned diner with coffee, soft drinks, sandwiches, cakes and light meals. Located close to the river pier, this is a good choice before setting off on the next leg of your day trip. *102/1 Phra Arthit Rd, Banglamphu.* ☎ *02280 7879.* Sun–Thu 10am–8:30pm; Fri–Sat 10am–10pm. $.

❻ **Royal Barges Museum.** If it's before 4pm, you still have time to visit Thailand's famous historical royal barges, which have been housed at this museum under the care of the Royal Thai Navy since 1932 when Thailand changed from

The Royal Barges Museum.

an absolute monarchy to a constitutional one. The 50m-long boats have participated in royal ceremonies since the 18th century. They were damaged by bombing during WWII, but caught the eye of current monarch HM Bhumibol who lovingly restored them to their former glory. Like everything connected with the monarchy in Thailand, much pomp, pageantry, and solemn respect is displayed. You can see the king's own barge, *Suppanahongse,* which is carved out of a single teak tree. Its bow is adorned with a golden swan. The best opportunity to see these majestic boats on the river (complete with trumpets and 30 oarsmen) is during the Royal Kathin Festival, which takes place every few years at auspicious times. ⌚ *45 min. West bank of Chao Phraya River (south of Phra Pinklao Bridge), Bang Phlat.* ☎ *02 424 0004. www.thailandmuseum.com. Admission adults 100 baht, kids 50 baht. Daily 9am–5pm. Ferry: Express boat from Phra Arthit pier (N13) to Phra Pin Klao Bridge pier (N12), plus a 10-min walk.*

7 ★★★ Wat Arun. If it's just before sunset, catch the splendor of Wat Arun, the "Temple of Dawn." This Khmer-style stupa looks somewhat grey from a distance. However, once you get up close you'll see the walls of the temple are actually a mosaic of glass cuttings, Chinese porcelain and ceramic tiles. In the morning or sunset light, the pieces glisten and the temple sparkles, often appearing to be shades of orange or purple. The architectural design of Wat Arun is inspired by Hindu mythology. In the temple's niches you'll see the Hindu god Indra sitting astride Erawan, the three-headed elephant. And if you look closely you'll see there are tridents of Shiva on top of each spire. The temple itself has high vertical stairs, which can be daunting to climb. If you do manage to scale them, you will be rewarded with wonderful views of the Bangkok skyline across the river. ⌚ *45 min. Arun Amarin Rd, Thonburi.* ☎ *02 891 1149. www.watarun.org. Admission 50 baht.*

Each Buddha in the long row at Wat Arun is slightly different than the next.

Daily 7am–6pm. Ferry: Take a cross-river ferry from Tha Tien pier (N8) to Wat Arun pier.

8 ★★ Jim Thompson Thai Silk. You've taken in temples and Thai history all day; now it's time for some shopping. And what better way to remember Bangkok than with some fine silk products? For the best in quality silk shopping, visit the main retail outlet where you can buy clothes, curtains, pillowcases, scarves, or just the fabrics themselves. The silks are irresistible and your friends will love you for buying them such a present.
30 min. 9 Surawong Rd, Bangrak. ☎ *02 632 81004. www.jimthompson.com. Daily 9am–9pm. Sala Daeng BTS or Silom MRT station.*

9 ★ Patpong. There's no getting away from the fact that Bangkok is synonymous with the sex

A young woman demonstrates the traditional way to spin silk at Jim Thompson Thai Silk.

The always bustling Patpong night market.

industry. Sex tourism is undoubtedly a thriving business in this city and certain areas (Nana Plaza, Soi Cowboy and Patpong for starters) are lined with door-to-door go-go bars, sex shows, prostitution, massage services, and the like. Despite the seedy nature of this underworld, many tourists can't resist having a peek at what goes on there. Two roads, Patpong 1 and Patpong 2, are probably the most tourist- and female-friendly. The streets have a nighttime market selling souvenirs and kitsch, so female visitors should not feel particularly unsafe or unwanted. In fact, many couples and groups of gals like to visit the go-go bars. King's Castle and King's Corner are two of the most reputable joints on Patpong Road, where female visitors and foreign couples are commonplace. You can sit quietly at the back and nurse a beer while entranced men ogle go-go dancers from around the stage. ***Warning:*** In the street, touts will approach you and invite you to see their seedy shows, which involve nudity and sex acts. Even if they say it's free, you will have to pay a cover charge for these shows and you may also get an extortionate bill for drinks. Bars above the ground floor level have a particularly bad reputation for ripping off tourists and are best avoided. However, there's a galaxy of open-air bars and cafes where you can soak up the atmosphere and watch the red-light district in action without getting involved. 🕓 *1½ hr. Patpong Rd, Bangrak. Daily 7pm–1am. BTS SkyTrain: Sala Daeng or MRT subway: Silom.*

Royal Kathin Festival

The Kathin ceremony is a royal barge procession for the presentation of new robes to Buddhist monks. Thailand's traditional handmade wooden barges are world famous because of the artistic craftsmanship they embody. The royal barge procession on the Chao Phya River is exceptionally glittering and majestic. On the occasion, the royal barges will, in a stately procession, transport His Majesty the King from Vasukri Royal Pier along the Chao Phraya River to Wat Arun where His Majesty will present saffron robes to the monastic community.

The Best in 2 Days

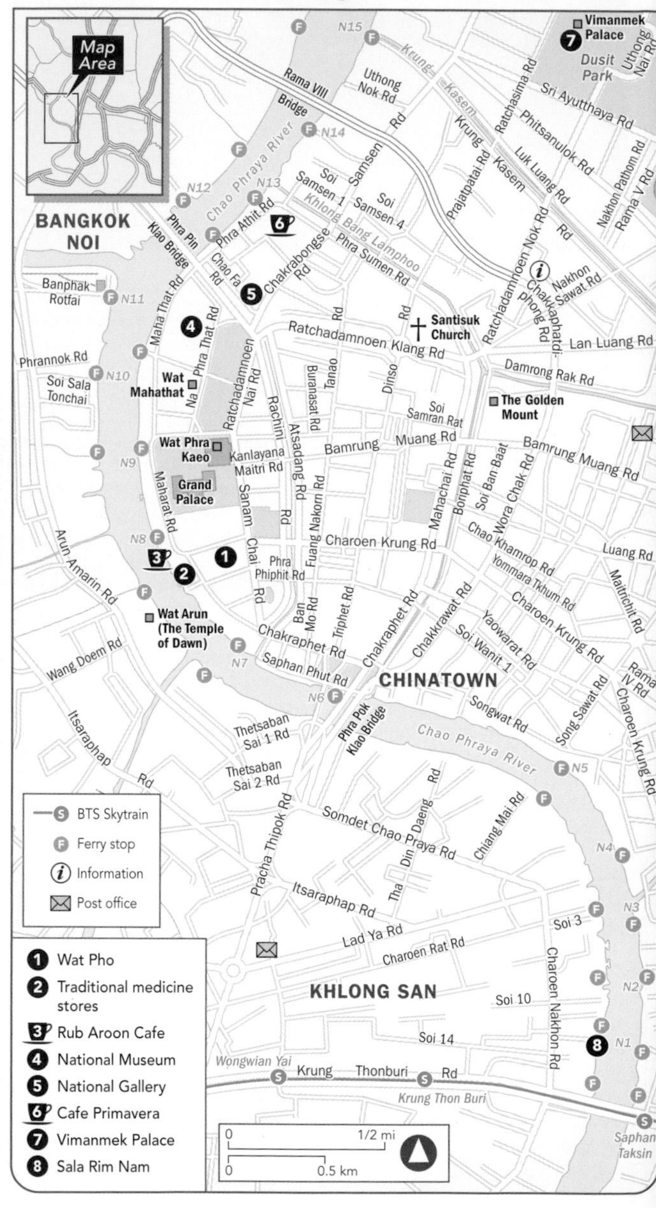

On day 2, we are going to delve a little deeper into Thai culture. Start the day by booking the evening's entertainment in advance (depending on availability you might want to swap nights two and three around—go to Thai boxing tonight instead and see the culture show tomorrow night). Whatever you choose, you're in for another great day out! If you would like to begin the day with an herbal Thai massage at Wat Pho, have a very light breakfast. And remember there's a dress code for Buddhist temples. **START: Express boat to Tha Tien pier (N8).**

❶ ★★★ Wat Pho. Bangkok's largest and oldest surviving temple is Wat Pho. In many ways, this temple is more impressive than those of the Grand Palace—less colorful and dazzling, certainly, but more tranquil, more spiritual, and more captivating. It is here in Wat Pho that you might discover your hidden Buddha. Dating as far back as the 16th century, the temple complex was favored by several Siamese kings who maintained their residence next door at the Grand Palace. Known to Thais as Wat Phra Chetuphon, the site includes nearly 100 towering *chedi* and some 394 bronze Buddha images, mostly retrieved from the ancient ruins of Siam's previous capital, Ayutthaya, and the spiritual city of Sukhothai. Among the treasures in Wat Pho is the famous Reclining Buddha, a 46m-long, gold-covered statue of the Buddha in repose, apparently passing into nirvana. The soles of the Buddha's feet are inlaid with intricate mother-of-pearl designs, while the walls of the room are lined with 108 collection bowls—believed to be the most auspicious number. Just outside the hall housing the Reclining Buddha is a Bodhi tree that is said to have grown from a cutting of the one in India under which the Buddha meditated. In the main pavilion you'll find the centerpiece is a bronze meditating Buddha. It is another item that was salvaged from the ruins of

Worshippers leave flower garlands as offerings on the ancient statues of Wat Pho.

Ayutthaya. You can follow a mural carved into the outer base and inner doors of the pavilion that depicts scenes from the epic tale, *The Ramakien.* *🕓 1½ hr. Soi Chetuphon, Rattanakosin. Admission 100 baht. Daily 8am–5 pm ☎ 02 225 5910. www.watpho.com. Ferry: Tha Tien pier (N8).*

❷ Traditional medicine stores. Fresh from your massage and spiritual journey around Wat Pho, you should be feeling healthy, soulful, and relaxed. Take a stroll along Maharat Road and take in the aromas of lemongrass, Kaffir

Thai Massage

In between the main pavilion of Wat Pho and the hall where the Buddha reclines is a traditional medicine and massage school (☎ 02 622 35501; daily 8.30am–6pm). This is one of the most popular attractions in Thailand as it is regarded as the home of Thai massage. The room contains plaques showing the body's acupressure points. The practitioners of this ancient art are said to be among the world's best, so if you have the time and can stand a little stretching and the sensation of hot stones bathed in herbs being ground into your muscles, then a Wat Pho herbal massage is not to be missed.

lime, green tea, pickled snake, and many other wild concoctions from the Chinese traditional medicine stores. Many of the pharmacists, or alchemists, can speak English and will be ready to offer a herbal remedy, whatever your ailment. Of course, you may want to buy some ginseng roots, balms, essential oils, or the like, but remember the import restrictions you may face when returning home. You might want to check your government's website on customs regulations regarding bringing home raw foods, plants, drugs, and medicines. ***Maharat Rd. No credit cards. Ferry: Tha Tien pier (N8).***

Monks praying at Wat Pho.

3 **Rub Aroon Cafe.** This teak house used to be an herbal dispensary. Now a pleasant cafe, it's a great spot to escape the heat either inside under the ceiling fans or on the footpath under a parasol, taking in the street atmosphere. It offers vegetarian and vegan dishes, as well as coffee, tea, and fruit shakes. *310–312 Maharat Rd.* ☎ *02 622 2312. Daily 8am–6pm. Ferry: Tha Tien pier (N8). $.*

4 ★★ **National Museum.** Now that you have a taste for Thai culture, you shouldn't miss the Bangkok National Museum, which is host to perhaps the greatest collection of historical and archaeological artifacts, cultural art, and Buddhist exhibits in Southeast Asia. Two of the museum buildings—the Wang Na Palace and the Buddhaisawan Chapel—are architectural wonders in themselves, dating from the 18th century. Take, for instance, the black-and-gold motif lacquered doors to the palace or the murals in the chapel—stunning examples of Thai art. While historians will spend days in the museum, others can be inspired by just a quick inspection of some of the biggest attractions. Unfortunately, some parts of the museum have scant information about the exhibits in English. Most of the exhibits run in chronological order, from prehistoric earthenware and bronze items to early carvings, weapons, and relics, to modern Buddhist art. Inside the chapel you'll find the *Phra Buddha Sihing,* a Buddha image shrouded in mystery. Some claim it comes from Sri Lanka, others that it was rescued from 13th-century Sukhothai, a religious center in central Thailand. The image is paraded through the streets of the capital every April during the Songkran Festival. Another exhibit worth looking out for is that of the royal funeral chariots, which are made of gilded teak. *1 hr. 1 Na Phra That Rd, Rattanakosin.* ☎ *02 224 1333. Admission 200 baht. Wed–Sun 9am–4pm. Ferry: Tha Phra Chan pier.*

5 ★ **National Gallery.** Situated in a splendid colonial house that was once home to Thailand's Royal Mint, the National Gallery sits in notable contrast to the National Museum in that it is modern and displays contemporary art, featuring exhibitions from mainly local but also international artists. What is particularly pleasant about the gallery is the natural light, the cool breeze from the air-conditioning and the high ceilings, making this an ideal spot to rest and cool down. *1 hr. 4 Chao Fa Rd, Banglampmphu.* ☎ *02 282 2639. Admission 200 baht. Wed–Sun 9am–4pm. Ferry: Phra Arthit pier (N13).*

A statue of the god Vishnu stands guards outside the National Museum.

An exhibit of contemporary Thai art at the National Gallery.

6 ★ **Cafe Primavera.** You can't walk more than 10 paces without bumping into a noodle stall in this area. On nearby Khao San Road there are also the fast food joints we all recognize. But for a hearty lunch or just a coffee and a snack, Cafe Primavera gets my vote. It's a stone's throw from Phra Sumen Fort (see p 60, bullet 11), and has great oven-baked pizzas, homemade ice-cream and lovely smiling staff. *56 Phra Sumen Rd, Banglamphu. ☎ 02 281 4718. Daily 9am–11pm. Ferry: Phra Arthit pier (N13). $$.*

7 ★★★ Vimanmek Palace.

Still got your ticket from the Grand Palace? Good! You get free entry. The centerpiece of the immaculate Dusit Park is this magnificent golden teak mansion, which was reassembled here in 1901 by royal order after being shipped over from the island of Ko Sichang. Amazingly, the entire three-story structure was built using wooden pegs and no nails. It was the favorite retreat of King Chulalongkorn (1853–1910). The palace was the first building in Thailand to have electricity and an indoor toilet. Follow the teak corridors around 81 royal rooms, taking in the exhibits and furnishings and the distinctly "Victorian" sense of interior design. Compulsory guided tours leave every 30 minutes; try to time your visit to catch free performances of Thai dance and martial arts in the lakeside pavilion at 10:30am and 2pm daily. Remember, this is a royal palace, so dress respectfully. *🕓 1 hr. Rajvithi Road, Dusit. ☎ 02 281 5454. www.vimanmek.com. Admission 100 baht. Tues–Sun 9:30am–4:30pm. Ticket booth opens*

Vimanmek Palace.

9am. Last ticket sold 3:15pm. No metro or ferry.

8 ★★★ Thai culture show/ dinner theatre. I'll assume you've had a fulfilling day and have rested up at your hotel, booked your tickets, and scrubbed up in your finery for tonight. No trip to Thailand is complete without an evening of fine dining with delicious Thai food and stage performances of traditional Thai dance, song, mime, and drama. My suggested dinner theater venues is on the banks of the river, and is superb, so have a show with your meal! **8A** Natayasala: Traditional Thai Puppet Theatre, also known as Joe Louis, hosts traditional and modern interpretations of Thai puppetry. There's also a gourmet Thai restaurant and bar, Sala Rim Nam at the Mandarin Oriental. *Joe Louis at Asiatique: The Riverfront, S13 2194 Charoenkrung Rd ☎ 02 688 3322. www.joelouistheatre.com. Free shuttle boat from pier at BTS SkyTrain station, Saphan Thaksin. Sala Rim Nam: Private boat for guests leaves from Mandarin Oriental, 48 Oriental Ave, Bang Rak; ☎ 02 659 9000; www.mandarinoriental.com; tickets from 2400 baht (w/dinner); nightly 7:30pm; Nearest BTS SkyTrain, Saphan Taksin station.*

King Chulalongkorn (1853–1910)

Thais still revere King Chulalongkorn, or Rama V. Photographs of him—easily recognizable by his flamboyant mustache—are on walls all over Bangkok. As a child he was tutored by Anna Leonowens, made famous in the movie *The King and I*. An admirer of British administration, King Chulalongkorn modernized the country, while avoiding the colonial desires of Britain and France. He is fondly remembered for introducing governmental and social reforms, and for abolishing slavery in Siam. King Chulalongkorn designed Dusit Park, which is the site of Vimanmek Palace (see p 22).

The Best in 3 Days

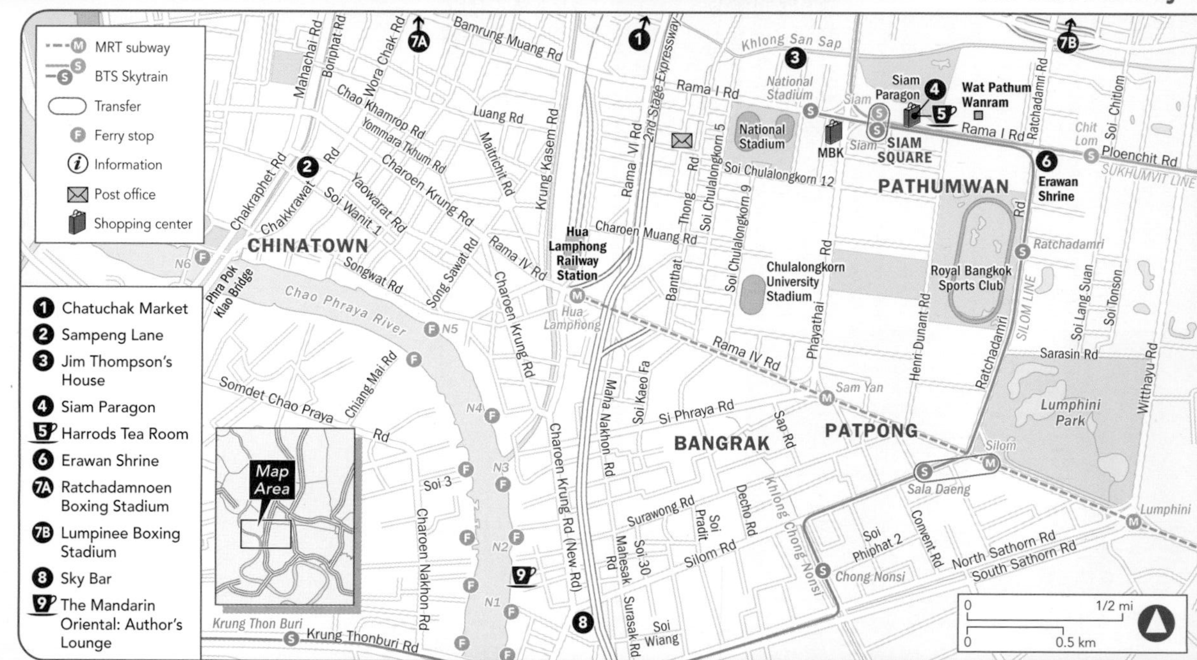

Today we're going to avoid temples, do some shopping and rub shoulders with both ordinary Thai folks and high-society types. We're going to visit the former home of Bangkok's most famous foreigner and end the day with sunset cocktails at one of the most breathtaking locations you've ever seen. *Chok dee!* (Good luck!) **START: If it's Saturday or Sunday we're going to Chatuchak Market, so take the metro to Mo Chit or Kampaeng Phet. If it ís a weekday, get a taxi to Sampeng Lane in Chinatown.**

❶ ★★★ Chatuchak Market, commonly known as JJ. Said to be the world's largest flea market; perhaps half a million people visit every weekend. Situated in the northern suburbs of the city and with no less than 15,000 stalls, it covers an area equivalent to five football fields. JJ is a maze of merchandise with a cacophony of characters and an unexpected twist at every corner. You can find everything here—from clothes, plants, and household goods to live snakes, exotic fish, Buddhist art, herbal medicine, CDs, and hill-tribe handicrafts. Every possible type of Thai food is for sale—some of it still alive and twitching! If you have an eye for antiques, look around the stalls close to the entrance at BTS SkyTrain station, Kamphaeng Phet. Note that the Children's Discovery Museum (see p 42, bullet ❷), the Queen Sirikit Park and the Botanical Garden adjoin Chatuchak Market on its northern side, so there are alternatives for family members. 🕓 *2 hr. Phahonyothin Rd, Chatuchak. No credit cards. Sat & Sun 9am–6pm. BTS SkyTrain: Mo Chit or MRT subway, Kamphaeng Phet.*

Dozens upon dozens of happy little Buddhas for sale at the Chatuchak Market.

❷ ★★ Sampeng Lane. (Also known as Soi Wanit.) Not as good a shopping experience as Chatuchak by any means, but a great chance to experience the hustle 'n' bustle of a Thai market and see the strong work ethic of the local people. This is Chinatown, one of the original foundations of Bangkok. Sampeng Lane is a sheltered alleyway about 1.5km long. Pedestrian traffic is slow and labored and you'll have to squish and squeeze your way past shops and stalls selling sweets, dried fruit, cheap jewelry, gold and gems, clothes, toys, steaming dim sum, and much more. It's a kaleidoscope of chaos and a feast for the senses. *Sampeng Lane. Daily 6am–9pm. Nearest MRT subway station to Chinatown is Hua Lamphong. Nearest ferry, Rachawongse (N5).*

❸ ★ The Jim Thompson House. American Jim Thompson was head of the OSS (forerunner to the CIA) in Thailand in 1945. He became enamored with Thailand

The festive Jim Thompson House museum, restaurant and shop.

and, in particular, silk. He founded the first Thai silk export company and was a celebrated socialite in Bangkok until his mysterious disappearance in Malaysia in 1967. His former home, a complex of six traditional teak houses, has been preserved and now acts as a museum, housing his collection of antiques, artwork, and elegant furniture. There's also a restaurant, exhibition space, and shop. *6 Soi Kasemsan 2, Rama I Rd. ☎ 02 216 7368. www.jimthompsonhouse.org. Admission 150 baht. Daily 9am–6pm (last tour at 6pm). BTS SkyTrain: National Stadium.*

❹ ★★ **Siam Paragon.** This mega-luxurious shopping mall has something for everyone. First, there are outlets for Jimmy Choo, Hermès, Versace, Gucci, and many other designers. There are Jim Thompson silk retailers, beauty parlors, IT, sports and bookstores, and several boutiques on the fourth floor selling chic Thai crafts and furnishings. On the top floor you'll find an entertainment center with cinemas and tenpin bowling. And, best of all, you can visit Siam Ocean World (see p 44, bullet ❼), a tunneled aquarium with 3000 species of exotic fish and sea animals. *Cnr Rama I & Phayathai rds, Siam Square. ☎ 02 610 8000. www.siamparagon.co.th. Daily 10am–10pm. BTS SkyTrain: Siam.*

5 **Harrods Tea Room.** Just to show you really have entered another world at Siam Paragon, at the luxurious Harrods Tea Room you can enjoy a British afternoon tea complete with finger sandwiches, scones and clotted cream. It's popular venue with locals and Asian tourists wanting a taste of old England in Bangkok! *Ground Floor, Siam Paragon, Siam Square. Daily 10am–10pm. BTS SkyTrain: Siam. $.*

Bangkok's cutting-edge luxury mall, the Siam Paragon.

6 ★★ Erawan Shrine. You've already seen your fair share of temples in Bangkok, but this strange little altar—sandwiched between shopping centers and towering hotels—is nonetheless quite magical. The shrine itself represents the four-headed Hindu god of creation, Brahma, and was erected in 1956 after a series of fatal mishaps befell the construction of the original Erawan Hotel. Suddenly, all mishaps ceased, the hotel's business started booming and devotees began to flock in droves to the shrine in mystic reverence. As you approach the busy junction where the Erawan Shrine stands, you will smell the billows of incense and might hear music, as those whose wishes come true pay respect by hiring traditional dancers. For the non-Buddhist/Hindu visitor, it's a colorful photo op, if not a mind-blowing sight with pin-striped businessmen praying for success, university students hoping for romance, and housewives imploring the gods for winning lottery numbers. *Outside the Grand Hyatt Erawan Bangkok (see p 140), Ratchadamri & Ploenchit rds, Pratunam. Daily 6am–10pm. BTS SkyTrain: Chit Lom or Ratchadamri.*

Lord Brahma watches over the faithful visiting the Erawan Shrine.

7 ★ Thai boxing. Thailand's national sport is *muay Thai*, a bloody contest of kickboxing, often fought by wiry little 50kg guys whose power and flexibility are remarkable. Thai boxing draws huge crowds who are as much part of the spectacle as the fighters. Screaming, betting, drinking, and jumping up and down in excitement are all par for the course. An evening usually involves eight bouts each with a maximum of five rounds, accompanied by traditional

Thai Silk

The art of weaving silk arrived in Thailand from China over 2000 years ago. Threads of silk are extracted from the cocoons of silkworms, which feed exclusively on mulberry leaves. The threads are reeled together into fibers by hand before being boiled and bleached to remove the natural yellow of silk yarn. The silk is then dyed before being hand-woven on a wooden loom. This labor-intensive system ensures that each Thai silk product is unique. While a little more coarse than its shiny Chinese counterpart, Thai silk has a more subtle luster, an ideal material for making women's dresses and scarves and men's shirts, and is a luxurious fabric for furniture.

Night-time cocktails at Sky Bar set high standards.

Thai music and some Sumo-esque rituals. Although you'll rarely see any serious injuries, some might find the sport too violent. There are two main stadiums in Bangkok: **7A Ratchadamnoen Boxing Stadium**, which is the national Thai boxing arena with championship bouts; and **7B Lumphini Boxing Stadium**, a brand new purpose built stadium for 5,000 spectators. *See p 131.*

8 ★★★ Cocktails at Sky Bar. Precariously situated like a diving board over a swimming pool on the 63rd floor of lebua Hotel is the Sky Bar. The spine-chilling views of the city below warrant at least enough time to enjoy a cocktail, a martini, or a glass of wine to keep your knees from turning to jelly. *63rd floor, lebua at State Tower Hotel, 1055 Silom Rd, Bang Rak. ☎ 02 624 9555. www.thedomebkk.com. Daily 6pm–1am. BTS SkyTrain: Saphan Taksin.*

There are photo-ops galore at the Grand Palace.

9 ★★★ The Mandarin Oriental: Author's Lounge. For years the Oriental was acknowledged as "The World's Greatest Hotel" and many, including myself, would argue that it has lost little of its timeless charm. Even if you are not staying at the Mandarin Oriental (see p 142) you will still want to take a look at it. Walk through the cool and tropical—but not ostentatious—lobby, past the boutiques and you'll come into a lounge with ceiling fans, French windows and a Kiplingesque air of British-Raj India. This is the Author's Lounge, where many of the greats, including Joseph Conrad, W Somerset Maugham, and Noel Coward, penned their works. Soak up the atmosphere with coffee and cake or high tea and scones served on pristine china. *🕓 45 min. 48 Oriental Ave, Bang Rak. ☎ 02 659 9000. www.mandarinoriental.com. BTS SkyTrain: Saphan Taksin. Ferry: Oriental pier (N1). $$.* ●

2 The Best Special-Interest Tours

Bangkok Food Safari

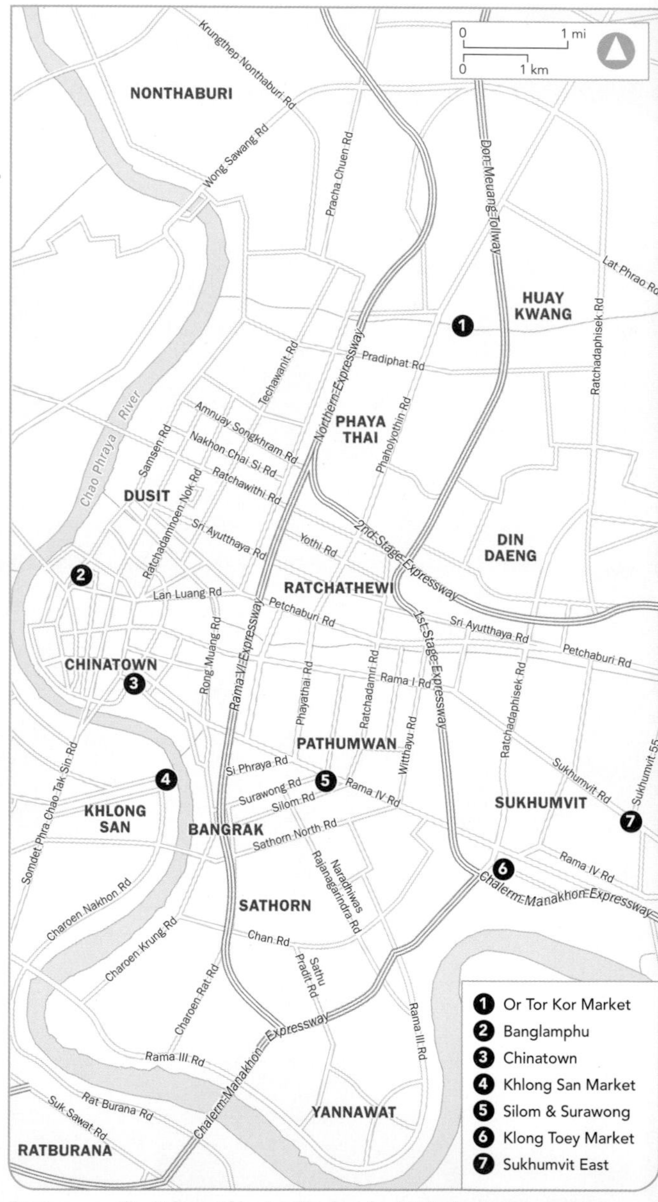

Previous page: Fine Italian marble gives Benchamabophit Wat its dazzling good looks.

You can't walk more than 100m in Bangkok before you trip over a marketplace or a little stall on wheels offering noodles, spicy papaya salad, grilled chicken, sticky rice, pork skewers, fresh orange juice, coconut desserts, or any one of a million dishes sizzling away in woks. Rather than concentrate on three hearty meals a day, Bangkokians tend to eat every few hours and, in between times, they love to snack. Whatever time of day, you'll see woks and stoves set up along the pavement and Thais of all classes sitting on little plastic stools at metal tables gratefully tucking in to whatever's on offer. There's a fantastic selection of lip-smacking street food available all over Bangkok—most dishes cost no more than 30 or 40 baht. Just let your nose do the walking. **START: Kampaeng Phet metro station.**

❶ **Or Tor Kor Market.** A cleaner, vacuum-packed, covered version of the bustling Bangkok street market, this is clearly a more up-market place to shop (and perhaps 25 to 50% more expensive). Fruit, veg, meat, fish, sweets, condiments, and spices are all available, but in a smell-free environment. *Directly outside Kamphaeng Phet MRT exit 3, opposite to Chatuchak Market. Daily 6am–8pm. MRT subway: Kamphaeng Phet.*

❷ **Banglamphu.** Backpackers love street food and the streets near Khao San Road are jam-packed with stalls selling *pat-thai* (fried noodles, vegetables, and peanuts) for 30 baht, fresh orange juice and sugar cane juice (25 baht), and even deep-fried insects and scorpions. Pick up a nice dessert, such as coconut pudding in a banana-leaf cup, on Tani Road. *Khao San, Samsen & Tani rds. Daily 10am–1am. No SkyTrain or subway. Nearest ferry: Phra Arthit pier (N13).*

If you're squeamish about goods sitting out unwrapped and unrefrigerated, the upscale Or Tor Kor Market is where to shop.

Papaya Salad (Som-Tam)

Aside from the ubiquitous noodle stalls, the most popular street food in Bangkok is arguably *som-tam*. Recognizable by her large wooden or earthenware mortar and pestle, the *som-tam* vendor is an artist in her own right. She surrounds herself with a variety of ingredients and pounds them in the mortar one by one—cherry tomatoes, chillis, palm sugar, dried prawns, pickled crab, peanuts, snake beans, garlic, lime juice, fish sauce, and the main ingredient, long shards of green papaya. Tell her how spicy you want it. I always ask for my *som-tam* without the salty prawns and crab, and then eat it with a 10-baht portion of sticky rice and some fried chicken. The best 50-baht takeaway you can get!

A plate of Som Tam (papaya salad).

A street vendor selling fried cockroaches and other insects. Will these photo-snapping tourists buy any?

There's enough food for an army at the street stands of Yowarat Road in Chinatown.

❸ ★ **Chinatown.** A veritable festival of street food; just meander along Yaowarat Road in the evening and let the aromas lure you in. Bird's nest soup and shark fin soup are popular. Apart from the many seafood dishes, you should try 1000-year-old eggs, medicinal teas, boiled cockles, Thai porridge *(joak)*, Chinese cakes *(kanom piah)*, roasted chestnuts, fried banana and, my favorite, fried wonton. Chinatown hosts an annual vegetarian food festival in September/October. *Yaowarat, Charoen Krung & Chakkrawat rds. Daily 11am–11pm. Ferry: Rachawongse (N5). Nearest MRT subway: Hua Lamphong.*

❹ **Khlong San Market.** Away from the baying hordes, this open-air market is just a short ferry ride across the Chao Phraya River. University students tend to come here for lunch. Half the market is dedicated to ladies' clothes and accessories, the other half to food—hot-off-the-wok chilli sensations, fruit such as apples, pears, rose-apples and pineapples, spicy salads, and hot, fried doughnuts. Ask for *ho mok pla*—little curried fish curry souffles in banana-leaf cups—they're delicious. *Charoen Nathorn Rd, Thonburi. Daily 7am–10pm. Ferry: cross the river from Sri Phraya pier (N3) to Klong San pier.*

❺ **Silom & Surawong.** Woks sizzle with chilli and garlic until the wee hours at this popular traveler hangout. I particularly recommend a dish of braised pork and rice (35 baht) from the English-speaking vendor who occupies a space on the lane next to Montien Hotel. *Surawong, Patpong, Silom, and particularly Convent rds. Daily 10am–3am. BTS SkyTrain: Sala Daeng, MRT subway: Silom.*

❻ ★ **Klong Toey Market.** This crowded, pungent marketplace offers bowls of coconut soup, fried rice, *kwit-diao* (noodle soup) with prawns, fruit and spices—but visitors will be more intrigued by the array of fresh produce.

Today's catch is laid out at Klong Toey Market.

Many of Bangkok's restaurants buy here wholesale so the place is buzzing almost 24-hours a day, 7 days a week. ***Cnr Ratchadaphisek & Rama IV rds, Klong Toey. Daily 6am–2am. MRT subway: Klong Toey.***

❼ ★★ **Sukhumvit East.** On the north side of the Thong Lor BTS station, you'll see stalls selling a kaleidoscope of exotic fruit—rambutans, mangoes, durians, mangosteens, jackfruit and more. On the opposite side of the street, Soi 38 is one of Bangkok's gems. Mobile stalls offer Chinese and Thai favorites, including dim sum, *khao mun gai* (chicken and rice), sticky rice and mango in coconut sauce (delicious!), pork satay, and oyster omelets. ***Sukhumvit Rd sois 55 and 38. Daily noon–9pm. BTS SkyTrain: Thong Lor.***

Enjoy fresh fruit at Bangkok's markets.

Buddhist Temples of Old Bangkok

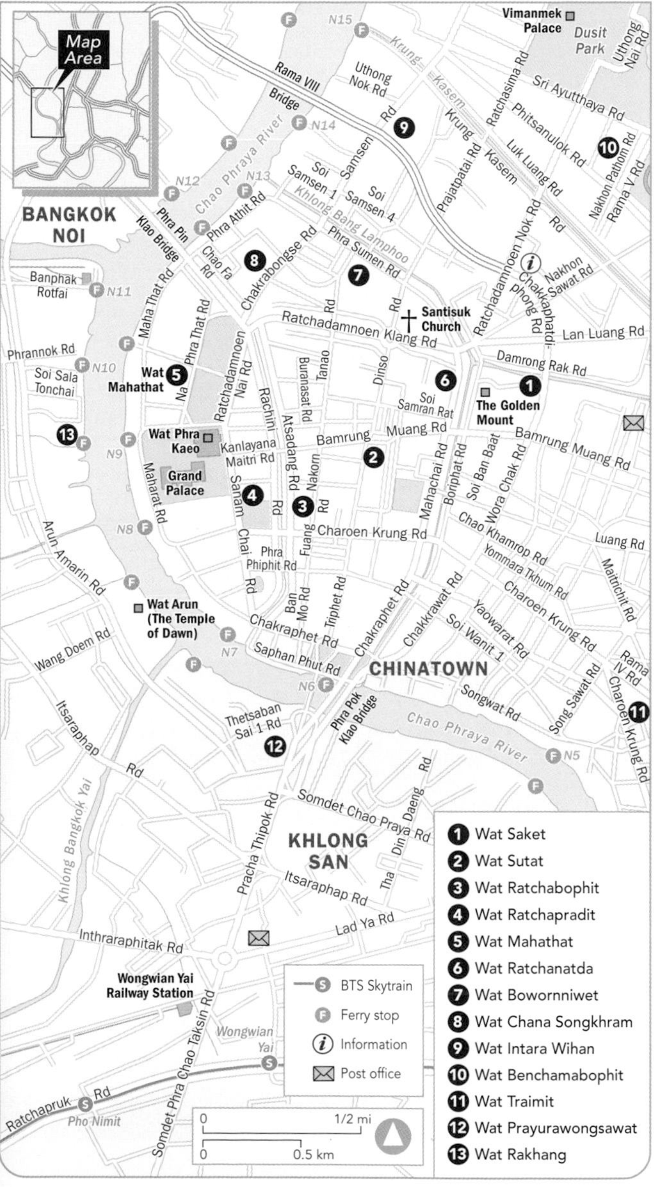

Virtually every neighborhood in Thailand has its own Buddhist temple where locals pray. Locals also subsidize the temple and often help with repairs. In fact, you could say the local temple is a spiritual community center. The best place to see a stunning variety of old temples and architectural styles is the Old City in Bangkok. Please remember that these are holy places and you must observe the dress code—no shorts, short skirts or sleeveless shirts—and be respectful while you are in the compound. These are also places to relax, gather thoughts, contemplate life and meditate. Buddhist temples can be fascinating places, evoking a deep sense of tranquility and awareness among visitors. **START: Catch a taxi or a tuktuk to Wat Saket.**

❶ **Wat Saket.** Adjoining the 78m Golden Mount (see p 53, bullet ❶), this simple Buddhist temple tells much of Bangkok's history. Built in the late 18th century by King Rama I just outside the new city walls, Wat Saket served as the capital's crematorium and, over the next century, was the pyre for some 60,000 plague victims. The golden stupa was added some years later, built on rubble dredged from the canal nearby. Later, King Rama V reportedly placed relics (said to be the Buddha's teeth) in the *chedi.* Wat Saket hosts an annual 9-day and -night temple fair in November. *344 Chakkraphat-diphong Rd (between Boriphat & Lan Luang rds), Phra Nakorn.* ☎ *02 621 0576. Admission free. Daily 8:30am–5pm. No SkyTrain, subway, or ferry.*

❷ **Wat Sutat.** Situated across from the Giant Swing (see p 54, bullet ❸) in the Old City, this temple is one of Bangkok's oldest. It is built in traditional Rattanakosin (Bangkok) style, with a high roof

Flags flutter atop Wat Saket, also known as the Golden Mount.

A line up of golden Buddhas await the faithful at Wat Sutat.

and pointed finials. On the east gable you'll see a representation of the god of the sun, while the west gable sports the god of the moon. *146 Bamrung Muang Rd, Phra Nakorn. ☎ 02 2221 4026. Admission 20 baht. Daily 8:30am–9pm. No SkyTrain or subway. Nearest ferry: Tha Tien pier (N8).*

❸ **Wat Ratchabophit.** If you have visited several Thai temples already, you will quickly notice the difference in style at Wat Ratchabophit. The main buildings are linked by a circular courtyard—probably a Chinese design. The exterior of the temple is glazed with handpainted tiles, which are definitely Thai, but then suddenly there rises a Gothic spire from one of the *chedis.* Architects might call it a cultural mishmash, but to me it's very appealing. *Fuang Nakorn Rd, Rattanakosin. Admission free. Daily 8am–5pm. Ferry: Tha Tien pier (N8).*

❹ **Wat Ratchapradit.** Built by King Mongkut (Rama IV), who was played by Yul Brynner in the Hollywood epic *The King and I*, this temple has certain Khmer architectural features, including the faces on the side towers, reminiscent of those found at the Bayon in Cambodia. Its white walls are decorated in mother-of-pearl and marble tiles and it certainly glistens in the sunlight. Wat Ratchapradit also has some beautiful murals. Look out for a painting of King Mongkut studying an eclipse through a telescope. *Cnr of Rachini Rd & Saranrom Royal Park, Rattanakosin. ☎ 02 223 8215. Admission free. Daily 8am–6pm. Ferry: Tha Tien pier (N8).*

❺ **Wat Mahathat.** Originally built to house a relic of the Buddha, Wat Mahathat is nowadays the headquarters of Thailand's largest monastic order and Vipassana meditation center. Classes in this

Carved soldiers guard the doors of Wat Ratchabophit.

meditation technique are held daily (see p 48, bullet ❶), often with English-language instruction. Fortune tellers often set up stalls inside the compound. Running along the northern wall outside the temple is the Amulet Market (see p 14, bullet ❹), where you can buy antique Buddha images and lucky charms. *Phra That Rd (near Sanam Luang), Rattanakosin.* ☎ *02 222 6011. Admission free. Daily 7am–5pm. Ferry: Tha Chang (N9).*

❻ **Wat Ratchanatdaram.** I find this Indian-style temple, with its 37 steel spires pointing to the sky, quite spectacular. It was built by King Rama III for his granddaughter in the 19th century. The large white temple is set in a compound with immaculate gardens and bonsai trees. You can easily find shade in one of the open-air *salas*. There's also a small Buddhist market in the compound where you can buy Hindu and Buddhist images and lucky charms. *Mahachai Rd, Phra Nakorn.* ☎ *02 224 8807. Admission free. Daily 8am–5pm. No SkyTrain or subway. Nearest ferry: Tha Tien pier (N8).*

❼ **Wat Bowon Niwet.** Founded in 1826, this temple also serves as a Buddhist university. At one time it was the traditional temple of members of the royal family when they entered monkhood. Nowadays you'll notice there are always foreign/western monks and many religious ceremonies are conducted in English. The temple contains murals depicting western life in the 19th century. In the compound you'll also find a pond full of giant turtles and catfish and an herbal medicine center. *248 Phra Sumen Rd, Banglamphu.* ☎ *02 281 2831. Admission free. Daily 8am–5pm. Ferry: Phra Arthit pier (N13).*

❽ **Wat Chana Songkhram.** This Buddhist temple from the Ayutthaya period was presented to a group of ethnic Mon monks by King Rama I. Inside the *ubosot* (ordination hall) you'll find a statue of King Taksin the Great, and there's an interesting motif of the Hindu god Vishnu mounted on the

The spires of Wat Ratchanatdaram are dazzling at sunset.

A stone sculpture of a Qing Dynasty Chinese nobleman stands in the courtyard of Wat Bowon Niwet.

bird Garuda. The temple monks are a happy bunch here and lay out market stalls to tempt tourists, no doubt due to the fact that the temple walkway provides a shortcut for foreign backpackers every day between Khao San Road and the river ferry pier. ***Chakrabongse Rd, Banglamphu.*** ☎ ***02 281 8244. Daily 8am–4pm. Admission free. Ferry: Phra Arthit pier (N13).***

❾ Wat Intara Wihan. Another temple of the Ayutthaya era, Wat Intara Wihan is famous for its 32m-high image of the Buddha standing on a lotus leaf and holding an alms bowl, known as *Luangpor Toh*. This amazing statue took 60 years to build. It was commissioned by Rama IV in 1867, but not finished until the reign of Rama VII. The image was constructed of brick and stucco and decorated in glass mosaics and 24-carat gold. The temple draws crowds in early March when, for 10 days, it hosts a festival to honor Luangpor Toh. ***114 Wisutkasat Rd, Bangkhunphrom.*** ☎ ***02 628 5550 2. Daily 8:30am–8pm. Admission free. Ferry: Thewet pier (N15).***

❿ Wat Benchamabophit. (The Marble Temple or simply Wat Ben.) I always feel like I'm in a theme park when I come here. Not because there's anything false or tacky about the Marble Temple—it's simply so picturesque I wonder if it's real. Commissioned by King Chulalongkorn in 1899, it is built of fine Italian white marble, which can be blinding on a sunny day. Unusually for a Thai temple, it features stained glass windows. You can also find a large bodhi tree—representing the spot where the Buddha attained enlightenment—brought in from Bodgaya in India. ***69 Rama V Rd, Dusit. Admission free. Daily 6am–5pm. No subway or ferry. Nearest BTS SkyTrain station: Phaya Thai then a taxi.***

⓫ Wat Traimit. Visitors both local and foreign flock here to see the outstanding 3m-high Golden Buddha image. It is the largest solid-gold Buddha in the world, weighing some five tons, worth in the region of US$14 million, and is one of the country's greatest treasures. The image is over 700 years old, but it was not until 1957 that it was rediscovered. It had been encased in plaster—probably to hide it from Burmese invaders when it was smuggled out of Sukhothai. It was not until it was dropped by a crane while being moved that its golden majesty was uncovered. Within the compound, you can find some strange electronic fortune-telling machines, too, with prophesies in English, Thai and Chinese. ***Cnr Mittaphap Thai-China & Yaowarat rds, Chinatown.*** ☎ ***02 222 9775. Admission 20 baht Daily 8am–5pm. MRT subway: Hua Lamphong.***

The splendid exterior of Wat Traimit.

⓬ Wat Prayura Wongsawat. Built in the style of the old Thai capital, Ayutthaya, Wat Prayura-wongsawat (or Wat Prayoon) has a towering white *chedi* that many people pass every day by river, but few take the time to visit. The temple has two curiosities. The first is a huge mound built in the center of the compound that apparently represents the shape King Rama III witnessed when he watched a candle melting one night. Nowadays it is covered in shrines. The other interesting sight is the pond, or moat around the *chedi*, which is filled with turtles that feed on papaya. Strange, but true. *Thetsaban Sai 1, Thonburi. ☎ 02 465 0439. Admission free. Daily 8am–8pm. Ferry: Memorial Bridge pier (N6) & walk across the bridge.*

⓭ Wat Rakhang. Built during the Ayutthaya period (1677–1767), Wat Rakhang was declared a royal temple by King Taksin when he established his capital at Thonburi. While the temple was being renovated in the late 18th century, a brass bell was unearthed. King Rama I found the bell so melodious he had it moved to Wat Phra Kaeo (see p 11, bullet ❸) and five bells were given to Thonburi in exchange. 'Rakhang' means 'bells', and today a small belltower houses the five brass bells in the garden. I think the most interesting building is a small red house amongst the trees in the garden which used to be the home of King Rama I. Known as the *ho trai* (the library), the teak house is now a scripture hall with artifacts from the reign of King Rama I, as well as his interred ashes and a mural depicting the Thai epic, *The Ramakien*. *250 Arun Amorin Rd, Thonburi. ☎ 02 418 1079. Admission free. Daily 8am–5pm. Ferry: Tha Chang pier (N9).*

While it's not the biggest, Wat Rakhang's Buddha image has a symmetry and serenity to it that's quite striking.

Bangkok for Kids

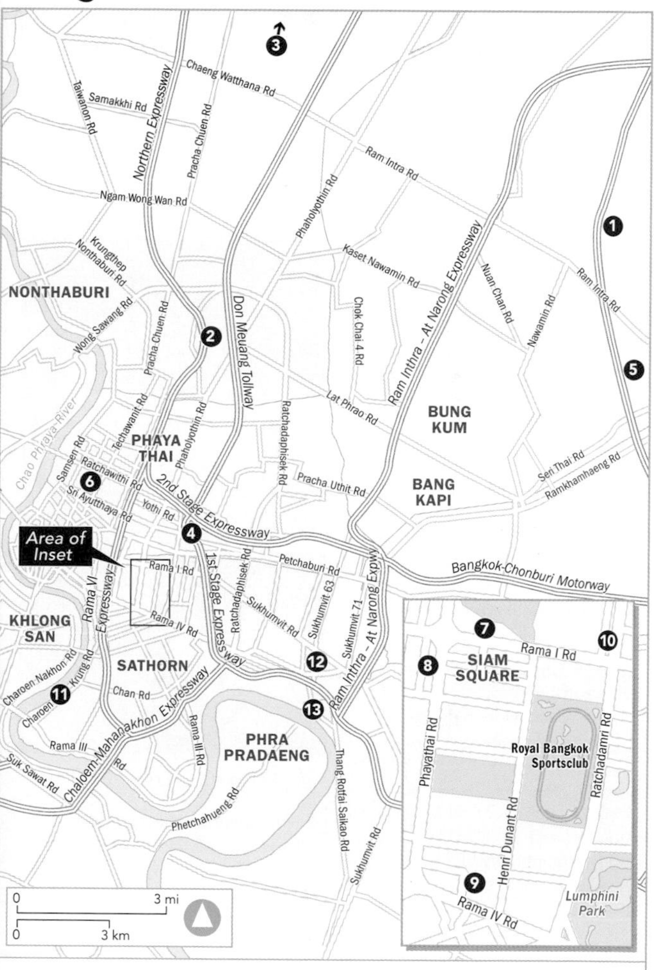

1 Safari World
2 Children's Discovery Museum
3 Dream World
4 Bangkok Dolls Museum
5 Siam Park City
6 Dusit Zoo
7 Siam Ocean World
8 Kim Bowl
9 Snake Farm
10 Bangkok TK Park
11 Joe Louis Puppet Theatre
12 Bangkok Planetarium & Science Museum
13 Combat Zone Paintball

Bangkok used to be a tough city with children—it's often hot and crowded, and most of the attractions involve walking around Buddhist temples and historical landmarks. However, in recent years Bangkok has exploded with family-friendly activities and now has some great zoos, safari parks, water parks, fun fairs and theme parks, most of which are in the suburbs and which operate all year round. Shopping malls usually provide some entertainment activities (see p 67) and there are seaside resorts within a few hours' drive that are safe for swimming (see p 145). **START: Catch a taxi or a tuktuk to Safari World.**

1 ★ Safari World. Very commercial in a theme-park kind of way, so kids love it! There's no end to the entertainment—jungle cruises, aquariums, dolphin shows, Hollywood cowboy movie shows, sea lion performances, crocodile wrestling, and much more. A full day out for all the family. *99 Payaintra Rd, Samwatawantok, Klongsamwa. ☎ 02 9144 1001 9. www.safariworld.com. Admission (for both Safari & Marine parks) 1,200 baht adults, 900 baht kids. Daily 9am–5pm. No SkyTrain, subway, or ferry.*

The dolphin show at Safari World.

2 ★★ Children's Discovery Museum. Fantastic for kids who love to touch everything! This is interactive education for youngsters—mostly aimed at the 5 to 10 age group—where skills are sharpened through practical experience. Kids can walk in Velcro feet, stand inside a giant bubble, test their reaction times with knobs and levers, and generally learn how various things work in a fun way. There are paints and pencils, books, puppet shows, and a toddler playground. The museum is located inside Queen Sirikit Park, which has pleasant botanical gardens, fountains, and lotus ponds, and is very close to Chatuchak Market (see p 25, bullet 1), so there should be enough variety to keep everyone happy for a day. *Queen Sirikit Park, Kamphaenphet Rd, Chatuchak. ☎ 02 615 7333 or 02 272 4745. Tues–Fri 9am–5pm, Sat & Sun 10am–6pm. Admission free. BTS SkyTrain: Mo Chit or MRT subway: Chatuchak Park.*

3 ★★ Dream World. Dream World is Bangkok's biggest theme park, with roller-coasters and fast rides, parades with cartoon characters and lots of teddy bears, train rides around models of the Great Wall of China and the Taj Mahal, water-park slides and a Hollywood action-movie film set. All in all, it's similar to Siam Park, but oriented

Your kids will love the roller coasters at Dream World.

towards younger children. There are ice-cream parlors, restaurants and a host of booths around the park. It's situated outside the city; you should call ahead to organize packages, which include transfers from your hotel, lunch, and all the rides in the price. Otherwise, a taxi is the best alternative. *62 Moo 1, Rangsit-Ongka Rak Rd, Km 7, Thanyaburi, Pathumthani. ☎ 02 533 1152. www.dreamworld.co.th. Admission 450 baht, kids under 90cm (35 in) free; package with transfers from 1,200 baht. Mon–Fri 10am–5pm, Sat & Sun 10am–7pm. Bus: 538 from Victory Monument/Don Mueang Bus Terminal.*

❹ Bangkok Dolls Museum. Founded in 1957, with some exquisite handcrafted pieces, this is a doll factory, a museum and a retail shop rolled into one. It also has a short history of dolls and some collectors' items. *85 Soi Ratchataphan, Ratchataphan Rd, Pratunam. ☎ 02 245 3008. www.bangkokdolls.com. Admission free. Tue–Sun 8am–5pm. BTS SkyTrain: Victory Monument, plus a 1km walk.*

❺ ★★★ Siam Park City. This is Bangkok's best and most over-the-top amusement center and all-in-one theme park. What better way to cool down on a sweltering day than to get out of Bangkok and kick back at a water park? And when the kids finally get tired of sliding down the flumes, there's an amusement park, a botanical garden, an aviary, a zoo, a safari park, and a *Jurassic Park* theme park to choose from. For me, though, it's the water park that is the highlight, despite the screaming and shouting of a thousand kids. Check the website first for the best deals. If you only want to visit the water park, prices are 200 baht (adults) and 100 baht (children), then you have a pay-per-ride system. For those who want to make a full day of it, you can buy combination tickets (350 to 1000 baht), which include most, if not all, attractions. *203 Suan Siam Rd, Kanna Yaow, Min Buri. ☎ 029197200. www.siamparkcity.com. Admission 1,000 baht adults, 900 baht kids, family ticket 3,000 baht. Daily 10am–6pm. No SkyTrain, subway, or ferry.*

❻ ★★ Dusit Zoo. Thailand's top zoo has more than 300 species of animals, including rhinos, elephants, hippos, tapirs, gibbons, lions, tigers, crocodiles, and exotic birds. There are lots of lakes, which have pedalos and shaded places to sit and eat. It's very busy on weekends, so avoid it on Saturdays and Sundays if you can. *Ratchawithi Rd*

Visitors can feed the goats at Dusit Zoo.

(cnr Rama V Rd). ☎ 02 281 2000. www.dusitzoo.org. Admission 150 baht adults, 70 baht kids. Daily 8am–6pm. Ferry: Thewet pier (N15), plus a 1km walk.

7 ★ Siam Ocean World. Situated in the basement of the chic shopping mall Siam Paragon (see p 26, bullet 4), this huge neon-lit aquarium is a surprise. Siam Ocean World is an easily accessible attraction that's very popular on weekends. Sharks, exotic fish, penguins, rays, and otters abide down here. The show mainly entails feeding sessions, including shark feedings at 1pm and 4pm, but there's almost always something extra for young children, such as a "magic mermaid" show. The only distasteful part for me is that foreigners have to pay two to three times the admission fee. *Floor B1–B2, Siam Paragon, Siam Square, 991 Rama I Rd, Pathumwan. ☎ 02 687 2000. www.siamoceanworld.co.th. Admission foreigners 990 baht adults, 790 baht kids. Discounts for advance online bookings. Daily 9am–10pm. BTS SkyTrain: Siam.*

8 ★ Kim Bowl. Almost every shopping mall has 10-pin bowling on its top floor alongside video game machines and karaoke booths. Kim Bowl is my favorite

You don't usually find sharks at the mall, but you do at Siam Ocean World, which is set in the basement of the popular Siam Paragon.

because it's always like a party—there's food and drink, flashing lights, loud pop music, and 28 bowling lanes. Open 'til late and bags of fun! *7th floor, Mah Boon Krong Center, 444 Phayathai Rd, Pathumwan. ☎ 02 611 7171 4. Admission 70–90 baht. Sun–Thurs 10am–1am, Fri–Sat 10am–2am. BTS SkyTrain: National Stadium.*

❾ **Snake farm.** Thailand has more snakes per square mile than any other country—they are a common sight outside the cities. And believe me, if you ever find a snake coiled up inside your toilet, you'll never sit down without thoroughly checking under the rim again! Known officially as the Queen Saovabha Memorial Institute, the snake farm was opened in 1923 by this queen as an arm of the Thai Red Cross. Why? Because the institute specialized in the production of anti-venom. You can watch the snakes being 'milked' of venom and listen to a video explaining the institute's progress. That's where the education stops and the horror begins for the squeamish—after that, it's watching snakes being fed rats and other small animals, and a chance to get a photo with a giant python draped around your neck. *1871 Rama IV Rd, Lumphini. ☎ 02 252 0161. www.saovabha.com. Admission 200 baht adults, 50 baht kids. Weekdays: venom extraction, 11am, snake handling and photos with tame snake, 2:30pm. Weekends: snake handling and photos with tame snake, 11am. BTS SkyTrain: Sala Daeng or MRT Subway: Silom.*

⓫ **Bangkok TK Park.** A chance for your kids to get to know Thai children while you dredge the designer stores of CentralWorld mall (see p 74). "TK" stands for "Thailand Knowledge," and the center is half babysitting and half educational. There are lots of spatial awareness games for toddlers, with books, paints, and a play area for children. The activities mainly center around computers, video games, and new innovations, with general attractions for 10- to 13-year-olds. It's a smart, colorful, safe, supervised fun park for your children. *8th floor, CentralWorld, Rajdamri Rd, Pathumwan. ☎ 02 257 4300. Admission 20 baht. Tues–Sun 10am–8pm. BTS SkyTrain: Chit Lom.*

⓬ ★ **Joe Louis Puppet Theatre.** This is not Punch 'n' Judy—it's more of a cultural performance. Every night you can see a reenactment of the Hindu classic *Ramayana* featuring beautifully hand-carved puppets. *Asiatique: The Riverfront, S13 2194 Charoenkrung Road ☎ 02 688 3322. www.joelouistheatre.com. Free shuttle boat from pier at BTS SkyTrain station, Saphan Thaksin.*

⓭ **Bangkok Planetarium & Science Museum.** Currently not very high-tech, it has ambitions to become so. The planetarium offers visitors exhibits and shows in natural science, technology, the human body, astrology, astronomy, and, of course, outer space. The center is very popular with high school groups and certain times of the day are reserved for students. Check the website before you go. *928 Sukhumvit Rd (next to Ekkamai Bus Terminal). ☎ 02 391 0544. www.sciplanet.org. Admission30 baht. Tues–Sun 9am–4:30pm. BTS SkyTrain: Ekkamai.*

⓮ **Combat Zone Paintball.** For adventurous types ages 7 and older, this is Bangkok's premier paintball field and it's easy to get to. Book in advance; it's busy on weekends. *Two locations, Nawamin Rd and Srinakarin Rd, ☎ 02 748 0238. www.combatzone62.net. Admission 450 baht. Daily Mon–Fri 10am–midnight, Sat–Sun noon–midnight. BTS SkyTrain: Udom Suk station, then a taxi.*

Mind, Body & Soul

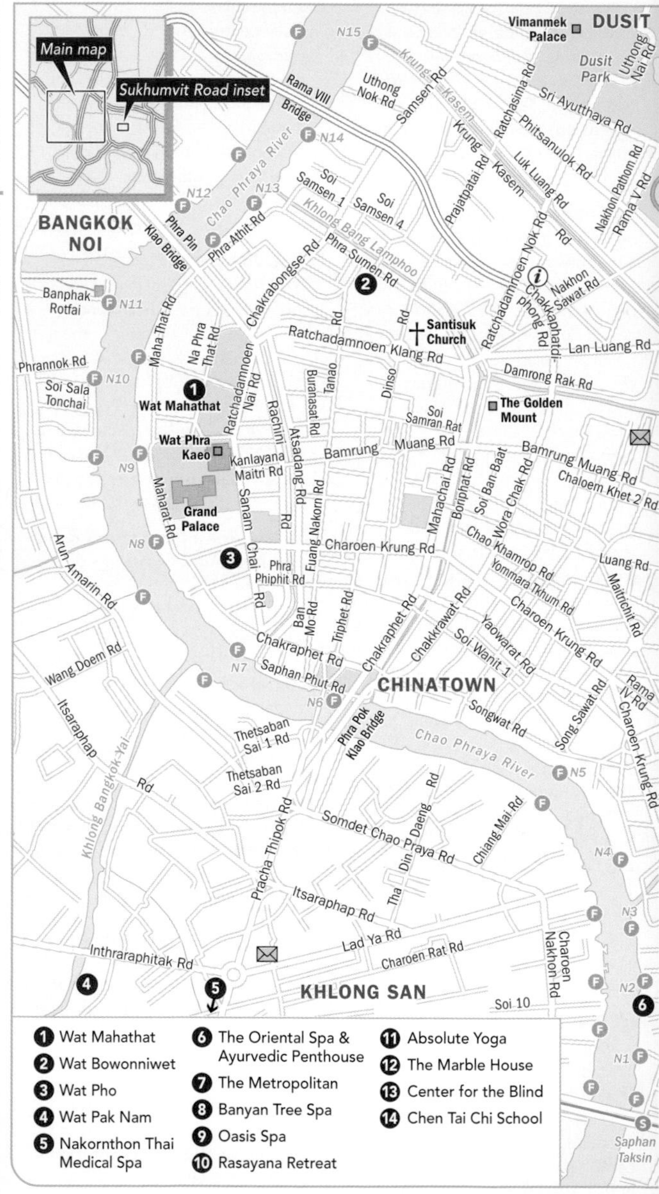

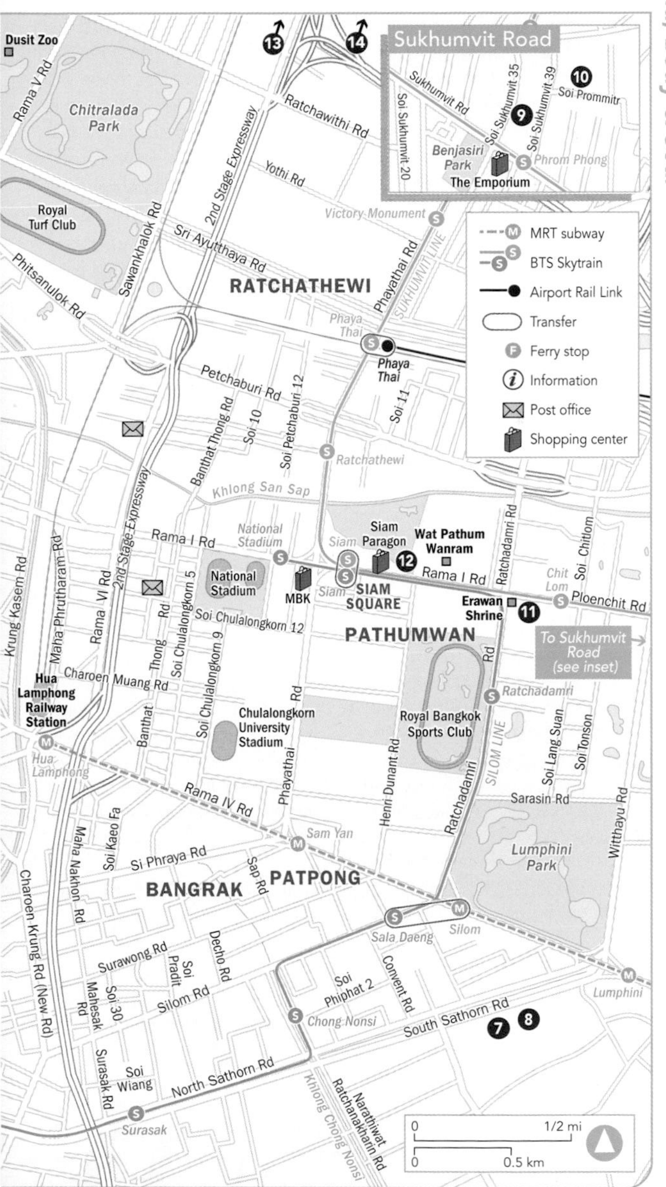

Sukhumvit Road
Dusit Zoo
Chitralada Park
Royal Turf Club
RATCHATHEWI
PATHUMWAN
SIAM SQUARE
BANGRAK
PATPONG
National Stadium
MBK
Siam Paragon
Wat Pathum Wanram
Erawan Shrine
Hua Lamphong Railway Station
Chulalongkorn University Stadium
Royal Bangkok Sports Club
Lumphini Park
Benjasiri Park
The Emporium
Phrom Phong
Victory Monument
Phaya Thai
Ratchathewi
Siam
Chit Lom
Ratchadamri
Sam Yan
Silom
Sala Daeng
Chong Nonsi
Surasak
Lumphini
Hua Lamphong
To Sukhumvit Road (see inset)
MRT subway
BTS Skytrain
Airport Rail Link
Transfer
Ferry stop
Information
Post office
Shopping center
0 1/2 mi
0 0.5 km

Thai culture is alive with holistic treatments and methods of relaxation for your mind, body, and soul. Of course, Thai massage is famous all over the world and the country has enjoyed a boom in recent years in spas and resorts offering full-body cleansing and pampering so good you'll think you're melting. For those with physical ailments, you might feel the time has come to try alternative medicines such as Chinese remedies, herbal solutions, or acupuncture. And for your troubled soul, where else would you turn to but a Thai meditation center? START: **Tha Phra Chan ferry stop.**

❶ ★ **Wat Mahathat.** Vipassana Meditation involves sitting silently in the Buddha position and following your breath coming in through your nostrils, traveling down to your stomach, and then leaving the body. It is the main practice employed by Buddhist monks for cleansing the mind. As the center of the Mahanikai school of Buddhism in Bangkok, this historical temple (see p 37, bullet ❺) is a serious place to take group classes in meditation, which are taught by English-speaking monks. You can sleep at the temple in humble dormitories or go in every day. *Mahathat Rd (near Sanam Luang), Rattanakosin. ☎ 02 222 6011. Courses free. Daily 7–10am, 1–4pm & 6–8:30pm. Ferry: Tha Chang pier.*

❷ **Wat Bowonniwet.** Established as a Buddhist university in 1826, this temple allows visiting foreigners to meditate, but does not provide courses. Within the grounds there is a picturesque pond teeming with turtles and catfish, as well as an herbal medicine center. *248 Phra Sumen Rd, Banglamphu. ☎ 02281 2831. Admission free. Daily 5am–8pm. Ferry: Phra Arthit pier (N13).*

❸ ★★★ **Wat Pho.** Thailand's most renowned center of Thai massage has a well-earned reputation spanning a great many years. Many of the top masseurs and masseuses in the country learn the craft at this massage school. Visitors to Wat Pho can try a traditional Thai massage for 300 baht per hour, a foot massage for 250 baht per hour or (I recommend) an Ayurvedic massage with hot herbs ground into your body for 500 baht per hour. This will be one of the most therapeutic events of your life. *Sanam Chai Rd, Rattanakosin. ☎ 02 226 0335 (temple) or 02 662 3533 (massage*

The renowned massage school at Wat Pho.

school). www.watpho.com and www.watpomassage.com. Daily 8am–5pm. Ferry: Tha Tien pier (N8).

❹ **Wat Pak Nam.** Perhaps it's better if you have practiced meditation before or can speak some Thai, because you listen to Buddhist sermons in Thai language as you practice at this temple. The meditation technique taught here is recorded in an English book, *Samma Samadhi*, and involves high levels of concentration, which teachers say will allow you "to develop penetrating insight." Not for the casual passerby. *Therdthai Rd, Phasi Charoen, Thonburi. ☎ 02 467 0811. www.watpaknam.org. Sermons: Mon–Fri 8am & 6pm; Sat & Sun 8am, 10am, 1pm & 6pm. No metro or ferry.*

❺ **Nakornthon Thai Medical Spa.** As opposed to luxury and relaxation, this medical spa concentrates more on wellness and is popular with elderly visitors. Traditional acupressure massage and herbal scrubs are the norm and the friendly staff also like to recommend herbs/diets for your benefit. It's also much cheaper than hotel spas. *12th floor, Nakornthon Hospital, 1 Soi Rama II Soi 56, Samaedum Bangkhunthain. ☎ 02 450 9999. www.nakornthonhospital.com. No metro or ferry.*

❻ **★★ The Oriental Spa & Ayurvedic Penthouse.** All the herbal oils, furnishings, techniques, and even most of the staff come from India at this chic and refined resort spa. Employing the holistic Ayurvedic practice of massaging and treating the whole body at once, this place assures a genuinely regal experience. You will carry the scents of amber, myrrh, marjoram, and nutmeg on your purified skin for weeks. *Mandarin Oriental Hotel, 48 Oriental Rd, Bangrak. ☎ 02 659 9000, ext 7440. www.mandarinoriental.com. Daily 9am–8:30pm. BTS Skytrain station: Saphan Taksin.*

Thai Massage at the Oriental Spa.

❼ **The Metropolitan.** This is a stylish, minimalist hotel that prides itself on health and holism—and not only in its organic, low-calorie restaurants, like Glow (p 98). It also includes accessories and activities such as spas, yoga, and meditation to protect your body and soul. *27 South Sathorn Rd. ☎ 02 625 3333. www.comohotels.com/metropolitanbangkok. 171 units. Doubles 10850 baht. AE, DC, MC, V. BTS SkyTrain: Chong Nonsi, MRT subway: Lumphini.*

❽ **Banyan Tree Spa.** An exquisite spa with views over Bangkok's business district, the Banyan Tree offers scrubs, beauty treatments and a choice of Thai, Swedish, or Balinese massage. The hotel (see p 137) also offers spa packages and in-room services for those who just can't get enough pampering. *21st floor, Banyan Tree Hotel, 21/100 South Sathorn Rd. ☎ 02 679 1052 4. www.banyantreespa.com. BTS SkyTrain: Sala Daeng or MRT subway: Lumphini.*

❾ **★ Oasis Spa.** This award-winning spa is renowned for elegance, graceful service, and the most soothing of treatments. Full- and half-day packages include oil massage, wrap, body scrub, facial, and hydrotherapy. You're sure to leave glowing. *Sub-soi 4, 64 Soi 31 (Soi Sawadee), Sukhumvit Rd, Phrakanong. ☎ 02 262 2122.*

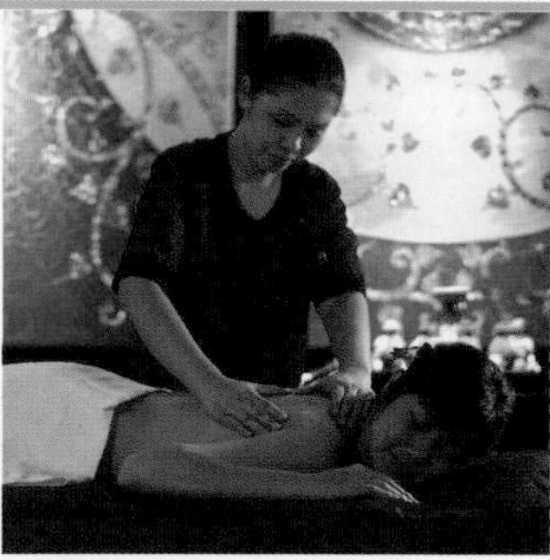

A masseuse at the Banyan Tree Spa.

www.oasisspa.net. Daily 10am–10pm. BTS SkyTrain: Phrom Phong.

⑩ ★★ **Rasayana Retreat.** Check in for a full day's cleansing with detox, colonic irrigation, therapeutic massage, salt baths, saunas, acupuncture, and even hypnotherapy. Very good value and highly recommended for those of us who eat, drink, and smoke too much or are stressed, sedentary, or suffer from insomnia. *57 Soi Prommitr, Sukhumvit Rd Soi 39, Wattana. ☎ 02 662 4803 5. www.rasayanaretreat.com. BTS SkyTrain: Phrom Phong.*

⑪ **Absolute Yoga.** Visitors can join in a session at any of the six Absolute studios in the city. Be aware that many Thais are very flexible, so even what is deemed a beginners class may be a high level. Daily classes in Bikram, Hatha, Pilates, and more. *4th floor, Amarin Plaza (access directly from Chit Lom BTS), Ploenchit Rd, Pathumwan. ☎ 02 252 4400. www.absoluteyogabangkok.com. Daily 7am–9:15pm. BTS SkyTrain: Chit Lom.*

⑫ ★★ **The Marble House.** Many of my friends in Bangkok come here every week, because it is no-frills but exotic, and professional but inexpensive. A full-body massage—from toenails to the tips of your hair—costs just 250 baht per hour. Oil massage, foot reflexology, and Ayurvedic massage cost a little more. Some of the masseuses might be half your height, but they're surprisingly strong and will stretch you into shape in no time. 488/1-2 Soi Siam Square 6 *(opp. Novotel Hotel), Rama I Rd, Pathumwan. ☎ 02 658 4124 5. Daily 9am–midnight. Metro: Siam.*

⑬ ★★ **Center for the Blind.** An excellent massage—and so much more. This is a half-day trip and a chance to get out of the city by river and meet blind people in a work environment—Thai massage being just one of their activities. In fact, traditionally in Thailand, many blind people become massage therapists—and darn good ones too. Many at the Center are old but strong as oxen and will really grind their thumbs and elbows into you. *78/1 Moo 1, Thiwanon Rd, Pak Kret, Nonthaburi. ☎ 02 583 7327. 120–160 baht for 1½ hr massage, 100 baht sauna (Sun only). Ferry: Express boat to Nonthaburi (N30) or boat to Pak Kret pier plus a 10-min taxi ride.*

⑭ **Chen Tai Chi School.** Although you can join in this graceful martial art for free any morning at Lumphini Park (see p 10, bullet ❶), it pays to learn the technique from professionals. English-language classes are available at Chen with special short-term courses for visitors. *Piyavan Tower, next to Ari BTS station. ☎ 086 014 4050. www.chentaichithailand.com. BTS SkyTrain: Ari.*

Masks used in a dance version of the epic poem and religious text the Ramayana.

3 The Best Neighborhood Tours

The Old City

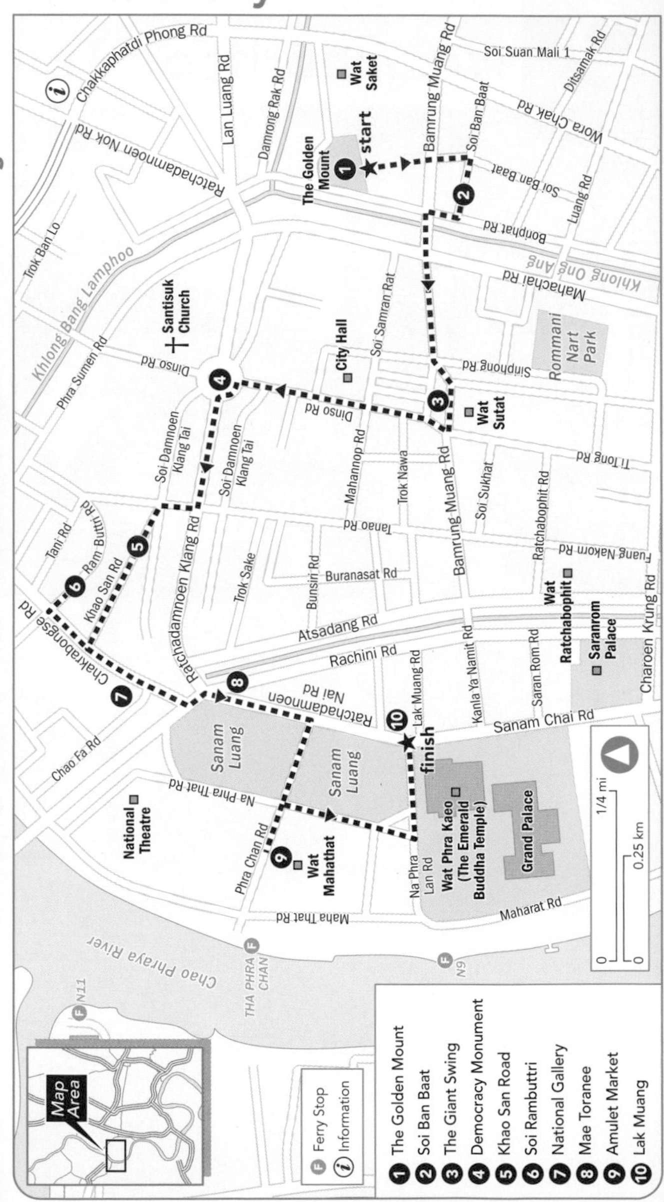

Previous page: Worshippers pray at the Lak Muang Shrine.

Bangkok's "Old City" is in so many ways the heart of Thailand. It is the historical soul of Siam and home of the country's kings of yesteryear. The "island" of Rattanakosin also hosts Thailand's national museum, art gallery, and several government ministries. King Rama I established Phra Nakorn as the Thai capital in 1782 and founded his palace on the artificial island of Rattanakosin—bordered to the west by the Chao Phraya River and to the east by the Khlong Lord canal. This walk allows you to witness firsthand the sites that gave birth to Bangkok in the 18th century and the national treasures that all Thais hold dear. START: **Taxi to the Golden Mount or canal boat to Phanfa and 5-minute walk.**

❶ ★★★ The Golden Mount. This magnificent Buddhist temple is built on an artificial hill and is one of the only vantage points from which to enjoy a panoramic view of the Old City, because of a strict ban on high-rise buildings in the area. A gradual, spiraling climb of 320 stairs takes you past small graves, Buddhist shrines, a tidy forest with a waterfall, and wild frangipani to the top. The original *chedi* collapsed long ago and the newer, larger golden dome you see today was commissioned by King Rama III, though it was not completed until the reign of King Rama V. In 1877, Rama V transferred a relic of the Buddha from the Grand Palace to Wat Saket, the temple just behind the Golden Mount. It was later enshrined in the pagoda at the top of the hill. Two decades later the British viceroy of India presented the Siamese king with more bones of the Buddha, which joined the original relic inside the Golden Mount. ⏲ *30 min; go weekdays as early as possible. 344 Chakkraphatdiphong Rd (off Boriphat Rd).* ☎ *02 621 0576. Admission free. Daily 8:30am–5pm. No SkyTrain, subway, or ferry.*

❷ ★★ Soi Ban Baat. Literally "Monks Bowl Village Lane," this street is where the traditional artisans of *baat*—Buddhist monks' alms bowls—have lived for two centuries. You can watch the *baat*-smiths at work, hammering out metal bowls in their shops. Go at sunrise to see Buddhist monks collecting alms. ⏲ *30 min. Community headman's workshop: 71 Soi Ban Baat.* ☎ *02 221 4466. No metro or ferry.*

The Golden Mount towers over the surrounding neighborhood offer visitors spectacular views.

3 The Giant Swing. In the 18th century, the giant swing that stood here was the focal point of a Brahmin festival, where volunteers would swing back and forth trying to snatch a bag of coins with their teeth. Competitors frequently fell and often died, and this pre-Olympic event was outlawed in the 1930s. Now there's just a timber frame to remind us. *In front of Wat Sutat, Bamrung Muang Rd (see p 36, bullet 2). No SkyTrain or subway. Nearest ferry: Tha Tien pier (N8).*

This giant swing was once the site of a life-and-death competition.

4 Democracy Monument. Designed by Italian sculptor Corrado Feroci and Thai architect Mew Aphaiwong in the 1930s, this monument became the rallying point for pro-democracy supporters in 1992 before the army suppressed the uprising and shot dead over 100 protesters. Some 250m west on this wide avenue is the October 14 Monument, which honors the victims of the 1973 mass uprising. *Ratchadamnoen Klang Rd. No metro or ferry.*

5 ★★★ Khao San Road. In the '60s and '70s, western hippies and travelers came to Thailand curious to see its culture. Khao San Road became a backpackers' Mecca and, ironically, curious locals started coming to this street just to see the strange tourists and their culture of walking around barefoot and stoned, dressed in sarongs, bikinis and tie-dye vests. Every 5 yards or so, another hostel, diner, cafe or bar blasts out music or videos—or both. It's like a scene from Dante's *Inferno*. Yet, Khao San Road's vibe is strangely infectious. It has that center-of-the-world ambience and you get the sense that anything could happen. It's often seedy and illicit, but in recent years has become

This powerful modern monument, a symbol of Democracy, is often the meeting place for political demonstrations.

Khao San Road is the Thai version of Times Square, Picadilly Circus, and the Las Vegas Strip all rolled into one.

popular with hip young Thais for its effervescent nightlife and air of reckless abandon. The 400m walk along Khao San usually takes at least an hour, as you have to walk a gauntlet of vendors, beggars, con artists, travel agents, hairdressers, tattoo artists, dentists, cobblers, and jewelers. You can shop for cheap clothes, jewelry, and CDs, sit at a cafe and people-watch, or just have a drink and enjoy the Mardi Gras atmosphere. It's quiet in the mornings, becoming steadily busier and crazier as the day goes on. ⏲ *1 hr. Ferry: Phra Arthit pier (N13).*

6 **Soi Rambuttri.** Just around the corner from Khao San Road is the green and leafy Soi Rambuttri. This pleasant street offers an array of cheap and cheerful street stalls where you can try a wide variety of local favorites such as spicy somtam papaya salad, grilled chicken and fish, and one dish wonders like pad Thai. Try grilled sticky rice and banana wrapped in a banana leaf for dessert. Delicious. You will also find laidback cafes and restaurants, along with book shops and clothing stalls, so save time for a little after lunch browsing. *Daily 24 hr. Ferry: Phra Arthit pier (N13).*

7 ★ **National Gallery.** Contemporary Thai art housed in an old colonial building. The tranquil ambience and air-conditioning offer blissful respite from the heat. *See p 21, bullet 5.*

8 **Mae Toranee.** Opposite the Royal Hotel is a small fountain dedicated to the Earth Goddess, whose statue sits inside the shrine washing her hair of evil spirits. *Opp Royal Hotel, Ratchadamnoen Ave. Ferry: Phra Arthit pier (N13).*

9 ★★★ **Amulet Market.** Throngs of religious devotees and the superstitious gather here to examine, discuss, and haggle for Buddhist amulets and lucky charms. *See p 14, bullet 4.*

10 **Lak Muang.** Just to the east of the Grand Palace is the site of a wooden pillar erected by King Rama I in 1782 to mark the founding of Bangkok and to protect the city. The shrine has great spiritual significance and you will see devotees making offerings or even hiring classical dancers to perform. The pillar also marks the center of the city, from which all mileages are taken. *Cnr Na Hap Phoei & Ratchadamnoen Nai rds. Admission free. Daily 6am–6pm. Ferry: Phra Arthit pier (N13).*

Chao Phraya River

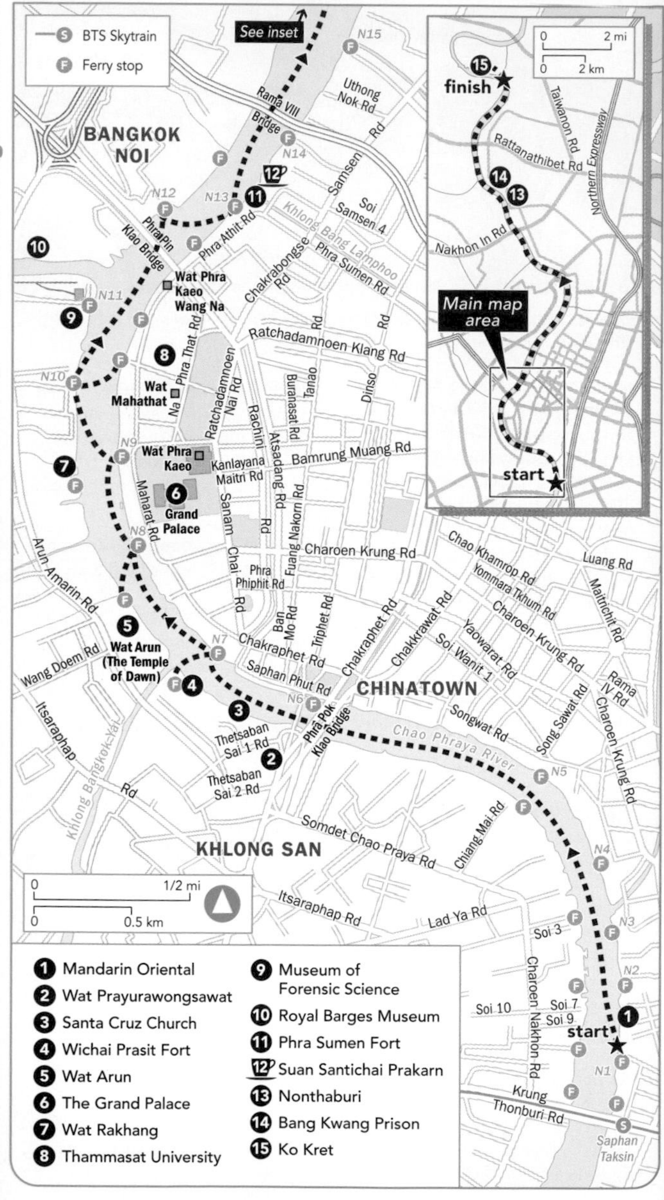

What a great way to see Bangkok! Avoid the traffic and the heat and catch the cool breeze as you skip along the Chao Phraya River, which runs from north to south and flows into the Gulf of Thailand. Much of Bangkok's history and many interesting sights lie along its banks. There's also a fantastic express boat service (see p 167), which allows you to jump on and off whenever you like. You just pay 15 baht for a ticket each time you jump on. Look out for the different colored flags on the boats which denote where they stop. There's also an official tourist boat with unlimited travel for 150 baht. **START: Metro to Saphan Taksin. Walk down to Sathorn ferry pier immediately below the metro station. You are on the east bank of the river and want express boats heading north. Buy a day pass or just pay as you go when you get on the boat. Note: Saphan Taksin is located immediately south (or just under) the bridge marked Krung Thonburi Road.**

❶ Mandarin Oriental. The first stop on the east bank is the world-famous Oriental Hotel. The colonial building is mostly shaded by palm trees, but you might catch a glimpse of the rich and famous dining on the hotel's riverfront terrace. On the opposite bank is the Royal Orchid Sheraton. Just after the Oriental, on your right, you pass the French and Portuguese embassies, the first foreign diplomatic residences in Thailand. As the river bends to the left you will see a six-story Chinese pagoda. *See p 142.*

❷ ★ Wat Prayura Wongsawat. As you pass under the first bridge, immediately on your left you'll see an impressive 60m-high white *chedi*. This temple has murals depicting the life of Buddha and its doors are decorated in mother-of-pearl. There's also a large pond where hundreds of turtles and fish swim. You can feed them—they like papaya! *See p 40, bullet ⓬.*

❸ ★ Santa Cruz Church. Just past the Memorial Bridge and opposite Pak Khlong flower market is the beige-and-pink Santa Cruz Church and convent with its octagonal dome on top. It was originally built in 1770 by Portuguese traders during the reign of King Taksin. The

The riverside terrace at the Mandarin Oriental is one of the most serene places in the city to relax and take in the views.

The dazzling white chedi of Wat Prayura Wonsawat.

present church was constructed in 1910 and has a beautiful Italian-style ceiling. Church services are held on Sundays. ⏱ *30 min. 112 Thetsaban Sai I Rd, Thonburi.* ☎ *02 466 0347 or 02 472 0153 4. Daily 5:30–8:30am & 6–8pm. Ferry: Rajinee pier (N7).*

❹ **Wichai Prasit Fort.** This was built during the reign of Narai the Great (1656–1688) to protect the city from Burmese invaders. One hundred years later, after repulsing the Burmese, King Taksin built the Wang Derm Palace in the same compound when he chose Thonburi (the town west of the river) as his capital. Nowadays the Thai navy fires the cannon from the fort to celebrate special ceremonies. It is the naval banner you can see on the flagpole on top of the fort. Wang Derm Palace is open to the public, but the fort is not. ⏱ *30 min. 2 Royal Navy Headquarters, Phra Ratcha Wang Derm, Arun Amarin Rd, Thonburi.* ☎ *02 475 4117 or 02 466 9355. Admission 50 baht. Daily 8:30am–5pm. Ferry: Rajinee pier (N7).*

❺ ★★★ **Wat Arun.** On the west bank, just north of the tall Wat Kanlayanamit temple, is my favorite temple in Thailand—the Temple of Dawn, known in Thai as Wat Arun. This Hindu-inspired Khmer stupa becomes very photogenic both at sunrise and at sunset when the stonework changes to a mauve or orange hue. *See p 15, bullet* ❼.

Travel Tip

You can get off the express boat and walk around ❷, ❸, ❹ and ❺ by changing at Rajinee pier (N7) and taking a small cross-river boat to Wat Arun for just 3.5 baht. It's an interesting walk south from Wat Arun, taking you through modest backstreets. You will first pass Wat Kanlayanamit with its 15m-high Buddha. Then, take the waterfront boardwalk towards Santa Cruz Church. Hidden from view from the river, there's a small red Chinese temple called Wat Sanjaomaeguanim. Built in the 18th century, it shares Buddhist, Taoist, and Confucianist influences. There are return boats to Rajinee from Wat Kanlayanamit pier.

Santa Cruz Church.

Wat Arun glows in the sunset.

6 ★★★ The Grand Palace. Just north of Wat Arun is Bangkok's oldest temple, Wat Pho (see p 48, bullet 3), across the river from Tha Tien ferry pier (N8). The following pier on the east bank is Tha Chang (N9), meaning "Elephant Pier," in reference to the days when flotillas of teak logs would be carried from the river to warehouses by the great tusked beasts. This is where to get off if you are visiting the Grand Palace. From the river you can get dazzling photographs of the golden spires, although much of the majesty is hidden behind a long white wall. On the west bank, you will see the imposing buildings of the Naval Harbour Department and the Quartermaster Department. *See p 11, bullet 3.*

7 Wat Rakhang. Sometimes called the Bell Temple for its collection of brass bells, this 18th-century *wat* houses an interesting teak library (where the ashes of King Rama I are interred) and murals depicting the Thai epic, "The Ramakien." *See p 40, bullet 13.*

8 Thammasat University. On the east bank of the river lies the historical area of Rattanakosin. There are several sights, but you need a separate day to take them in. If you were to jump off at Tha Chang pier, you could visit the National Gallery (see p 21, bullet 5), the Bangkok National Museum (see p 21, bullet 4), followed by Thammasat University, where many of the nation's elite were educated and which was the hub of political dissent in 1973 and 1976 when the army shot dead many students and protesters.

There are lots of photo ops at the Grand Palace.

Ready for a Detour?

Running off to the west is Klong Bangkok Noi, the "Small Bangkok Canal." This canal can be navigated as a detour of your Old City or Chao Phraya tour by renting a longtail boat (approximately 800 baht per hour—beware of attempts to grossly overcharge). It's a worthwhile trip. The canal winds its way in a 16km horseshoe around "Small Bangkok" and comes out again at Nonthaburi (⓭). You'll pass several fine Thai houses, some squalid suburban homes on stilts and lots of temples. It's a wonderful opportunity to witness firsthand the real lifestyles of average Bangkokians. You can rent longboats at Phra Arthit pier (N13) and sometimes at Tha Chang pier (N9).

2 Prachan Rd. ☎ 02 613 3333. Ferry: Tha Chang pier (N9) or change at Wang Lang pier (N10).

❾ Museum of Forensic Science. It's definitely not my cup of tea, but if you have a fascination for the macabre you might want to spend an hour or two studying pathology via the remains of accident victims and exhibits of human parts kept in formaldehyde, including non-separated Siamese twins. Not for the squeamish. *🕒 1 hr. Siriraj Hospital, Bangkok Noi. ☎ 02 419 7000. Admission free. Mon–Fri 8:30am–4:30pm. Ferry: Wang Lang pier (N10).*

❿ Royal Barges Museum. A chance to see Thailand's famous historical royal barges. Used in royal ceremonies since the 18th century, the 50m-long royal longtail boats have been housed here under the care of the Royal Navy since 1932. *See p 14, bullet ❻.*

⓫ ★ Phra Sumen Fort. One of the two remaining forts still standing in Bangkok, Phra Sumen was built in 1783 by King Rama I to protect the Old City. From the river you can see the battlements and cannons and an observation tower. The fort was established at the

An intricate detail on one of the royal barges.

The grounds of Phra Sumen Fort are a wonderful place for a picnic.

confluence of the river and Banglamphu Canal, which carves an arc around the Old City, exiting further south at Memorial Bridge. With the river to the west, this canal effectively makes Rattanakosin an island. *Cnr Phra Arthit & Phra Sumeru rds. Daily 8am–8pm. Ferry: Phra Arthit pier (N13).*

12 Suan Santichai Prakarn. This is a pleasant park to stretch your legs or relax and have a picnic. There are plenty of vendors around selling snacks and soft drinks. *Phra Arthit Rd. Ferry: Phra Arthit pier (N13). $.*

13 Nonthaburi. Next you go under the impressive Rama VIII Bridge (which looks like a giant golden harp lying on its side) and start heading northeast. You'll pass the Church of Holy Conception and St Francis Xavier Church, both further testaments to the prominent role of missionaries in 18th- and 19th-century Thailand. You'll notice that the river widens and becomes more industrial. You'll pass a jetty where old barges are moored, the Singha beer factory, and the Bang Kwang Chinese temple just before you pull into Nonthaburi Pier. Now you have to decide whether to carry on to 14 and 15 or call it a day. You can get taxis back to town from Nonthaburi Pier or just take another express boat heading south. *Ferry: Nonthaburi pier (N30).*

14 Bang Kwang Prison. The notorious "Bangkok Hilton" hosts hundreds of foreign inmates, usually incarcerated for drug offences. Read Australian prisoner Warren Fellows's "The Damage Done" for a chilling insight into prison life here. It is not uncommon for tourists to visit their compatriots and take them some food, toiletries, and magazines. *1 Nonthaburi Rd.* ☎ *02 525 0484. Mon–Fri 9:30–11:30am & 1:30–2:30pm. Ferry: Nonthaburi pier (N30).*

15 ★★★ Ko Kret. This enchanting little island on the river is home to hundreds of Mon—an ethnic group indigenous to Myanmar. Some islanders grow lychees and durian in large orchards on the southern part of Ko Kret. However, the most interesting and distinctive occupation of the Mon islanders is pottery-making. Perhaps 20 to 25 families maintain small factories where they sculpt red clay and fire earthenware in kilns, producing flowerpots, mortars, and larger water urns. The finished products have a red-black glaze; visitors are welcome to watch the potters and buy souvenirs. You can hire a bicycle here and ride around the island. *30 min. Ferry: Pak Kret pier (N33).*

Chinatown

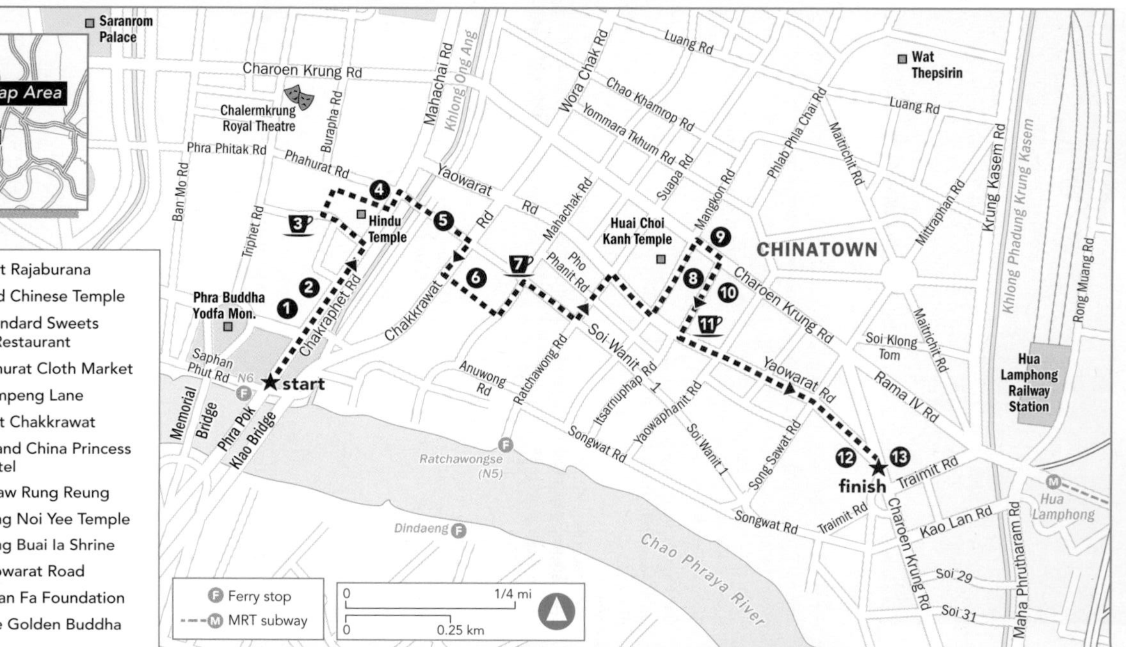
Saranrom Palace
Map Area
1 Wat Rajaburana
2 Red Chinese Temple
3 Standard Sweets & Restaurant
4 Pahurat Cloth Market
5 Sampeng Lane
6 Wat Chakkrawat
7 Grand China Princess Hotel
8 Chaw Rung Reung
9 Leng Noi Yee Temple
10 Leng Buai Ia Shrine
11 Yaowarat Road
12 Thian Fa Foundation
13 The Golden Buddha
Ferry stop
MRT subway
0 1/4 mi
0 0.25 km
Charoen Krung Rd
Chalermkrung Royal Theatre
Burapha Rd
Phra Phitak Rd
Phahurat Rd
Ban Mo Rd
Triphet Rd
Hindu Temple
Phra Buddha Yodfa Mon.
Saphan Phut Rd
N6
start
Memorial Bridge
Phra Pok Klao Bridge
Chakraphet Rd
Mahachai Rd
Khlong Ong Ang
Yaowarat Rd
Chakkrawat
Wora Chak Rd
Chao Khamrop Rd
Yommara Tkhum Rd
Suapa Rd
Mahachak Rd
Pho Phanit Rd
Huai Choi Kanh Temple
Mangkon Rd
Luang Rd
Phlab Phla Chai Rd
Maitrichit Rd
Wat Thepsirin
Mittraphan Rd
Krung Kasem Rd
Khlong Phadung Krung Kasem
Rong Muang Rd
CHINATOWN
Charoen Krung Rd
Anuwong Rd
Ratchawong Rd
Soi Wanit Rd 1
Itsarnuphap Rd
Yaowaphanit Rd
Soi Wanit 1
Song Sawat Rd
Songwat Rd
Ratchawongse (N5)
Dindaeng
Yaowarat Rd
Soi Klong Tom
Rama IV Rd
Hua Lamphong Railway Station
finish
Traimit Rd
Hua Lamphong
Kao Lan Rd
Maha Phrutharam Rd
Soi 29
Soi 31
Chao Phraya River

This 3- to 4-hour walk will take you on an adventure into the heart of Bangkok's Chinatown. It's where two great cultures, Chinese and Indian, meet in harmony with an explosion of colors, smells, and sights. Stroll through the bustling backstreets into the mystic temples and hidden shrines, and experience the lively banter of the marketplaces. Nothing here is polished for the tourist's benefit. I hope this walk will give you an insight into the real people of Bangkok, their rituals, idiosyncrasies, and hard-working lifestyles. **START: Express boat to Memorial Bridge pier (Saphan Phut).**

❶ **Wat Rajaburana.** This large, imposing Buddhist temple was built during the Ayutthaya period (1677–1767) by a Chinese merchant. I think it's a good introduction to temples, because the architectural style is typical of Bangkok Buddhist temples, with a high green roof accompanied by curved golden finials shaped like mythical *naga* serpents. On the east face under the awnings, you can see an intricate gilded facade guarded by three angels with a three-headed elephant known as Erawan, the Mount of Indra. *15 min. Cnr Triphet & Chakkraphet rds. Daily 5am–8pm.*

❷ **Red Chinese Temple.** You'll immediately notice the difference between a Thai temple and this typical Chinese shrine—*wat san chao,* as locals say. This temple represents the three main religions of China: Taoism, Buddhism, and Confucianism. *15 min. Chakkraphet Rd. Daily 6am–8pm.*

❸ **Standard Sweets & Restaurant.** Turn left 100m after the temple into a nice street lined with Indian shops selling spices, religious offerings, shawls and Indian foods. A simple diner sits next to another small red temple. It sells soft drinks, coffee, Indian masala tea, and Indian sweets such as *gulab jaman. Soi Pahurat, 95/46–47 Chakkraphet Rd. 086 708 1375. Daily 7am–7pm. $.*

Colorful cloth for sale at the Pahurat Market.

❹ ★ **Pahurat Cloth Market.** Walk past the Sikh temple, Siri Guru Singh Sabha, and you find that you are in the middle of "Little India." Turn right and follow the narrow lane of vendors selling everything from satin saris and made-to-measure suits to Indian spices and Ayurvedic cures. *15 min. Cnr Pahurat & Chakraphet rds. Daily 5am–9pm.*

❺ ★★ **Sampeng Lane.** (Also known as Soi Wanit.) The alleyway narrows and pedestrian traffic is slow and labored as you squish and squeeze your way past shops and stalls that sell sweets, dried fruit, cheap jewelery, gold, gems, clothes, toys, steaming *dim sum*, and much more. It's a kaleidoscope of chaos and a feast for the senses. ⌚ *30 min. Daily 6am–9pm.*

6 ★ kids Wat Chakkrawat. Take a breather from the claustrophobic market and step into the compound of this simple temple. There's a fenced pond behind the temple with two huge crocodiles, plus a stuffed one in a glass case! ⌚ *15 min. Wanit Rd. Daily 5am–7pm.*

7 ★★ Grand China Princess Hotel. After jostling your way through Sampeng Lane you surely deserve a break. Take the lift to the 25th floor of this hotel and you can sit in an air-conditioned restaurant that offers a magnificent 360-degree view of Bangkok. There are several hotels and rooftop restaurants higher than this, but the fact that you can see the Grand Palace and the Golden Mount from here makes this, in my opinion, the best view you can get of the city. The restaurant starts revolving at 6pm. The menu mainly offers Japanese, Chinese and seafood dishes. *215 Yaowarat Rd, Samphantawong.* ☎ *02 224 9977. Mon–Sat 11am– midnight, Sun 5pm–midnight. $$.*

8 Chaw Rung Reung. On the right side of Mongkol Road you pass some open-front stores selling foods and spices. Look for one with large sacks of tea outside. There's green, jasmine, masala, and many other authentic and aromatic teas. You can buy them by the half kilo. ⌚ *15 min. 609–611*

The otherwise plain temple of Wat Chakkrawat has splendidly carved gold doors.

Mongkol Rd. ☎ *02 224 5240. Daily 8am–7pm.*

9 ★★★ Leng Noi Yee Temple. Known in Thai as Wat Mangkol Kamalawat and in English as the Dragon Flower Temple, the magnificent Chinese Leng Noi Yee is the highest revered Mahayana Buddhist temple in Thailand. Built in 1871, the main shrine is guarded by gruesome giant "guardians of the world" statues. Much praying to various shrines and icons goes on inside the temple, so be respectful. There are young boys—resident Chinese monks—who do chores. You'll see that they wear saffron-colored pajamas as opposed to robes. The temple is usually very busy with worshippers lighting lots of incense and candles and offering fruit, flowers, and oil to the gods. One interesting thing to observe is people buying what looks like Monopoly money, which is then burned as an offering on the basis that they can take the money with them into their next lives. This temple is especially popular at Chinese New Year (January to February). *30 min. 423 Charoen Krung Rd. Daily 6am–6pm.*

⑩ **Leng Buai Ia Shrine.** With pungent whiffs of raw meat, fish, spices, and roasted chestnuts at every turn, Itsarnuphap Road is a bustling alleyway straight out of a Hollywood set. Just 100m or so on the left, tucked quietly behind the marketplace, is a humble wee Chinese temple. This temple is thought to be the oldest shrine in Thailand, dating back to 1658. It is designed in Tae Chew style, which is Fujian, the origin of many of Bangkok's Chinese immigrants. *15 min. Itsarnuphap Rd. Daily 7am–5pm.*

11 ★ **Yaowarat Road.** There are several modest diners at the corner of Yaowarat and Plaengnarm roads serving bird's nest and shark's fin soup (although animal rights activists won't thank you). If you feel like a stop, why not just choose a steaming bowl of noodles? On the main street of Chinatown you are greeted by large signs in Chinese characters hanging over the street. As you cruise down the broad avenue, you'll pass gold retailers and Chinese medicine shops. **$.**

⑫ ★ **Thian Fa Foundation.** You are welcome to take a peek inside this Chinese medicine hospital, which was founded in 1902. The treatment center, not surprisingly, has a shrine where patients pray for recovery. If you would like to say a prayer for good health—for yourself or for someone else—light an

Leng Buai Ia Shrine, thought to be the oldest shrine in Thailand, is tucked away off Itsarnuphap Road.

Yaowarat Road in Chinatown is busy and crowded, day and night.

incense stick and a candle at the Kuan Si Yim shrine, where the four-faced Buddha sits. ⏲ *15 min. 606 Yaowarat Rd.* ☎ *02 237 2190 4. Daily 7am–7pm.*

⓭ ★★ The Golden Buddha. The largest solid-gold Buddha image in the world is this 3m-high, 5.5 ton shimmering sculpture, which is housed in the 19th-century temple of Wat Traimit (see p 39, bullet ⓫) and is thought to date to the Sukhothai period (1238–1438). A new pavilion inside the compound, a *mondop*, recognizable by a towering golden spire, was completed the summer of 2009 to house the enormous Buddha. ⏲ *15 min. Wat Traimit, cnr Mittaphap Thai-China & Yaowarat rds. Daily 8am–5pm.* ●

4 The Best Shopping

Shopping Best Bets

Best **Antiques in an Antiquated House**
★★ House of Chao, *Decho Rd* *(see p 72)*

Best for **Buying an Engagement Ring in Secret**
Uthai's Gems, *28/7 Soi Ruam Rudi, Ploenchit Rd* *(see p 77)*

Best **Cameras**
★ Fotofile *MBK, Phayathai Rd* *(see p 73)*

Best **Cheap Clothes That Will Last for Years**
★ Pratunam Market, *cnr Phetburi & Ratchaprarop rds* *(see p 78)*

Best **Designer Labels**
★★ Siam Paragon, *cnr Rama I & Phayathai rds, Siam Square* *(see p 75)*

Best **English Language Books**
★ Kinokuniya, EmQuartier Shopping Complex *Sukhumvit* *(see p 73)*

Most Likely Place to **Get Lost for a Day**
★★★ Chatuchak Weekend Market, *Phahonyothin Rd, Chatuchak* *(see p 77)*

Best **IT Supplies**
Pantip Plaza, *604/3 Petchaburi Rd, Pratunam* *(see p 75)*

Best **Made-to-Measure Suits for Men**
★★ Marco Tailors, *430/33 Soi 7, Siam Square* *(see p 79)*

Best for **Protection Against Evil Spirits**
Amulet Market, *Maharat Rd* *(see p 72)*

Best **Selection of Silk**
★★ Almeta, *20/3 Soi Prasarnmitr, Sukhumvit Soi 23* *(see p 80)*

Best **Tie-Dye Shirts**
★ Khao San Road, *Banglamphu* *(see p 77)*

Best **Wedding Presents**
★★★ River City, *23 Trok Rongnamkhaeng, Bangrak* *(see p 72)*

Previous page: Central World shopping center.

Silk is a popular gift, like these silk suits from Jim Thompson.

Sukhumvit Road Shopping

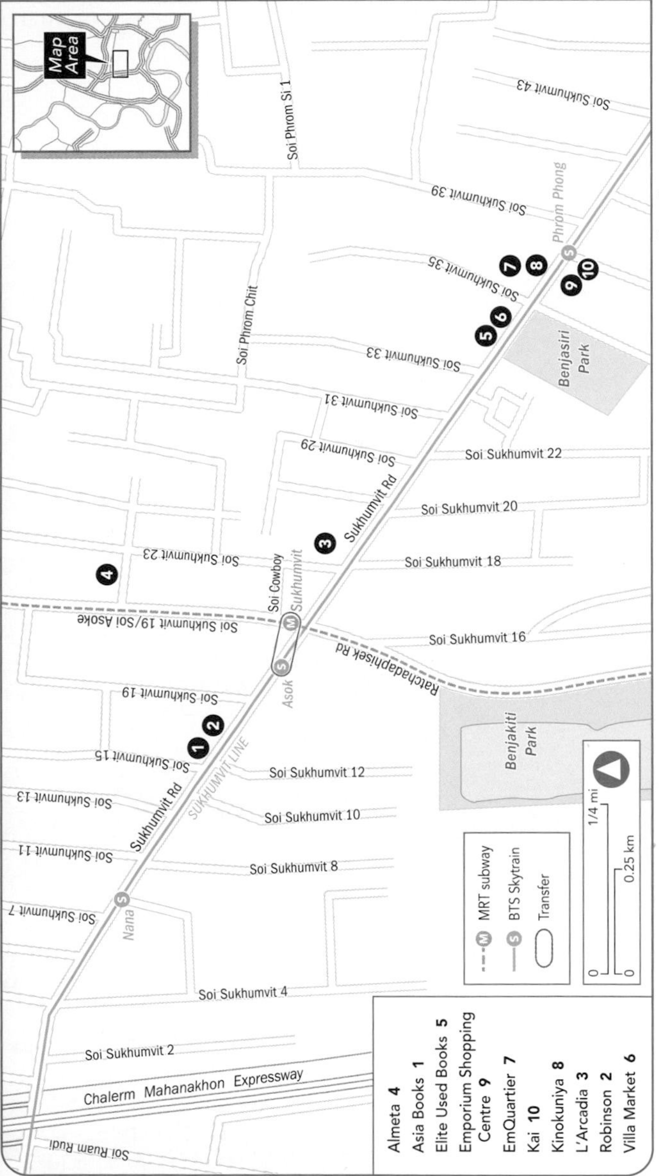

Central Bangkok Shopping

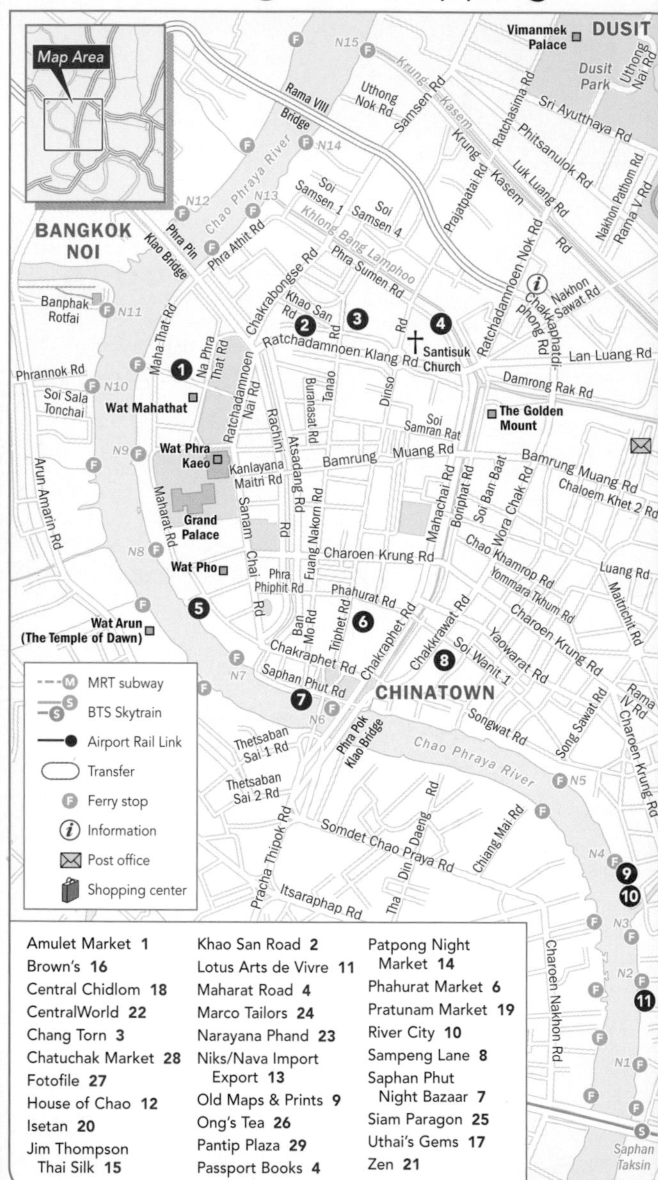

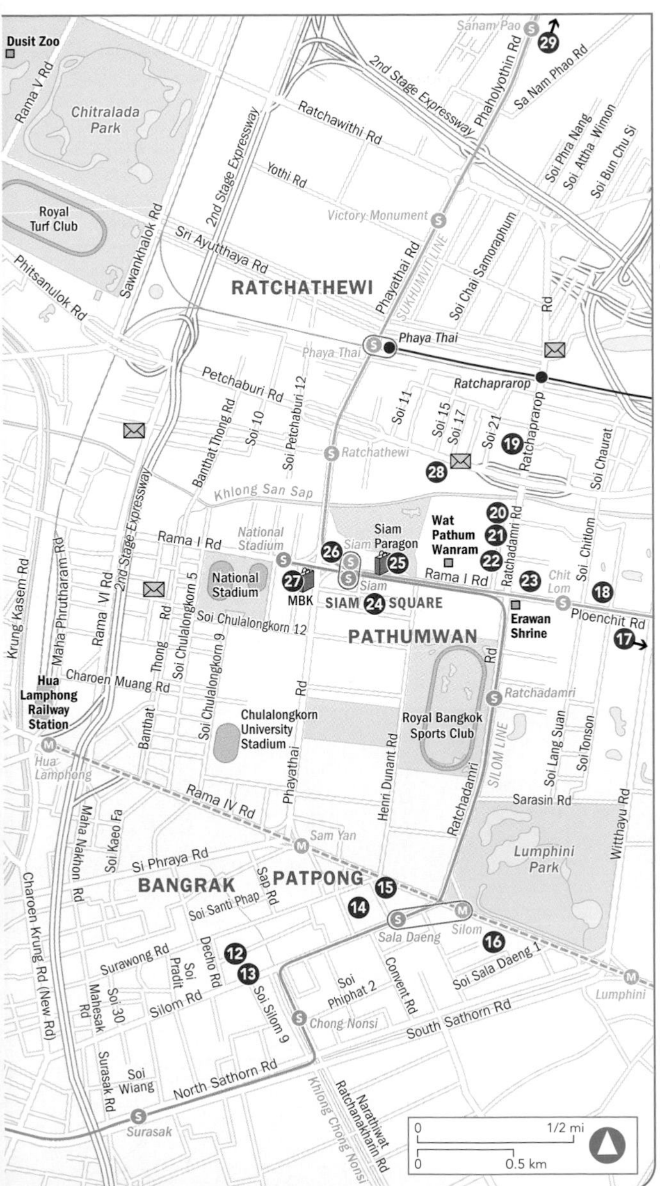

Dusit Zoo
Chitralada Park
Royal Turf Club
Rama V Rd
Phitsanulok Rd
Sawankhalok Rd
Sri Ayutthaya Rd
2nd Stage Expressway
Yothi Rd
Ratchawithi Rd
Phaholyothin Rd
Sanam Pao
Sa Nam Phao Rd
Soi Phra Nang
Soi Attha Wimon
Soi Bun Chu Si
Victory Monument
SUKHUMVIT LINE
Soi Chai Samoraphum
Phayathai Rd
RATCHATHEWI
Phaya Thai
Ratchaprarop
Petchaburi Rd
Banthat Thong Rd
Soi 10
Soi Petchaburi 12
Soi 11
Soi 15
Soi 17
Soi 21
Soi Chaurat
Ratchathewi
Khlong San Sap
National Stadium
Rama I Rd
Siam
Siam Paragon
Wat Pathum Wanram
Ratchadamri Rd
Soi Chitlom
Chit Lom
MBK
SIAM SQUARE
Erawan Shrine
Ploenchit Rd
PATHUMWAN
Soi Chulalongkorn 5
Soi Chulalongkorn 12
Soi Chulalongkorn 9
Krung Kasem Rd
Maha Phrutharam Rd
Rama VI Rd
Hua Lamphong Railway Station
Charoen Muang Rd
Chulalongkorn University Stadium
Royal Bangkok Sports Club
Ratchadamri
SILOM LINE
Soi Lang Suan
Soi Tonson
Hua Lamphong
Henri Dunant Rd
Rama IV Rd
Sarasin Rd
Witthayu Rd
Maha Nakhon Rd
Soi Kaeo Fa
Sam Yan
Lumphini Park
Si Phraya Rd
BANGRAK
PATPONG
Sap Rd
Soi Santi Phap
Charoen Krung Rd (New Rd)
Sala Daeng
Silom
Surawong Rd
Soi Pradit
Decho Rd
Soi Sala Daeng 1
Lumphini
Mahesak Rd
Soi 30
Silom Rd
Soi Silom 9
Soi Phiphat 2
Convent Rd
Chong Nonsi
South Sathorn Rd
Surasak Rd
Soi Wiang
North Sathorn Rd
Khlong Chong Nonsi
Narathiwat Ratchanakharin Rd
Surasak
0 1/2 mi
0 0.5 km
12 13 14 15 16 17 18 19 20 21 22 23 24 25 26 27 28 29

Bangkok Shopping A to Z

Amulets

Amulet Market RATTANAKOSIN Even if you're not interested in buying a little Buddha to hang around your neck, this street market is an interesting circus of superstition and magic as Thais consult astrologers to see which Buddhist amulets to wear to ward off ghosts, diseases, debt, and motorbike accidents. *Maharat Rd (north of the Grand Palace). Daily 7am–5pm. No credit cards. No BTS SkyTrain or MRT subway. Nearest ferry: Tha Chang. Map p 70.*

Antiques

★★ **House of Chao** SILOM I love this three-story colonial house. I just want to live here with all the antiques—from the chandeliers to the beds to the clocks and artwork. 9/1 *Decho Rd.* ☎ *02 635 7188. AE, MC, V. Nearest BTS SkyTrain station: Chong Nonsi. Map p 70.*

River City This complex houses the largest collection of Asian antiques shops in the city. Prices are high, but so is the quality. Daily 10am–10pm. *23 Trok Rongnamkhaeng, Si Phaya Pier, Yota Road (on the riverfront next to the Royal Orchid Sheraton), Bangkok.* ☎ *02 237 0077. www.rivercity.co.th. AE, MC, V. BTS SkyTrain: Saphan Thaksin. Map p 70.*

Books

Asia Books SUKHUMVIT This bookstore has a large selection of novels, travel guides, and international newspapers. There are also many other Asia Books locations throughout the city. *221 Sukhumvit Rd (between Soi 19 & Soi 21).* ☎ *02 252 7277. www.asiabooks.com. AE, DC, MC, V. BTS SkyTrain: Asok or MRT subway: Sukhumvit. Map p 69.*

Elite Used Books SUKHUMVIT Elite Used Books sells thousands of

Buddhist amulets are thought to ward off misfortunes.

Kinokuniya bookstore.

secondhand books in various languages at reasonable prices. *593–595 Sukhumvit Rd (between Soi 33 & Soi 35). ☎ 02 258 0221. No credit cards. BTS SkyTrain station: Phrom Phong. Map p 69.*

★ **Kinokuniya** SUKHUMVIT This is my favorite store for browsing. You can find almost everything here: all the latest releases, maps, guides, and books on Thailand. There's also a branch at Isetan CentralWorld and Siam Paragon. *3rd floor, EmQuartier Shopping Complex, 689 Sukhumvit Rd. ☎ 02 6109500 www.kinokuniya.com. AE, MC, MC, V. BTS SkyTrain: Phrom Phong. Map p 69.*

Passport Bookshop BANGLAMPHU Located in the heart of the Old Town, this small shop and café specializes in books about Southeast Asia and is loved by tourists and locals alike. There are new, secondhand, and handmade books from independent writers on sale here. *523 Prasumeru Rd. ☎ 02-629-0694. Open Tues–Sun, 10:30am–7pm. Nearest ferry: Phra Athit. Map p 70.*

Cameras

Fotofile SIAM This is the best camera shop in Bangkok and the choice of professional photographers. They stock an extensive range of equipment and the staff is very knowledgeable and helpful. *444 MBK Center 1st, 3rd, and 5th floors, Phayatai Rd. ☎ 02 620 9200. www.fotofile.net. Nearest BTS SkyTrain: National Stadium. Map p 70.*

Department Stores & Shopping Centers

kids **Central Chidlom** PATHUMWAN Seven air-conditioned stories of cosmetics, international fashion, and clothing stores, as well as children's toys, electronics, supermarkets, restaurants, and much more. *1027 Ploenchit Rd.*

Taking Antiques Home

The people of Thailand are understandably sensitive about antique Buddhist statues and art leaving the country. Certificates must be obtained from the Department of Fine Arts for authentic Buddha images (over 200 years old) that you plan to export. However, this law is essentially applied to antique Buddhas that may have been taken from temples rather than amulets and *objets d'art* you might find in a market.

If you need it you'll likely find it at Central Chidlom shopping center.

☎ *02 655 7777. www.central.co.th. AE, DC, MC, V. BTS SkyTrain: Chit Lom. Map p 70.*

Central Embassy PLOENCHIT This place bills itself as "an ultra-luxury lifestyle mall." Its eight floors of premium designer brands such as Alexander McQueen, Paul Smith, and Vivienne Westwood, with high-end restaurants and cinemas. *1031 Ploenchit Rd.* ☎ *02 119 7777. www.centralembassy.com. AE, MC, V. BTS SkyTrain: Ploen Chit.*

★ kids **CentralWorld** PATHUMWAN Billed as the largest lifestyle shopping destination in Asia, this mammoth mall includes department stores, designer boutiques, a food court, dozens of restaurants, cinemas, and a kids' entertainment zone. *Ratchadamri Rd.* ☎ *02 635 1111. www.centralworld.co.th. AE, DC, MC, V. BTS SkyTrain: Chid Lom. Map p 70.*

EM District SUKHUMVIT Situated on the side of Phrom Pong BTS station, the EM District includes The Emporium shopping mall, and the brand new EMQuartier mall where you will find high-end brands such as Jimmy Choo and Valentino, an excellent Kinokuniya bookstore, and more. There's also some great coffee shops and restaurants, cinemas and a fitness center. *622 Sukhumvit Rd, Soi 24.* ☎ *02 269 1000. www.theemdistrict.com. AE, DC, MC, V. BTS SkyTrain: Phrom Phong. Map p 69.*

Isetan PATHUMWAN This Japanese-owned department stores

More than just a mall, CentralWorld offers entertainment of all sorts, along with many eating options.

features luxe fashion, fragrances, jewelry, and housewares. There's also a Jim Thompson outlet, cafes, restaurants, and a supermarket. Located within CentralWorld. *4/1–2 Rajdamri Rd. ☎ 02 255 9898 9. AE, DC, MC, V. BTS SkyTrain: Chit Lom.* *Map p 70.*

Robinson SUKHUMVIT Rather than designer gear, Robinson pulls in shoppers for its reliable local brands and cheaper prices. There are also outlets on Charoen Krung Road, Rama 9, and Seacon Square. *259 Sukhumvit Rd (between Soi 17 & Soi 19). ☎ 02 651 1533. AE, DC, MC, V. BTS SkyTrain: Asok or MRT subway Sukhumvit.* *Map p 69.*

★★ **kids Siam Paragon** PATHUMWAN The trendiest place to be seen is this luxurious mega-complex. It features über-chic fashion stores, perfumeries, Starbucks, gourmet cafes, and more. Note that there are cinemas and kids' entertainment on the top floor and Siam Ocean World is downstairs—great for those who are unwilling to shop for hours. *Rama I. ☎ 02 690 1000. AE, DC, MC, V. BTS SkyTrain: Siam.* *Map p 70.*

Terminal 21 SUKHUMVIT An airport-themed shopping experience with zones for London, Rome, Tokyo, and San Francisco and dozens of small shops run by local designers. The mall pulls in a young and trendy crowd. It has direct access from the BTS SkyTrain station. *288 Sukhumvit Soi 19. ☎ 02 651 2888. www.terminal21.co.th. AE, DC, MC, V. BTS SkyTrain: Asoke or MRT subway: Sukhumvit.*

Zen PATHUMWAM Specializing in women's stores, this is where you'll find local and international labels at cheaper prices. *Located within CentralWorld, 4/1–2 Ratchadamri Rd. ☎ 02 255 9669. AE, DC, MC, V. BTS SkyTrain: Chit Lom.* *Map p 70.*

Electronics

Pantip Plaza PATHUMWAN Not where I would personally hang out at weekends, but if you love electronics and computers, this will be

Arguably Bangkok's hippest mall, many spend the entire day at Siam Paragon, shopping, eating, and seeing all its sights.

Looking for the kinds of goods you'd find in San Francisco? Head for the Golden Gate Bridge (pictured) at Terminal 21.

heaven. There are hundreds of vendors selling pirated software, and bargains with on-the-spot servicing and upgrading. *604/3 Petchaburi Rd, Pratunam. ☎ 02 251 9008. Most stores accept MC & V, but some are cash only. BTS SkyTrain: Ratchathewi or Chit Lom, then a taxi. Map p 70.*

Fashion

Brown's LUMPHINI Hallelujah! A full range of "outsize" clothing for women who find Thai sizes too petite. Brown's also has an outlet at Emporium. *1st floor, U Chia-Liang Building, Rama IV Rd, opp. Lumphini Park. ☎ 02 632 4424. AE, DC, MC, V. BTS SkyTrain: Sala Daeng or MRT subway: Silom. Map p 70.*

Kai SUKHUMVIT Leading fashion designer Chatri Teng-Ha creates provocative and bold attire for ladies. Kai specializes in delicate fabrics such as cotton, linen, and chiffon in subtle shades. *1st floor, Emporium, Sukhumvit Rd, Soi 24. ☎ 02 664 8000 ext. 1533. AE, DC, MC, V. BTS SkyTrain: Phrom Phong. Map p 69.*

Food & Drink

Ong's Tea PATHUMWAN Take a break at Ong's and sample some of his majestic tea leaves from China, Japan and, of course, Thailand. Ceramic tea ceremony sets are available. *4th floor, Siam Discovery Centre, Rama I Rd. ☎ 02 658 0445. AE, MC, V. Metro: Siam. Map p 70.*

★★ **Villa Market** SUKHUMVIT This supermarket is my—and many other expats'—favorite retreat in Bangkok when in desperate need of cheeses, olives, wines, salami, tortillas, Vegemite, and other imported goodies from afar. There are several outlets of this place around town. *595 Sukhumvit Rd, Soi 33. ☎ 02 662 1000. www.villamarket.com. AE, DC, MC, V. BTS SkyTrain: Phrom Phong. Map p 69.*

A mecca for gadget geeks, Pantip Plaza is floor after floor of electronics.

VAT Refunds

As a tourist, you can get 7% of the cost of your purchases refunded at customs when you are leaving Thailand. But you have to jump through a few hurdles: the refund only applies at shops that have "VAT refund for tourists" signs; each purchase must cost more than 2000 baht and the total must be more than 5000 baht. You must present your passport, fill in a VAT refund form with the sales assistant, and show your goods to officials at the airport.

Handicrafts

★ Narai Phand PRATUNAM You can find an eclectic variety of good-quality handicrafts and artifacts, perfect to take home to friends and family. *7th floor, President Tower (Inter-Continental Hotel), 973 Ploenchit Rd. ☎ 02 656 0398 9 or 02 656 0400. www.naraiphand.com. AE, DC, MC, V. BTS SkyTrain: Chit Lom. Map p 70.*

Jewelry & Gems

Uthai's Gems PLOENCHIT Due to the dark nature of this business, I am loath to recommend tourists to the seedy world of gemstones. However, Uthai appears to be the most honest broker in Bangkok, and can custom design jewelry for you with rubies, sapphires, and emeralds. *28/7 Soi Ruam Rudi, Ploenchit Rd. ☎ 02 253 8582. AE, MC, V. BTS SkyTrain: Ploen Chit. Map p 70.*

Maps

★ Old Maps & Prints BANGRAK I love this little cubbyhole; it stocks some great old maps of Thailand and Asia, navigational charts, and engravings. Heaven for map lovers! *4th floor, River City Complex, Sri Phaya Pier, Yotha Rd. ☎ 02 237 0077 8. www.classicmaps.com. AE, MC, V. BTS SkyTrain: Saphan Taksin. Map p 70.*

Markets

Asiatique An extremely popular open air shopping center on the banks of the Chao Phraya. Spend a night browsing 1,500 shops with fashions and accessories, gifts, crafts, retro homewares, and more. There are also many restaurants, bars, a ferris wheel, and a theater with ladyboy cabaret. *2194 Charoenkrung Rd, Bangkok. ☎ 02 108 4488. www.thaiasiatique.com. Daily 5pm–midnight. BTS SkyTrain: Saphan Thaksin then free shuttle boat.*

★★★ Chatuchak Market CHATUCHAK Perhaps half a million people visit this market every weekend. With 15,000 stalls, you can expect to find everything—from clothes, plants, and household goods to live snakes, Buddhist antiques, herbal medicines, CDs, and hill-tribe handicrafts. *Phahonyothin Rd. No credit cards. BTS SkyTrain: Mo Chit or MRT subway: Kamphaeng Phet. Map p 70.*

★ Khao San Road BANGLAMPHU It's hippy heaven on Bangkok's backpacker boulevard. Trendy T-shirts, floppy hats, baggy pants, secondhand books, cheap jewelery, CDs, fake student cards, and some of the best wee souvenirs you can buy for less than 100 baht. *Khao San Rd. No credit cards. Nearest ferry: Phra Athit. No metro. Map p 70.*

Browsing is fun but frenetic at always-crowded Chatuchak market.

★★ Patpong Night Market SILOM Competing with go-go bars and seedy shows on Thailand's most famous street are countless stalls of Thai souvenirs and counterfeit goods, especially watches and designer labels. This is the place to get haggling. *Silom and Patpong rds. No credit cards. BTS SkyTrain: Sala Daeng or MRT subway: Silom. Map p 70.*

★ Phahurat Market PHAHURAT Little India meets Chinatown at this colorful market. Silks, textiles and saris are for sale, as well as Indian spices. *Cnr Phahurat & Thiphet rds. No credit cards. Nearest ferry: Saphan Phut. Map p. 70.*

★ Pratunam Market PRATUNAM This is the place to get cheap clothes, whether it be fake designer gear or sturdy local garments. *Cnr Phetburi & Ratchaprarop rds. No credit cards. Nearest BTS SkyTrain: Ratchathewi or Chit Lom then a taxi. Map p 70.*

Sampeng Lane CHINATOWN This narrow alley is everything you would expect of a Chinese backstreet—bustling, colorful, and loud. However, you might find a gemstone or an herbal concoction that you cannot resist. *Soi Wanit 1, Ratchawong Rd. No credit cards. MRT subway: Hua Lamphong. Nearest ferry: Ratchawongse. Map p 70.*

Saphan Phut Night Bazaar CHINATOWN Located on either side of the Memorial Bridge on the Chao Phraya River, this 24-hour down-to-earth market offers late-night snacks, cheap clothes, and other discounted goods. *Saphan Phut Rd. No credit cards. No SkyTrain or MRT. Ferry: Saphan Phut. Map p 70.*

Talaat Rot Fai It takes a little effort to get here, but it's worth it. There are hundreds of stalls selling fashion, trendy housewares, and gifts, and warehouses packed with furniture, ceramics, and even vintage cars. There's also a car boot sale area. There are many restaurants and food stalls, so make a night of it. *Wed and Fri–Sun nights from 6pm till*

Bolts of fabric on sale at the Pratunam Market.

Handcrafted jewelry and housewares at Lotus Arts de Vivre.

late. Nearest BTS SkyTrain: Udom Suk then a taxi. Near Seacon Square on Sri Nagarindra Rd.

Menswear

★★ Chang Torn BANGLAMPHU There are a lot of Indian tailors around Banglamphu offering great deals on suits (with free ties and shirts included). However, you must be very careful—many of the stores are fronts for sweatshops and the quality is poor. Chang Torn is experienced, unassuming, and reliable. Prices are higher than at many other tailors, but it's well worth it. *95 Tanao Rd. ☎ 02 282 9390. MC, V. No SkyTrain or MRT. Map p 70.*

★★ Marco Tailors SIAM SQUARE The best in made-to-measure men's cotton suits, especially for conservative styles. Note that you will need 2 weeks and two fittings. *430/33 Soi 7, Siam Square. ☎ 02 251 7633. AE. BTS SkyTrain: Siam. Map p 70.*

Objets d'Art

★★ Lotus Arts de Vivre BANGRAK You will be dazzled by the exquisite and intricately designed jewelry and home decor at this high-end boutique. There is also a branch at Four Seasons Hotel on Ratchadamri Road. *Mandarin Oriental Hotel, 48 Oriental Ave. ☎ 02 236 0400. www.lotusartsdevivre.com. AE, DC, MC, V. BTS SkyTrain: Saphan Taksin. Map p 70.*

★★★ River City BANGRAK This is a high-end complex,

Bargaining

Haggling is fun! It's an acceptable part of Thai culture, so don't take it as an affront. Smile and be playful. My personal tip is not to start haggling until you are sure you want to buy something, otherwise the canny market vendors will simply throw an inflated price at you to get a reaction. "What?" you scream. "500 baht just for this?" "Okay," mellows the salesperson. "So, how much do you want to pay?" And next thing you know you are haggling for an Akha hill-tribe hat that you will never wear. Remember: you can bargain at any outdoor market or Chatuchak, but not in department stores.

The Conscientious Shopper

Many visitors to the Land of Smiles worry how much blood, sweat and tears go into the making of the cut-price clothes and handicrafts they buy. Some believe Bangkok's suburbs to be dark slums where tiny orphans toil in sweatshops night and day. In fact, such a Dickensian scenario is rarely reported in Thailand nowadays, but there's no 100% guarantee. The copyright laws are not enforced, so you will come across counterfeit DVDs, sunglasses, designer handbags, and much more at marketplaces. That is not to say they're poor quality—many of the fake items are excellent and will last years—but of course if it's cut-price and bootlegged, it's made by lowly paid factory workers. Tailors that offer made-to-measure suits will often send the measurements to factories to make them. Many factory workers are Burmese migrants, but a few are children.

If you want to guarantee that your purchases help the people who make the products, look out for OTOP or Royal Project signs. OTOP—One *Tambon* (village), One Product—is a system of encouraging rural villages to undertake community projects producing handicrafts, furniture, woodcrafts, lacquerware, ceramics, candles, and more. Profits from sales return to the respective villages. Royal Projects mainly center on agriculture. Hill-tribe villages in northern Thailand have been pushed to abandon opium production in favor of growing coffee, strawberries, and other organic fruit and vegetables. These cooperative projects are sanctioned by the Thai royal family.

managed by the Mandarin Oriental, that offers *objets d'art*, antiques, and handicrafts to treasure. *23 Trok Rongnamkhaeng, Si Phaya Pier, Yotha Rd.* ☎ *02 237 0077. www.rivercity.co.th. AE, MC, V. BTS SkyTrain: Saphan Taksin. Map p 70.*

Silk

★★ Almeta SUKHUMVIT The creator of à la carte silk shopping, Almeta offers a choice of some 50,000 colors and weaves in the finest Thai and Chinese silk for gorgeous made-to-measure gowns, kimonos, and suits. *20/3 Soi Prasarnmitr, Soi Sukhumvit 23.* ☎ *02 204 1413. www.almeta.com. AE, DC, MC, V. BTS SkyTrain: Asok or MRT subway: Sukhumvit. Map p 69.*

★★ Jim Thompson Thai Silk BANGRAK You still can't beat Jim Thompson's after all these years. It's a wonderland of lustrous colors and fabrics. Everybody in your life deserves a silken gift from JT's. *9 Surawong Rd.* ☎ *02 632 8100 4. www.jimthompson.com. AE, DC, MC, V. BTS SkyTrain: Sala Daeng or MRT subway: Silom. Map p 70.*

Traditional Medicines

Maharat Road RATTANAKOSIN A series of small, dark Chinese stores line the street and entice passers-by with jars of exotic creatures and the aromatic scents of magical herbs and spices. *Running along the river, west of Wat Pho, near Tha Tien pier. No credit cards. No metro. Nearest ferry: Tha Tien pier N8. Map p 70.* ●

5 The Great Outdoors

Lumphini Park

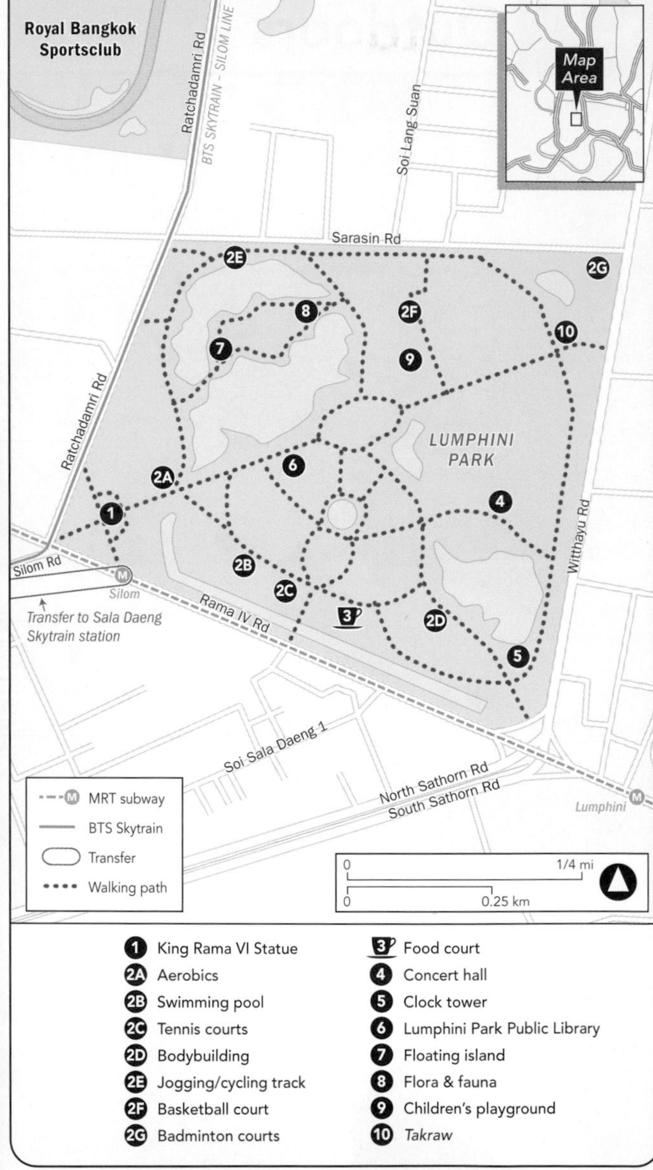

Previous page: Geese shaped paddleboats wait for rowers at Lumphini Park.

An oasis of greenery in the heart of Bangkok's business and shopping districts, Lumphini Park is where hundreds of Bangkokians seek refuge every day. It's a hive of activity with Tai Chi, aerobics, bodybuilding, and jogging all happening first thing in the morning. In the evening, office workers shed their ties and don shorts to play *takraw*—a Thai version of foot-tennis with a rattan ball—and work-out at mass aerobics sessions, while children go boating on the lake and young lovers stroll hand-in-hand. In the cooler months of November to February, you can also listen to the Bangkok Symphony Orchestra at the Sunday evening "Concert in the Park." This charming park, often referred to as the "Lungs of Bangkok,' is open every day from 4am to 9pm. START: **Metro to Silom.**

❶ **King Rama VI Statue.** King Rama VI, or King Vajiravudh, presented Lumphini Park (which is named after the Nepalese village where the Buddha was born) to the people of the city in 1925. A statue of the king stands outside the southwestern entrance to the park, near the junction of Ratchadamri and Rama IV roads. ⌚ *5 min. BTS SkyTrain: Sala Daeng or MRT subway, Silom.*

❷ **Sports.** Feel free to join in group 2A **aerobics**, usually held every day at 6am and 6pm. Sessions are free, but you should drop some coins in a collection box. There's a 2B **swimming pool** (daily 7am–7:30pm), which costs just 40 baht for a year's membership. Unfortunately, foreigners are obliged to produce their passports and a medical certificate to gain a membership. There are four all-weather 2C **tennis courts** (daily 7am–8pm; 35 baht per hour), however, you have to bring your own racket. There's a small outdoor 2D **bodybuilding** zone with free weights, which costs just 25 baht for an hour. An asphalt 2E **jogging/ cycling track** winds its way for about 3km to 4km around the park. Behind the children's playground you'll find a 2F **basketball court.** In the northeastern corner of the park, you'll find 2G **badminton courts,** which are free to the public. Again, you must bring your own equipment. ⌚ *1½ hr.*

King Rama VI is the first figure visitors see when they enter Lumphini Park.

3 **Food court.** The only place in the park that sells food is this small plaza. There's a selection of about 10 stalls selling noodles, rice dishes, sweets, and snacks. There are also stalls on the roadside just outside the park. You can also buy soft drinks (but not alcohol, which is forbidden in the park).

Anyone, tourists included, can join the daily aerobics classes at Lumphini Park.

❹ **Concert in the Park.** There are free concerts by the Bangkok Symphony Orchestra at 5:30pm every Sunday from the end of November to the beginning of February at this outdoor amphitheater. ☎ *02 255 6617/8, www.bangkoksymphony.org.* 🕓 *1 hr.*

❺ **Clock tower.** This Chinese-style structure was built for the 1925 trade fair. It is situated at the southwestern corner of the park (near Lumphini subway station). You can rent paddleboats here (80 baht per hour) and buy food for feeding the fish. 🕓 *5 min.*

❻ **Lumphini Park Public Library.** This was the first public library in Thailand. It has 30,000 books and has opened audio and visual exhibits and services to the public. 🕓 *15 min.*

❼ **Floating island.** So called because it is artificial, this shaded area is ideal for picnics, sunbathing, or finding some cool shade. There's a small botanical garden and usually lots of elderly Thai-Chinese chatting away, cooking lunch, playing chess, or practicing martial arts. 🕓 *30 min.*

❽ **Flora & fauna.** King Rama VI arranged for examples of native plants from all regions of the

A concert in the park.

Bangkok's 'Green Lung'

Lumphini Park truly is one of the few outdoor places in Bangkok where it is possible to escape the noise and traffic of the city. You can rent a rowboat to paddle around the lake, or simply find a spot to yourself and relax before the heat of the day kicks in. On Saturday and Sunday evenings you can enjoy a pleasant stroll in the park before heading for street food and nightlife on Silom Road and Patpong.

country to be planted here as an educational exercise. Many trees and shrubs are marked with the names. Birdwatchers will be pleased to know that migrating birds head for the forests and ponds in Lumphini Park every year. You might see or hear oriental magpie robins, coppersmith barbets, pied fantails, mynas, bulbuls, doves, flycatchers, and warblers around the lakes. ⏲ *30 min.*

❾ **Children's playground.** This is a safe, enclosed area for young children and toddlers with rides, slides, and climbing frames. ⏲ *30 min.*

❿ ***Takraw.*** Near the northeastern corner of the park you can find teenagers playing football, basketball and, most interestingly, the Thai national sport of *takraw*. It's like volleyball with no hands, usually played between two teams of three players each. They use a hard rattan ball and you will be amazed by the flexibility and agility of many players as they overhead-kick the ball and still land on their feet. ⏲ *30 min.*

It's not unusual to see friends competing at board games in the park.

Dusit Park

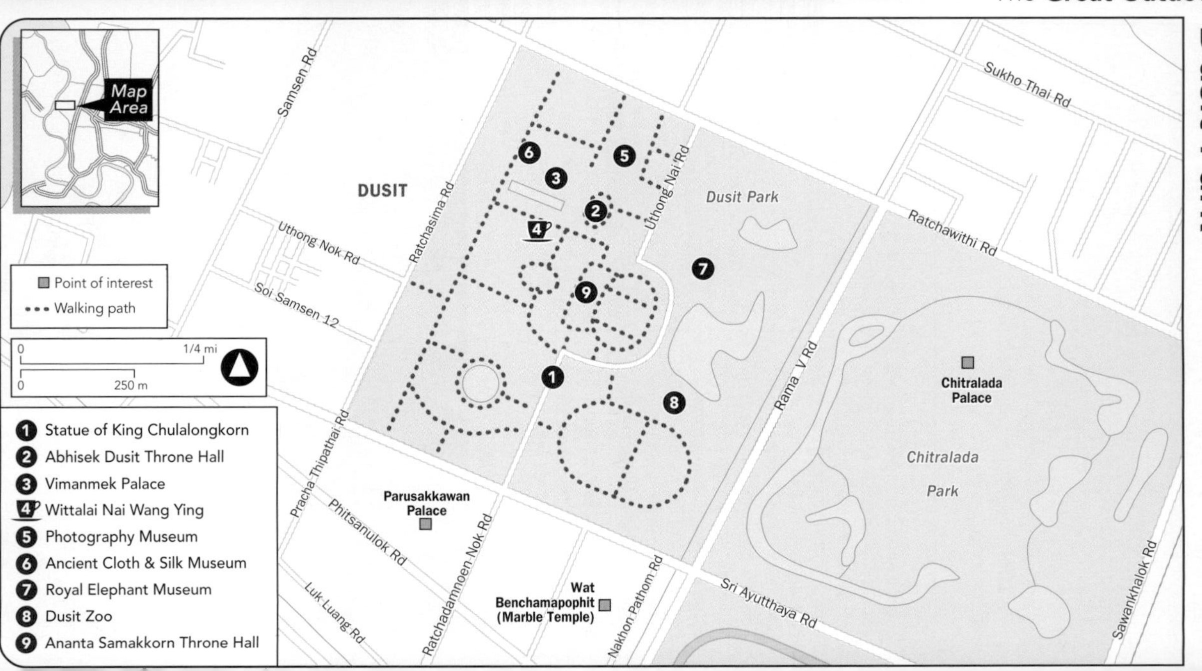
Map Area
Samsen Rd
DUSIT
Sukho Thai Rd
Ratchasima Rd
Uthong Nok Rd
Soi Samsen 12
Uthong Nai Rd
Dusit Park
Ratchawithi Rd
Rama V Rd
Chitralada Palace
Chitralada Park
Pracha Thipathai Rd
Phitsanulok Rd
Parusakkawan Palace
Ratchadamnoen Nok Rd
Wat Benchamapophit (Marble Temple)
Nakhon Pathom Rd
Sri Ayutthaya Rd
Sawankhalok Rd
Luk Luang Rd
Point of interest
Walking path
0
1/4 mi
0
250 m
1 Statue of King Chulalongkorn
2 Abhisek Dusit Throne Hall
3 Vimanmek Palace
4 Wittalai Nai Wang Ying
5 Photography Museum
6 Ancient Cloth & Silk Museum
7 Royal Elephant Museum
8 Dusit Zoo
9 Ananta Samakkorn Throne Hall

In my opinion, Dusit Park is Bangkok's most underated attraction. The gardens are delightful, the architecture sublime. Inspired by his travels to Europe, King Chulalongkorn (also known as King Rama V; 1868–1910) designed Dusit Park and ordered that manicured gardens and stately homes be built within its grounds. He then moved his entire family there from the Grand Palace. Today, the Thai king lives at Chitralada Palace, next to Dusit Park. Visitors have to pay 100 baht (50 baht for kids) to enter the park, which includes admission to the stately attractions within. However, if you're canny, you'll visit the Grand Palace first, keep the ticket and use it to get free admission to Dusit Park and its sights. Please note that if you wish to visit Vimanmek Palace, you have to wear long sleeves and no shorts or skirts above the knees. *Nearest BTS SkyTrain: Phaya Thai then a taxi. Nearest ferry: Thawhet N15* START: **Express boat to Tha Thewet pier. Walk/taxi to junction of Ratchadamnoen Road and Sri Ayutthaya Road.**

❶ Statue of King Chulalongkorn. You will see the dashing mustachioed portrait of King Chulalongkorn—perhaps the most fondly remembered of Thailand's kings—adorning the walls of half the houses in Thailand. He was a great modernizer and had a penchant for all things European. He abolished slavery, introduced a cabinet-style government and skillfully avoided French and British colonialism. He died in 1910 aged 57, having fathered at least 77 children to four queens and numerous concubines. This memorial of King Rama V on horseback overlooks the entrance to the park. *🕔 5 min.*

❷ ★ Abhisek Dusit Throne Hall. The red-tile Moroccan villa just across a canal from the Vimanmek Palace used to host state functions for foreign ambassadors during the early part of the 20th century. It was restored and reopened by the current king and queen in 1993 and now houses arts and crafts produced in Thailand under a royal foundation. *Admission 100 baht. Tues–Sun, 9:30am–4:30pm. Last ticket 3:15pm. 🕔 30 min.*

❸ ★★★ Vimanmek Palace. Resembling a Victorian mansion, this beautiful three-story golden teak mansion was built using wooden pegs instead of nails. Compulsory guided tours leave every 30 minutes; try to time your visit to catch free performances of Thai dance and martial arts in the lakeside pavilion at 10:30am and 2pm daily. *☎ 02 628 6300. www.vimanmek.com. Tues–Sun, 9:30am–4:30pm. Last ticket, 3:15pm. 🕔 1 hr.* *See p 22, bullet ❼.*

❹ Wittalai Nai Wang Ying. Of the two canteens in the park, this one at the Women's College is the better option, with tasty Thai dishes, drinks, desserts and cakes. *1st floor, Administration Building (behind Tourist Information). ☎ 02 628 6300, ext 5185. Daily 10:30am–3:30pm. $.*

❺ Photography Museum. Most of the photographs here were taken by the current king, Bhumibhol, who is an avid photographer. Many of the pictures are of the

Handsome Vimanmek Palace.

royal family. 🕔 *30 min. Tues–Sun, 9:30am–4:30pm. Last ticket, 3:15pm.*

6 Ancient Cloth & Silk Museum. If you have time, take a quick stroll around this charming French-style building and see different silks and textiles from around Thailand, and the robes of kings Rama IV and V. *Tues–Sunday, 9:30am–4:30pm. Last ticket, 3:15pm.* 🕔 *15 min.*

7 Royal Elephant Museum. Formerly a stable for three albino elephants, this small exhibition tells the tales and superstitions regarding elephants in Thailand, especially white elephants, which are considered holy and must be presented to the king. *Tues–Sun, 9:30am–4:30pm. Last ticket, 3:15pm.* 🕔 *30 min.*

8 ★★ kids Dusit Zoo. Just east of Dusit Park, with an entrance to the north, is Thailand's best zoo. Over 300 species of animal live here. Avoid visiting on weekends—it gets crowded. ☎ *02 281 2000. www.dusitzoo.org. Daily 8am–6pm.* 🕔 *2 hr.* *See p 43, bullet 6.*

9 ★ Ananta Samakkorn Throne Hall. This exquisite marble hall was built in Italian Renaissance style by the king in 1907 to receive foreign dignitaries. Check out the frescoes on the domed ceiling depicting the succession of Thai kings. *Admission 150 baht.* ☎ *02 283 9411. www.artsofthekingdom.com. Daily 10am–5pm. Tickets until 4:20pm.* 🕔 *15 min.* ●

Children love visiting the giraffes at Dusit Zoo.

6 The Best Dining

Dining **Best Bets**

Best **Anniversary Present**
★★★ The Manohra $$$$ *Anantara Riverside Bangkok Resort, 257 Charoen Nakorn Rd (p 102)*

Most Authentic **Chinatown Experience**
★ Hua Seng Hong $$$ *371–373 Yaowarat Rd (p 98)*

Best **Asian**
★★ You & Mee $$ *Grand Hyatt Erawan Hotel, 494 Ratchadamri Rd (p 108)*

Best **Classic Indian**
★ Rang Mahal $$$$ *Rembrandt Hotel, 19 Soi 18, Sukhumvit Rd (p 104)*

Best Place to **Dine Like a Siamese King**
★ Benjarong $$$$ *Dusit Thani Hotel, 946 Rama IV Rd (p 95)*

Best **Ribs and Burgers**
Smokin' Pug $$ *88 Surawongse Rd. (p 106)*

Most **Creative Dining**
★★ L'Atelier de Joël Robuchon Bangkok $$$$ *96 Narathiwas Ratchanakharin Rd (p 100).*

Best **Homemade Italian Meal**
★★★ Appia $$$ *Soi 31, Sukhumvit Rd (p 94)*

Best **Japanese**
★★★ Koi $$$$ *26 Soi 20, Sukhumvit Rd (p 100)*

Best **Meal for $1**
Kuaytiaw Reua Tha Siam $ *Siam Square Soi 3, Rama I Rd (p 100)*

Best **Meal for $30**
★★★ Eat Me $$$ *Soi Phiphat 2 (p 98)*

Best **'Once-in-a-Lifetime' Dinner for Two**
★★★ Le Normandie $$$$$ *Mandarin Oriental Hotel, 48 Oriental Rd (p 100)*

Most **Romantic Dinner**
★ Deck by the River $$$ *Arun Residence, 36–38 Soi Pratoo Nok Yooung, Maharaj Rd (p 97)*

Best **Steak**
New York Steakhouse $$$$ *JW Marriott Hotel, 4 Soi 2, Sukhumvit Rd (p 104)*

Best **Traditional Thai Dinner for Two**
★ Thiptara $$$$ *Peninsula Hotel, 333 Charoen Nakorn Rd (p 107)*

Best **Views of Bangkok by Night**
★★ Sirocco $$$$$ *The Dome at State Tower, 1055 Silom Rd (p 106)*

Sukhumvit Road Dining

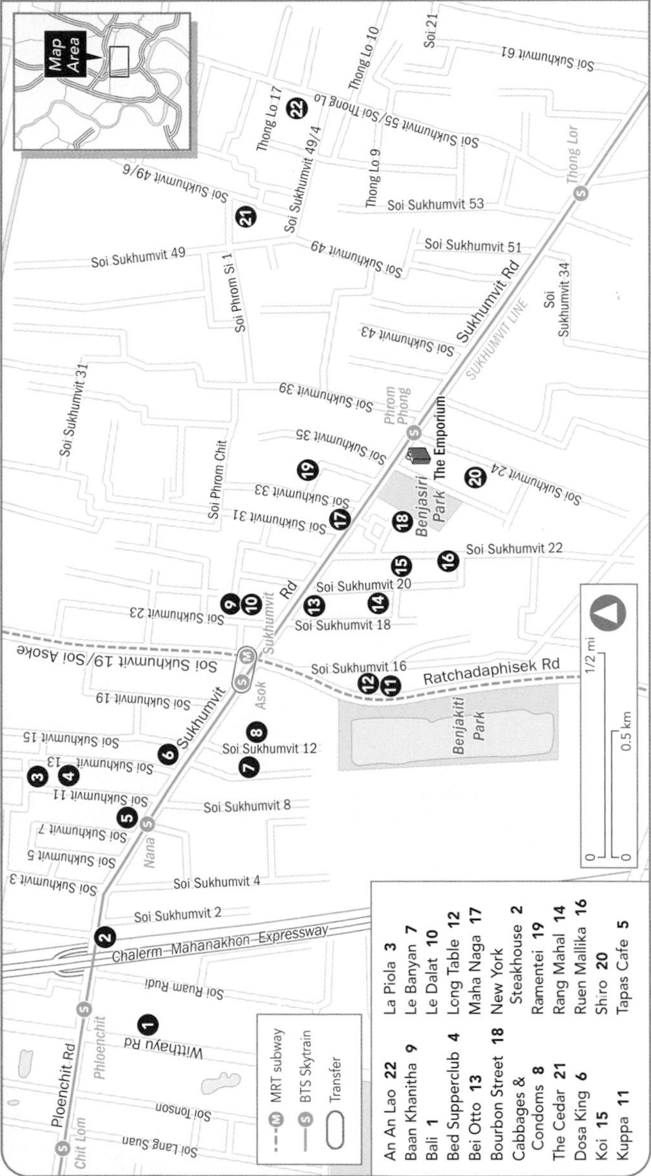

Central Bangkok Dining

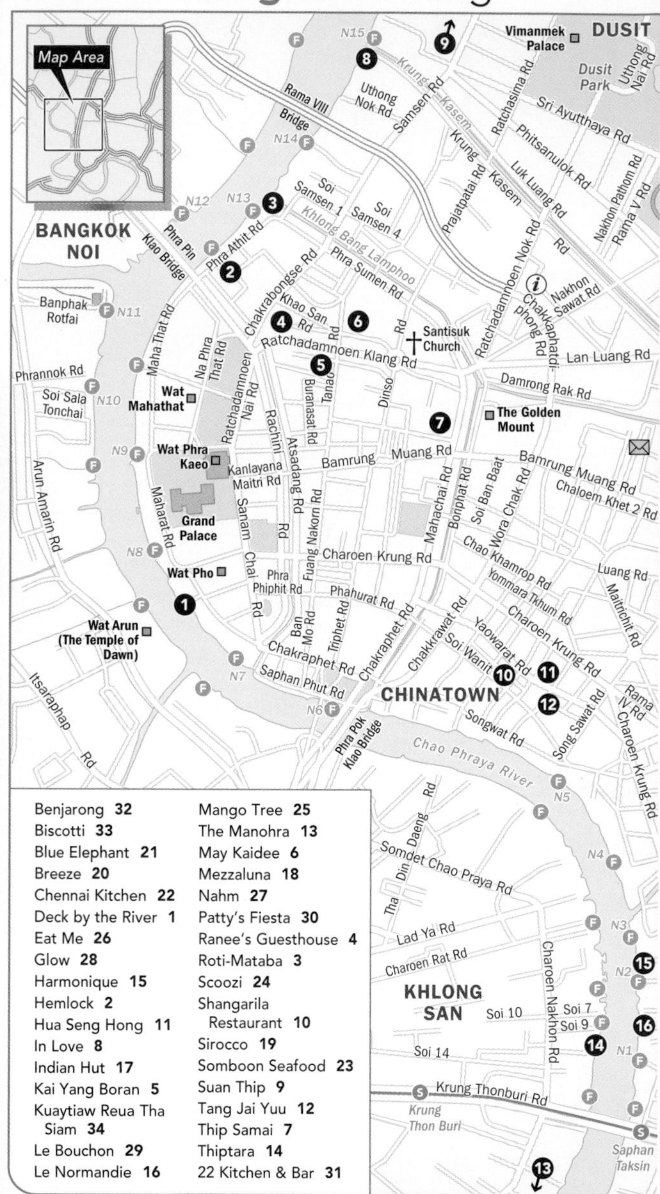

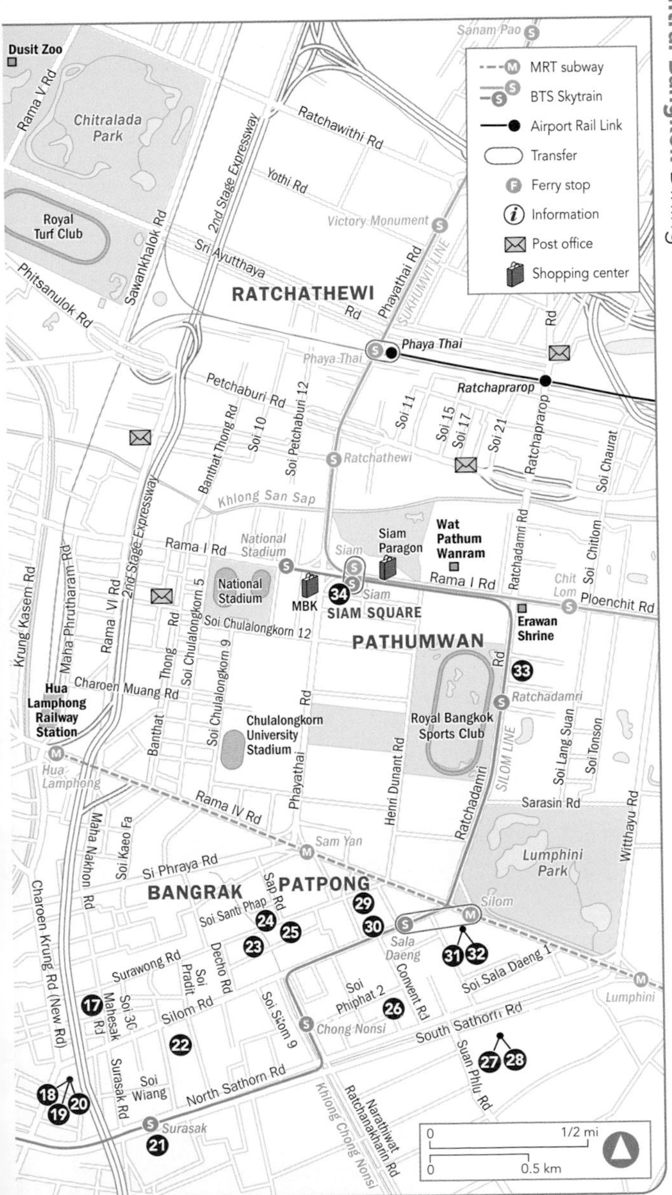
MRT subway
BTS Skytrain
Airport Rail Link
Transfer
Ferry stop
Information
Post office
Shopping center
Dusit Zoo
Chitralada Park
Royal Turf Club
RATCHATHEWI
PATHUMWAN
SIAM SQUARE
BANGRAK
PATPONG
Ratchawithi Rd
Yothi Rd
Sri Ayutthaya Rd
Petchaburi Rd
Rama I Rd
Ploenchit Rd
Rama IV Rd
Si Phraya Rd
Surawong Rd
Silom Rd
North Sathorn Rd
South Sathorn Rd
Phaya Thai
Ratchaprarop
Victory Monument
Sanam Pao
Ratchathewi
National Stadium
Siam
Siam Paragon
MBK
Wat Pathum Wanram
Erawan Shrine
Chit Lom
Ratchadamri
Royal Bangkok Sports Club
Chulalongkorn University Stadium
Hua Lamphong Railway Station
Hua Lamphong
Sam Yan
Silom
Sala Daeng
Lumphini Park
Lumphini
Chong Nonsi
Surasak
Khlong San Sap
Khlong Chong Nonsi
SUKHUMVIT LINE
SILOM LINE
0 1/2 mi
0 0.5 km

Bangkok Dining A to Z

★★ An An Lao KLONG TOEY *CHINESE* Ever heard of Betong chicken? (Neither had I.) The recipe comes from a Chinese town in southern Thailand—the savory chicken is served cold and complemented with watercress. You know this place must be good when you see Chinese people queuing up to come in. *122 Soi Sukhumvit 26 Rd. ☎ 02 261 8188. www.ananlao.com. Meals 350 baht. AE, MC, V. Lunch & dinner daily. BTS SkyTrain: Phrom Phong Lo. Map p 91.*

★★★ Appia SUKHUMVIT *ITALIAN* Styled as a Roman trattoria, the Italian cuisine here is rustic, featuring homemade pastas, stews, and roasted meats such as porchetta stuffed with fennel, garlic, and rosemary. Also on the menu: seafood, cold cuts, cheeses, and a good selection of wine. *Tues–Sun 6pm–11 pm, Sat–Sun 11:30am–2:30pm. 20/4 Sukhumvit Soi 31. ☎ 02 261 2056. www.appia-bangkok.com. Dishes from 220 baht. AE, MC, V. BTS SkyTrain: Phrom Pong.*

★★ Baan Khanitha SUKHUMVIT *THAI* As good an introduction to traditional Thai cuisine as you can get. Signature dishes include prawns in tamarind sauce, soft-shell crab curry, pomelo salad, and roast duck and grape red curry. There's other locations on Sathorn Road, Sukhumvit 53, and Asiatique. *36/1 Soi 23, Sukhumvit Rd. ☎ 02 258 4128. www.baan-khanitha.com. Meals 700–900 baht. AE, MC, V. Lunch & dinner daily. BTS SkyTrain: Asok or MRT subway: Sukhumvit. Map p 91.*

★ Bei Otto SUKHUMVIT *GERMAN* Solid portions of pork knuckle, sauerkraut, liver sausage, potato salad, and frothy white beer make this is a favorite for those craving a rice-free meal. Otto's also has a good delicatessen and bakery attached. *1 Soi 20, Sukhumvit Rd, Klong Toey. ☎ 02 260 0869. www.beiotto.com. Meals 800–1000 baht. AE, MC, V. Lunch & dinner daily. BTS SkyTrain: Asok or MRT subway Sukhumvit. Map p 91.*

An An Lao gets a mix of Thais, tourists, and Chinese ex-pats.

You'll feel like you've been transported to Rome at Appia, an Italian trattoria.

★ **Benjarong** BANGRAK *MODERN THAI* Recently revamped, this restaurant combines traditional flavors with innovation and modern presentation. Dine indoors or in a lush garden. *Dusit Thani Hotel, 946 Rama IV Rd, cnr Silom Rd, Lumphini. ☎ 02 200 9000. Meals 1000 baht. AE, DC, MC, V. Lunch & dinner daily. BTS SkyTrain: Sala Daeng or MTR subway: Silom. Map p 92.*

Biscotti PATHUMWAN *ITALIAN* This is Italian with elegance, from the polished wooden floors to the open-view kitchen and chef's table and the delicate little antipasti offerings such as tuna tartare, duck-liver terrine, and roasted scallops. *Anantara Siam Bangkok Hotel, 155 Ratchadamri Rd. ☎ 02 126 8866. http://siam-bangkok.anantara.com. Meals 1000 baht. AE, DC, MC, V. Lunch & dinner daily. BTS SkyTrain: Ratchadamri. Map p 92.*

Blue Elephant SATHORN *ROYAL THAI* A very dignified colonial-style enterprise, which has even exported this cuisine (originally created only for the Thai royal family) to branches in Europe and the Middle East. The menu includes a selection of delicate culinary delights from around Thailand. *233 South Sathorn Rd. ☎ 02 673 9353. www.blueelephant.com. Set menus*

Street Stalls?

Travellers love to scare each other with ghastly tales of exotic street food that crawled off the plate or that left a customer in a hotel toilet for 2 weeks. The truth is there's not much wrong with Bangkok's street fare. It's nearly always hygienic, cheap, and pretty darn tasty. You don't have to walk far in this city before your senses get hit by sizzling spices, garlic, ginger, barbecued pork, and noodles. Most Bangkokians gather for street food with friends and colleagues at lunchtime and after work. You should pull up a plastic stool and give it a go!

A dish of See Krong Mee Krob Wan at Benjarong.

1300–1450 baht. AE, DC, MC, V. Lunch & dinner daily. BTS SkyTrain: Surasak. Map p 92.

Bourbon Street Restaurant & Oyster Bar SUKHUMVIT *AMERICAN* This is as much a social club as a restaurant and has a faithful following for its Tex-Mex dishes, barbecued ribs and New Orleans/ Creole-style crayfish, gumbo and jambalaya. 9/39-40 Soi Tana Arcade, *Soi 63, Sukhumvit Rd, Klong Toey. ☎ 02 381 6801. www.bourbonstbkk.com. Meals 500–800 baht. AE, DC, MC, V. Breakfast, lunch & dinner daily. BTS SkyTrain: Ekkamai. Map p 91.*

A historic colonial building houses the Blue Elephant restaurant.

Breeze BANGRAK *NEW ASIAN* You enter via a neon-lit glass walkway 51 stories above the city. If that doesn't take your breath away, the prices certainly will. Breeze is unashamedly ostentatious. The menu includes signature jasmine tea smoked Wagyu beef ribs and the desserts to die for. *lebua at State Tower, 1055 Silom Rd, cnr Charoen Krung Rd. ☎ 02 624 9555. Meals 3000–5000 baht. AE, DC, MC, V. Dinner daily, 6pm–1 am. BTS SkyTrain: Saphan Taksin. Map p 92.*

Cabbages & Condoms SUKHUMVIT *THAI* Run by the Population and Community Development Association which promotes safe sex education in Thailand. The meals are certainly fresh and wholesome—the green curry, chicken wrapped in pandan leaves, and coconut soup are all delicious. *10 Soi 12, Sukhumvit Rd. ☎ 02 229 4610. http://www.pda.or.th/restaurant. Meals 400 baht. AE, DC, MC, V. Lunch & dinner daily. BTS*

SkyTrain: Asok or MRT subway: Sukhumvit. Map p 91.

★★ The Cedar SUKHUMVIT *LEBANESE* A renowned Middle Eastern restaurant, The Cedar has been around for some 30 years. The restaurant's interior is designed like a large Bedouin tent—quite funky. The menu offers solid Lebanese favorites such as falafel, humus, kebabs, and racks of lamb, but also has some Greek dishes—dolmades, feta, and moussaka. *6/1 Soi 49/9, Sukhumvit Rd, Klong Toey.* ☎ *02 391 4482. www.thecedar.20m.com. Meals 600–800 baht. AE, DC, MC, V. Dinner daily. BTS SkyTrain: Phrom Phong. Map p 91.*

Chennai Kitchen BANGRAK *INDIAN* This is about as authentic as Indian food gets. Forget the creamy kormas served in the U.S. and Britain. This is natural spiced southern Indian fare, which can be served on a banana leaf and scooped up with handfuls of roti and naan. And it's near the Hindu temple. *10 Pan Rd, Silom.* ☎ *02 234 1266. Meals 100 baht. No credit cards. Lunch daily. BTS SkyTrain: Chong Nonsi or Surasak. Map p 92.*

★ Deck by the River RATTANAKOSIN *THAI/INTERNATIONAL* With fresh, healthy Thai fare and a few western dishes, the Deck offers intimate dining on an open-air wooden terrace. Go at sunset to gaze at the changing hues of Wat Arun, the Temple of Dawn. *Arun Residence, 36–38 Soi Pratoo Nok Yooung, Maharaj Rd.* ☎ *02 221 9158. www.arunresidence.com. Meals 800–1400 baht. AE, MC, V. Lunch & dinner daily. No SkyTrain or MRT. Ferry: Tha Tien pier (N8) Map p 92.*

★ Dosa King SUKHUMVIT *INDIAN/VEGETARIAN* A small air-conditioned diner that caters to aficionados of Indian cuisine (and vegans) with authentic dishes from around the country. I recommend the *paneer tikka*, the *bhindi do piazza*, and, of course, the *Punjabi dosa*. *153/7 Soi 11/1, Sukhumvit Rd.* ☎ *02 651 1700. www.dosaking.net. Meals 500 baht. AE, MC, V. Lunch & dinner daily. BTS SkyTrain: Nana. Map p 91.*

Al fresco dining, with spectacular views, at Breeze Restaurant.

★★★ **Eat Me** BANGRAK *MODERN AUSTRALIAN* Dare I call this "haute cuisine for the budget diner?" I guess so. Personally, I love it. If you can live without chandeliers and silver service, and concentrate on the delicious Modern Australian–cum-Mediterranean cuisine, you're in for a treat—it's excellent value for money. Try the mouthwatering rack of lamb. *Soi Phiphat 2 (off Convent Rd), Silom. ☎ 02 238 0931. www.eatmerestaurant.com. Meals 600–800 baht. MC, V. Dinner daily. BTS SkyTrain: Sala Daeng or MRT subway: Silom. Map p 92.*

Gaggan PLOEN CHIT MODERN INDIAN Voted one of the top restaurants in Asia, Gaggan offers "progressive Indian cuisine" on a series of constantly changing seasonal menus. Modern gastronomy and stunning presentation. Prepare to be blown away. *Daily 6pm–11pm. 68/1 Soi Lang Suan, Bangkok. ☎ 02 652 1700. www.eatatgaggan.com. BTS SkyTrain: Ratchadamri.*

★ **Glow** SATHORN *HEALTH CUISINE* Fine dining with a holistic kick—chef Daniel Moran rustles up low-calorie, healthy haute cuisine. Try the chermoula crusted chicken and pumpkin puree with wild rice, nuts, and seeds. *Metropolitan Hotel, 27 South Sathorn Rd, Silom. ☎ 02 625 3366. www.comohotels.com. Meals 1000–2000 baht. AE, DC, MC, V. Breakfast, lunch & dinner daily. BTS SkyTrain: Sala Daeng or MRT subway: Silom. Map p 92.*

Harmonique BANGRAK *THAI* Mouthwatering seafood by the riverfront. Unfortunately, it's not well known and quite hard to find. Look for the big banyan tree by an old colonial mansion. Harmonique is in the courtyard. Try the *fish tom yum*—so good it'll make you cry! *22 Soi 34 (Soi Wat Muang Kae), Charoen Krung Rd. ☎ 02 237 8175. Meals 600–800 baht. AE, MC, V. Lunch & dinner Mon–Sat. BTS SkyTrain: Saphan Taksin. Map p 92.*

Hemlock BANGLAMPHU *THAI* Don't be put off by the modest shopfront exterior—this place is well known for its wholesome traditional fare, incorporating recipes from across Thailand that include plenty of herbs and spices. *56 Phra Arthit Rd. ☎ 02 282 7507. Meals 400–600 baht. Dinner daily. MC, V. No metro. Ferry: Phra Athit pier (N13). Map p 92.*

★ **Hua Seng Hong** CHINATOWN *CHINESE* This busy diner is what I imagine the backstreets of Hong Kong to have been like in the 1930s, with sizzling woks, skinned geese hanging from the ceiling, and the entire food production on display. I highly recommend the roast duck, *dim sum*, and bird's nest soup. *371–373*

Glow has a futuristic décor.

Anyone for Cricket?

At many marketplaces or along Sukhumvit and Khao San roads you may well encounter vendors offering deep-fried grasshoppers, grubs, scorpions, and beetles. In northeastern Thailand they are considered a good source of protein—and they don't taste that bad. If you want to take the plunge, I recommend the deep-fried crickets—they're just like crunchy, crispy chicken wings.

Fried crickets and other insects at a street stall.

Yaowarat Rd. ☎ 02 222 0635. www.huasenghong.co.th. Meals 500–600 baht. MC, V. Lunch & dinner daily. MRT subway: Hua Lamphong. Map p 92.

★★ In Love DUSIT *SEAFOOD* Refurbished in a chic minimalist design, In Love is an inexpensive option for soft-shell crab, king prawns, grilled fish, and spicy sauces, and commands a stunning view over the river. *Thewet pier, Krung Kasem, Thewet. ☎ 02 281 2900. Meals 500–700 baht. AE, MC, V. Lunch & dinner daily. No metro. Map p 92.*

Indian Hut BANGRAK *INDIAN* Plenty of vegetarian choices, Punjabi and Goan specialties, and hot vindaloo to choose from. Wine is available. *418 Surawong Rd, Silom. ☎ 02 236 5672. www.indianhut-bangkok.com. Meals 600–700 baht. AE, DC, MC, V. Lunch & dinner daily. BTS SkyTrain: Surasak. Map p 92.*

Issaya Siamese Club SATHORN *THAI* The first restaurant opened by Thailand's international celebrity chef, Ian Kittichai. The setting is a restored residential house. Expect Kittichai's signature Thai cuisine using traditional ingredients and flavors with modern cooking methods and creative presentation. Voted one of Bangkok's top tables. Lunch & dinner daily. *4 Soi Sri Aksorn, Chua Poeng Road, Sathorn. ☎ 02 672 9040. www.issaya.com. Dishes from 220 baht. AE, MC, V. BTS SkyTrain: Sala Daeng or MRT subway: Lumphini.*

Kai Yang Boran BANGLAMPHU *ISAAN* You must try north-eastern Thai (Isaan) food at least once! The sticky rice, chillis, papaya salad, fermented fish, and eye-watering sauces make for a distinctly unique Thai experience. *474–476 Tanao Rd. ☎ 02 622 2349. Meals 200–300 baht. No credit cards. Lunch & dinner daily. No BTS SkyTrain or MRT subway. Phra Athit pier (N13). Map p 92.*

★★★ Koi SUKHUMVIT *JAPANESE* As an aficionado of Japanese cuisine, it is with some gravitas that I pronounce Koi the number-one Japanese restaurant in town. It's chic, romantic, and thoroughly sensual. Apart from the sushi and (melt-in-your-mouth) sashimi, most dishes are done with an exquisite international touch. *26 Soi 20, Sukhumvit Rd. ☎ 02 258 1590. www.koirestaurantbkk.com. Meals 1600–2000 baht. AE, MC, V. Dinner daily. BTS SkyTrain: Asok or MRT subway: Sukhumvit. Map p 91.*

Kuaytiaw Reua Tha Siam SIAM SQUARE *THAI* *Kuay tiaw* (Thai noodle soup) is quick, cheap, and tasty, so if you are unsure about eating from street stalls, here is a clean diner with fresh vegetables where you can slurp up Thailand's most popular dish. *Siam Square Soi 3, Rama I Rd. ☎ 02 252 8353. Meals 40 baht. No credit cards. Breakfast, lunch & dinner daily. BTS SkyTrain: Siam. Map p 92.*

Kuppa SUKHUMVIT *THAI/INTERNATIONAL* There's a bit of everything here with Thai, Chinese, Italian, and French cuisines competing to sate your appetite. Kuppa is popular at lunchtime, perhaps because of the strong aromatic coffee that hostess Robin grinds up. *39 Soi 16, Sukhumvit Rd, Klong Toey. ☎ 02 663 0450. Meals 600–1000 baht. www.kuppa.co.th. AE, MC, V. Lunch & dinner Tues–Sun. BTS SkyTrain: Sukhumvit or MRT subway: Asok. Map p 91.*

★★ L'Atelier de Joël Robuchon Bangkok BANGRAK *FRENCH & INTERNATIONAL* The renowned Michelin star chef brings his unique dining concept to Bangkok. Chefs experiment and create, working on new ideas in front of customers seated at a high bar and open kitchen. Tasting menus, a la carte, and set menus are offered. *5th Floor, MahaNakhon CUBE, 96 Narathiwas Ratchanakharin Rd. ☎ 02 001 0698. www.robuchon-bangkok.com. Five-course tasting menu 5,000 baht. AE, DC, MC, V. Lunch & dinner daily. BTS SkyTrain: Chong Nonsi.*

★ Le Banyan SUKHUMVIT *FRENCH* Sophisticated and traditional, this is a good choice for dining alfresco by candlelight in a lush garden on a cool evening. The service is attentive and connoisseurs of fine French cuisine won't be disappointed. *59 Soi 8, Sukhumvit Rd. ☎ 02 253 5556. Meals 2000–3000 baht. AE, DC, MC, V. Dinner Mon–Sat. BTS SkyTrain: Nana. Map p 91.*

Le Bouchon PATPONG *FRENCH* This cozy wee bistro is curiously located in the heart of the red-light area, but manages to offer a romantic ambience. I recommend gorging on the starters—goat's cheese, pâté, frog's legs, niçoise salad, and much more. *37/17 Patpong Soi 2, Silom. ☎ 02 234 9109. lebouchonpatpong.com. Meals 800–900 baht. AE, DC, MC, V. Lunch & dinner daily. BTS SkyTrain: Sala Daeng or MRT subway: Silom. Map p 92.*

Le Dalat SUKHUMVIT *VIETNAMESE* This old Thai house is decorated with Vietnamese and Chinese antiques and has a charming air. I recommend *bi guon* (pork spring rolls), *naem nuang* (wrapped meatballs with mango), and Hanoi-style fish. *14 Soi 23, Sukhumvit Rd. ☎ 02 259 9593. www.ledalatbkk.com. Meals 1000–1500 baht. AE, DC, MC, V. Lunch & dinner daily. BTS SkyTrain: Asok or MRT: Sukhumvit. Map p 91.*

★★★ Le Normandie BANGRAK *FRENCH* Gracing the top floor of what is arguably the greatest hotel in the world, this dazzling restaurant is the epitome of fine dining.

Riverside dining is just one of the lures at La Normandie.

The superb menu is frequently updated by visiting Michelin chefs. Jackets are required for gents in the evening. *Mandarin Oriental hotel, 48 Oriental Rd. ☎ 02 659 9000. www.mandarinoriental.com. Meals 2500–5000 baht. Lunch Mon–Sat, dinner daily. AE, DC, MC, V. BTS SkyTrain: Saphan Taksin. Map p 92.*

Long Table. SUKHUMVIT *THAI* As the name implies, dining is at a long communal table, 24 metres (79 feet), to be precise, seating 44 diners. The menu is contemporary Thai and somewhat spiced down for the Westerner taste. Stunning city views and a chic bar mark this a great venue for

Watch the sun set at Long Table restaurant.

Dine inside or out at Maha-Naga.

special night out. *25th floor, the 48 Column Bangkok, Sukhumvit Soi 16.* ☎ *02 302 2557 9. www.longtable bangkok.com. Meals 1500–2000 baht. AE, DC, MC, V. Lunch daily. BTS SkyTrain: Asok or MRT subway: Sukhumvit. Map p 91.*

MahaNaga SUKHUMVIT *MODERN THAI* Creative Thai cuisine served in an elegant pavilion. Fountains, atmospheric lighting, a relaxed ambience, and Thai dishes such as chicken in zesty coconut milk soup with straw mushrooms and galangal spicy pomelo salad make for a romantic evening. *2 Soi 29, Sukhumvit Rd, Klong Toey.* ☎ *02 662 3060. www.mahanaga.com. Meals 1000–1200 baht. AE, DC, MC, V. Lunch & dinner daily. BTS SkyTrain: Phrom Phong. Map p 91.*

★★ **Mango Tree** BANGRAK *THAI* An excellent choice if you are in Bangkok for just one evening, because the food is rich and spicy (I recommend the duck dishes and *tom yum* soup) and the ambience is classical Siamese with traditional music and charming service. *37 Soi Tantawan (opp. Tawana Ramada Hotel).* ☎ *02 236 2820. www.coca.com/mangotree. Meals 750–850 baht. AE, DC, MC, V. Lunch & dinner daily. BTS SkyTrain: Sala Daeng or MRT subway: Silom. Map p 92.*

★★★ kids **The Manohra** CHAO PHRAYA *THAI* One night in Bangkok? Why not wine and dine by candlelight and moonlight on a

The Manohra is the rare dinner cruise on which the meal is as good as the scenery.

converted rice barge cruising on the Chao Phraya River? And an excellent dinner it is, too. The barge picks up diners at Thaksin pier and the Anatara; call to reserve. *Anantara Riverside Bangkok Resort, 257 Charoen Nakorn Rd, Thonburi. ☎ 02 476 0022. www.bangkok-riverside.anantara.com. Set menu 1990 baht (not including wine/drinks). AE, DC, MC, V. Cruises leave the Anantara at 7pm & Taksin pier at 7:30pm daily. BTS SkyTrain: Saphan Taksin. Map p 92.*

★ **May Kaidee** BANGLAMPHU *VEGETARIAN* Although tucked down an alley, everyone knows smiling May and her excellent vegetarian/vegan diner with lots of coconut curries and sour soups to choose from. May offers a Thai vegetarian cooking school for foreigners. There's also a branch at 33 Samsen Road. *Behind Burger King, Tanao Rd. ☎ 086 398 4808. www.maykaidee.com. Dishes from 100 baht. No credit cards. Breakfast, lunch & dinner daily. No metro. Ferry: Phra Arthit pier (N13). Map p 92.*

★ **Mezzaluna** BANGRAK ECLECTIC FINE DINING Chef Ryuki Kawasaki's recipes are elegant, complex, and visually stunning. A favorite: Nova Scotia lobster glazed in lobster jus with sea urchin, heart of palm, corn puree, bisque jelly, popcorn foam, and curry oil. There's also a primo selection of caviar and oysters. The restaurant's high ceilings allow for panoramic views across Bangkok, but unlike its brothers in the Tower Club at Lebua, Breeze, and Sirocco, this is fine dining indoors, so you don't get quite the same feeling of vertigo. *Tower Club at Lebua, 1055 Silom Rd, cnr Charoen Krung Rd. ☎ 02 624 9555. www.lebua.com/mezzaluna. Meals 2000–2500 baht. AE, DC, MC, V. BTS SkyTrain: Saphan Taksin. Map p 92.*

★ **Nahm** SATHORN *THAI* Aussie chef David Thompson's take on

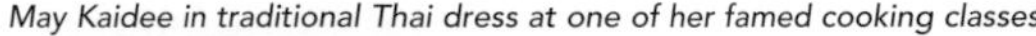

May Kaidee in traditional Thai dress at one of her famed cooking classes.

Grilled prawns with peanut relish at Nahm.

Thai food has seen Nahm voted one of the top 50 in restaurants in Asia. Expect well-executed dishes that draw on Thailand's rich culinary traditions, from the kitchens of the royal palace to street food stalls, all served in the sleek surroundings of the Metropolitan Hotel. *Metropolitan Hotel, 27 South Sathorn Rd, Silom. ☎ 02 625 3388. www.comohotels.com. Meals 2000–3000 baht. AE, DC, MC, V. Breakfast, lunch & dinner daily. BTS SkyTrain: Sala Daeng or MRT subway: Silom. Map p 92.*

New York Steakhouse SUKHUMVIT *AMERICAN* If you are homesick for a thick, juicy steak, barbeque pork ribs or other comfort foods, this is a dream come true. Dress up—the place is posh! *2nd floor, JW Marriott Hotel, 4 Soi 2, Sukhumvit Rd. ☎ 02 656 7700. Meals 1500 baht. AE, DC, MC, V. Dinner daily. BTS SkyTrain: Nana. Map p 91.*

★ kids **Patty's Fiesta** PATPONG *MEXICAN* For me, Mexican should never be a fine-dining experience, but more of a slapstick colorful cantina with a mariachi band, margaritas, sizzling fajitas, and a carnival ambience. And that's Patty's! It's in Patpong, too, so expect *muchisimo* revelry. *109–111 Patpong Soi 1 (cnr Silom Rd), Bangrak. ☎ 02 632 7898. Meals 800–900 baht. AE, DC, MC, V. Lunch & dinner daily. BTS: Sala Daeng or MRT subway: Silom. Map p 92.*

Ramentei SUKHUMVIT *JAPANESE* Fans of *ramen* (Japanese meat-based noodle soups) flock to this bustling diner, which is popular with Japanese expats at lunchtime. *593/23–24 Soi 33/1, Sukhumvit Rd. ☎ 02 662 0050. www.ramentei-bkk.com. Meals 200 baht. No credit cards. Lunch & dinner daily. BTS SkyTrain: Phrom Phong. Map p 91.*

Ranee's Guesthouse BANGLAMPHU *VEGETARIAN* A backpacker's favorite. I often head to Ranee's not only for the shaded courtyard and the healthy Thai vegetarian dishes, but also for the freshly baked breads and cakes. *77 Trok Mayom, behind Chakrapong Rd. ☎ 02 282 4072. Meals 300 baht. No credit cards. Breakfast, lunch & dinner daily. BTS SkyTrain or MRT subway. Ferry: Phra Arthit pier (N13). Map p 92.*

★ **Rang Mahal** SUKHUMVIT *INDIAN* Fine dining and Indian cuisine are not often found together in Thailand, but this rooftop restaurant is elegant and chic, and offers a sumptuous selection of culinary delights from every corner of India. Try the tender grilled lamb marinated in rum, herbs and spices. *Top floor, Rembrandt Hotel, 19 Soi 18, Sukhumvit Rd. ☎ 02 261 7100. www.rembrandtbkk.com. Meals 1000 baht. AE, MC, V. Lunch & dinner daily. BTS SkyTrain: Asok or MRT subway: Sukhumvit. Map p 91.*

Thai Dining Etiquette

Thai people have high standards of hygiene and politeness. A few rules of thumb:

- Several dishes are ordered together and placed in the center of the table. It is common for everyone tucks in with their own spoon and fork but in posher restaurants there is more likely to be a serving spoon in each dish.
- Chopsticks are used in Chinese restaurants or to eat noodles; plain rice and Thai food is eaten with a spoon and fork; only sticky rice is eaten with your hand.
- If you invite others to dinner, it will probably be assumed that you are paying. In a small group, the most senior person normally picks up the tab.
- Tipping is not obligatory. Most people will leave a small tip after a large meal but not for cheap dishes such as noodles.

Rasa Khas SUKHUMVIT *INDONESIAN* To my knowledge this is the sole Indonesian restaurant in Bangkok and it has quickly developed a grateful following. Fruity favorites such as the jackfruit curry and *gado-gado* (vegetables in a peanut satay sauce) make for a distinctly different Asian option. 86 Sukhumvit 23, Khlong Toei Nuea ☎ *02 108 5437. www.rasakhas.com. Meals 300 baht. AE, MC, V. Lunch & dinner Tues–Sun. BTS SkyTrain: Asok or MRT subway: Sukhumvit.*

A chef serves up Northern Indian delicacies at Rang Mahal.

★ **Roti-Mataba** BANGLAMPHU *MUSLIM* A popular backpacker haunt offering halal meat, Thai massaman curry, and stuffed Indian pancakes. *136 Phra Arthit Rd. ☎ 02 282 2119. www.roti-mataba.net. Meals 250–350 baht. No credit cards. Breakfast, lunch & dinner Tues–Sun. No BTS SkyTrain or MRT subway. Ferry: Phra Arthit pier (N13). Map p 92.*

kids **Ruen Mallika** SUKHUMVIT *THAI* An old Siamese teak house converted into a pleasant tourist-friendly restaurant serving the full range of traditional Thai favorites, beautifully presented by charming wait staff. *Soi Sedhi, 89 Soi 22, Sukhumvit Rd, Klong Toey. ☎ 02 663 3211. www.ruenmallika.com. Meals 800–900 baht. AE, DC, MC, V. Lunch & dinner daily. BTS SkyTrain:*

Asok or MRT subway: Sukhumvit. Map p 91.

Scoozi BANGRAK *ITALIAN* If you're on the lookout for pizza, Scoozi has 20 outlets in Bangkok all serving thin-crust pizzas baked in wood-fired ovens, as well as antipasti, pasta, soup, and salad. *174/3 Surawong Rd, Silom. ☎ 02 234 6999. Meals 800–900 baht. AE, DC, MC, V. Lunch & dinner daily. BTS SkyTrain: Chong Nonsi. Map p 92.*

Shangarila Restaurant CHINATOWN *CANTONESE* A banquet-sized eating hall for banquet-sized portions of steaming *dim sum* and fried Cantonese specialties. *306 Yaowarat Rd. ☎ 02 224 5933. Meals 500 baht. MC, V. Lunch & dinner daily. Nearest MRT subway: Hua Lamphong. Map p 92.*

Shiro SUKHUMVIT *JAPANESE* You'll get good value at this modest Japanese diner, which has a small sushi bar and tables for dining. Delicate sashimi, good sushi platters, fried fish, and warm soups make for an especially great lunch. *21 Soi 24, Sukhumvit Rd, Klong Toey. ☎ 02 258 7016. Meals 500–600 baht. AE, MC, V. Lunch & dinner daily. BTS SkyTrain: Phrom Phong. Map p 91.*

★★ Sirocco BANGRAK *INTERNATIONAL* Of the Tower Club's trinity of high-end restaurants (Sirocco, Breeze, and Mezzaluna), I would say Sirocco is the best. It's majestically situated on the edge of a glass tower high above the city, but still manages to offer the relaxing ambience of a live jazz venue. An exquisite Chef's Menu includes Atlantic scallops, goose rillettes, and aged U.S. beef. There's also a selection of caviar and oysters State Tower and Tower Club at lebua. *1055 Silom Rd, cnr Charoen Krung Rd. ☎ 02 624 9555. www.lebua.com. Meals 2000–3000 baht. AE, DC, MC, V. Lunch & dinner daily. BTS SkyTrain: Saphan Taksin. Map p 92.*

Smith SUKHUMVIT *INTERNATIONAL* Another restaurant by Ian Kittichai of Issaya Siamese Club, this time a nose-to-tail concept. The décor is industrial chic while the menu serves up calf's tongue, pig's trotters, mini haggis, hanger steak, and burgers. There's also a Chef's Table, cooking school, and a shop. *1/8 Sukhumvit Soi 49, Bangkok. ☎ 02 261 0515. www.smith-restaurant.com. Dishes from 180 baht. AE, MC, V. Tues–Sat 5pm–midnight; Sun 11am–midnight. BTS SkyTrain: Thong Lor.*

Smokin' Pug BANGRAK *AMERICAN* Tuck into a full rack of baby back ribs, pulled pork sandwiches, cornbread, slaw, smoky beans, mac'n'-cheese, all washed down with craft beers. Top notch nosh! *BTS SkyTrain: Sala Daeng or MRT subway: Silom. 88 Surawongse Rd. www.facebook.com/smokinpug. ☎ 083 029 7598 9125.*

★ Somboon Seafood BANGRAK *SEAFOOD* I would call this a seafood warehouse, with masses of tables overflowing with lobster shells and beer bottles, dozens of wait staff crisscrossing the floor and an aquarium of live crabs, prawns, fish, and crustaceans for you to peruse. Do not miss the fried curry crab! Seven branches including Ratchadaphisek Road, Sukhumvit Soi 103 and Samyan. *169/7–11 Surawong Rd (cnr Ratchanakharin Rd), Silom. ☎ 02 233 3104. Meals 600–1000 baht. No credit cards. Dinner daily. BTS SkyTrain: Chong Nonsi. Map p 92.*

Barbecued salmon on pressed potato with tomato salsa at 22 Kitchen.

★★ Suan Thip NONTHABURI *THAI* I was once out in Nonthaburi and found this wonderful restaurant, serving excellent traditional Thai food set in a lush garden on the river. Try the massaman chicken curry. *Changwattana Pak Kret 3 Rd (Soi Wat Koo), Bang Pood. ☎ 02 583 3748. www.suanthip.com. Meals 500–600 baht. AE, DC, MC, V. Lunch & dinner daily. No metro. Map p 92.*

Tang Jai Yoo CHINATOWN *CHINESE* My Chinese-Thai friends love this place for the seafood and, in particular, the barbecue-grilled fresh fish (chosen from a fish tank). *85–87 Yaowaphanit Rd. ☎ 02 224 2167. Meals 500–600 baht. No credit cards. Lunch & dinner daily. MRT subway: Hua Lamphong. Map p 92.*

★ Tapas Cafe SUKHUMVIT *SPANISH* Every time I walk in here, there's a fiesta atmosphere. Maybe it's the open-plan design, the fruity sangria, or the salsa and Latino tunes. All your Spanish favorites—Serrano ham, Manchego cheese, and chorizo sausage—are available on the extensive menu. *1/25 Soi 11, Sukhumvit Rd. ☎ 02 651 2947. www.tapasiarestaurants.com. Meals 600–900 baht. AE, MC, V. Lunch & dinner daily. BTS SkyTrain: Nana. Map p 91.*

Thip Samai PHRA NAKORN *THAI* I have no idea why, but visitors to Thailand seem to go nuts for *pad Thai* (fried egg noodles and peanuts). If you suffer from a similar disposition, you will be drawn to the renowned Thip Samai. *313 Maha Chai Rd, opp. Golden Mount. ☎ 02 221 6280. Meals 50 baht. No credit cards. Dinner daily. No metro. Map p 92.*

★ Thiptara THONBURI *THAI* This is Thai home-style cooking at its finest, served delightfully in open-air teak pavilions by candlelight with a panoramic view of the city and the Chao Phraya River by night. Don't miss the *polamai nam* *pung*, a feast of Thai fruits roasted in honey, chili, and vanilla. ***Peninsula Hotel, 333 Charoen Nakhon Rd.*** *☎ 02626 1849. Meals 1400–1600 baht. AE, DC, MC, V. Dinner daily. BTS SkyTrain: Saphan Taksin then a free hotel ferry from the pier. Map p 92.*

★★★ **22 Kitchen & Bar** BANGRAK *PACIFIC COAST* The renowned Dusit Thani's latest dining concept focuses on an eclectic seafood menu with flavors of Hawaii, Mexico, and Japan. A great place to relax with a cocktail and enjoy panoramic city views. ***22nd floor, Dusit Thani Hotel, 946 Rama IV Rd, cnr Silom Rd, Lumphini.*** *☎ 02 200 9000. www.dusit.com. Meals 2000–2500 baht. AE, DC, MC, V. Lunch Mon–Fri, dinner Mon–Sat. BTS SkyTrain: Sala Daeng or MRT subway: Silom. Map p 92.*

★★ **You & Mee** PATHUMWAN *ASIAN* Pop in for a comforting bowls of noodle soup or fried noodles at this relaxed venue in a five-star hotel. There's also a lunchtime curry buffet, and a popular evening *khao tom* rice soup buffet. ***Grand Hyatt Erawan Hotel, 494 Ratchadamri Rd.*** *☎ 02 254 1234. www.bangkokgrand.hyatt.com. Meals 300 baht. Lunch & dinner daily. BTS SkyTrain: Chit Lom.* ●

Twinkling lights, orchids, and river views make for a romantic meal at Thiptara.

7 The Best Nightlife

Nightlife Best Bets

Best **Aussie Pub**
The Office Bar & Grill, *Soi 33, Sukhumvit Rd (p 117)*

Best **Blues Bar**
★★★ Ad Here the 13th, *13 Samsen Rd (p 119)*

Best **British Pub**
Black Swan, *326/8–9 Sukhumvit Rd (p 115)*

Best **Champagne at Sunset**
★★★ Moon Bar at Vertigo, *21/100 South Sathorn Rd (p 115)*

Best **Chance to Bump into Supermodels**
★★★ Sing Sing Theatre, *26 Soi 11, Sukhumvit Rd (p 121)*

Best **Jam Sessions**
★★ Overtone Music Cave, *29/70–72 Royal City Ave (p 120)*

Best **Jazz Club**
★ Brown Sugar, *Wanchad Junction (p 119)*

Best **Margaritas**
Vesper, *10/15 Convent Rd (p 118)*

Best **Party Atmosphere**
★★★ Tawandang German Brewery, *Rama III Rd, Levels, Sukhumvit Soi 11 (p 120)*

Best **Jazz Lounge**
Bamboo Bar, *Mandarin Oriental Hotel, 48 Oriental Ave (p 119)*

Best **Trance/Techno Club**
★ Lava Club, *Khao San Rd (p 120)*

Best **Views of Bangkok by Night**
★★★ Sky Bar at Sirocco, *63rd floor, lebua at State Tower, 1055 Silom Rd (p 117)*

Best **Wine Bar**
★ Scarlett, *188 Silom Rd (p 122)*

Preceding page: Kao San Road is just one of Bangkok's many nightlife districts.

You can't beat the views at the Moon Bar (see p. 115)—and the drinks aren't bad, either.

Greater Bangkok Nightlife

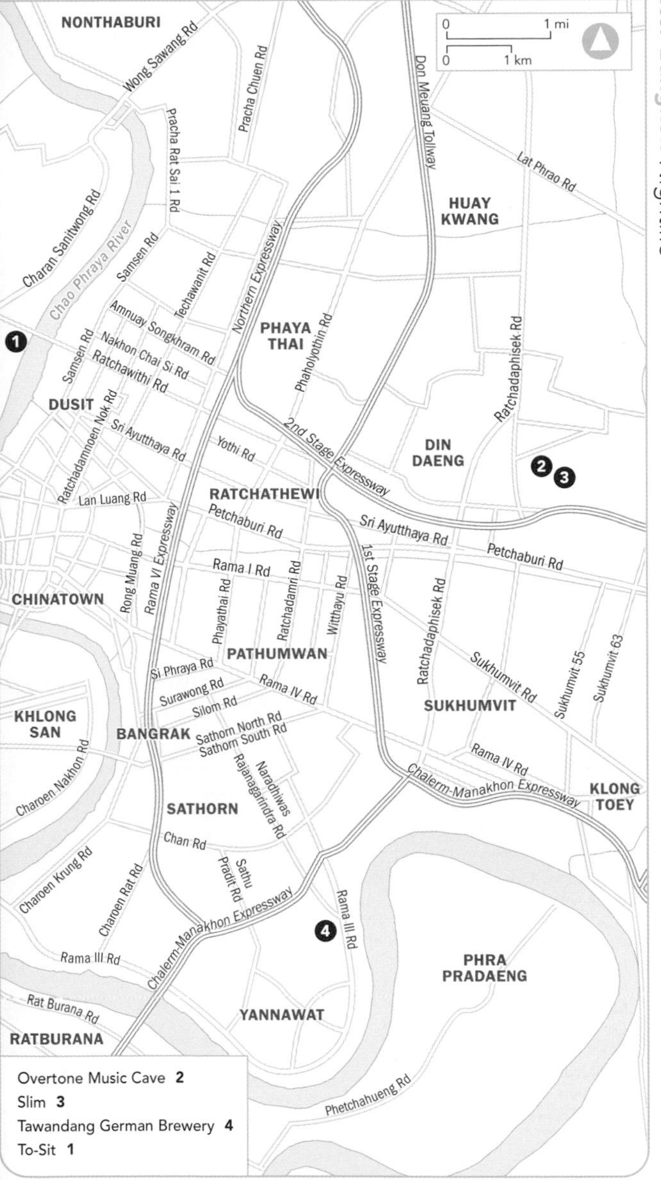

Central Bangkok Nightlife

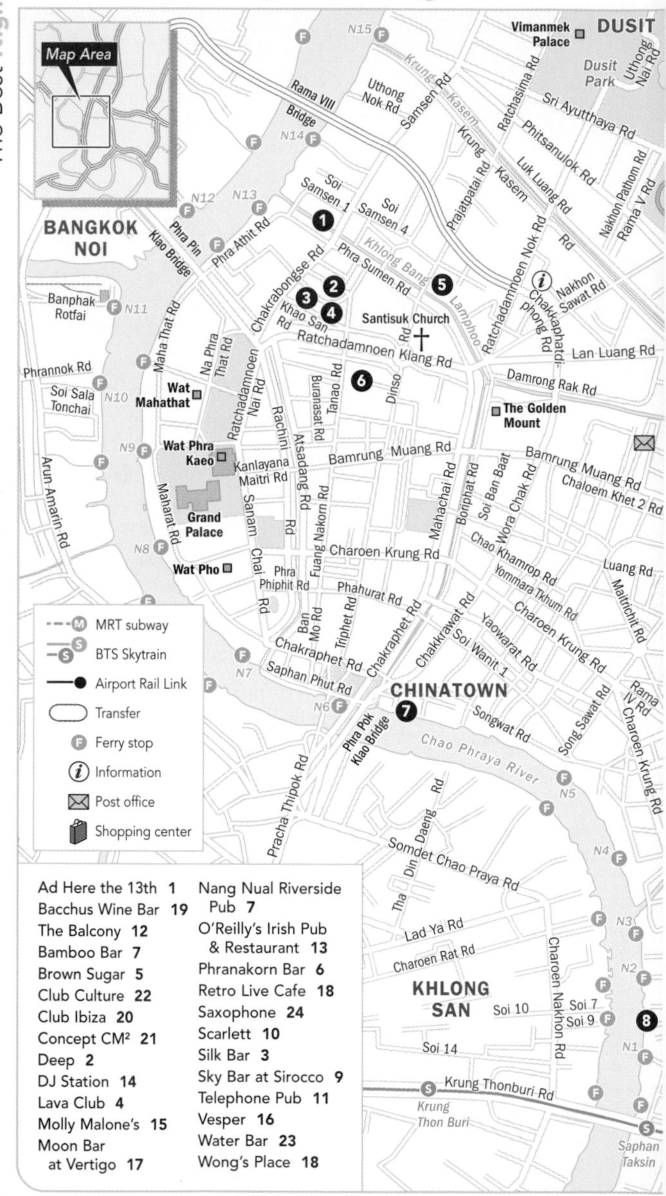

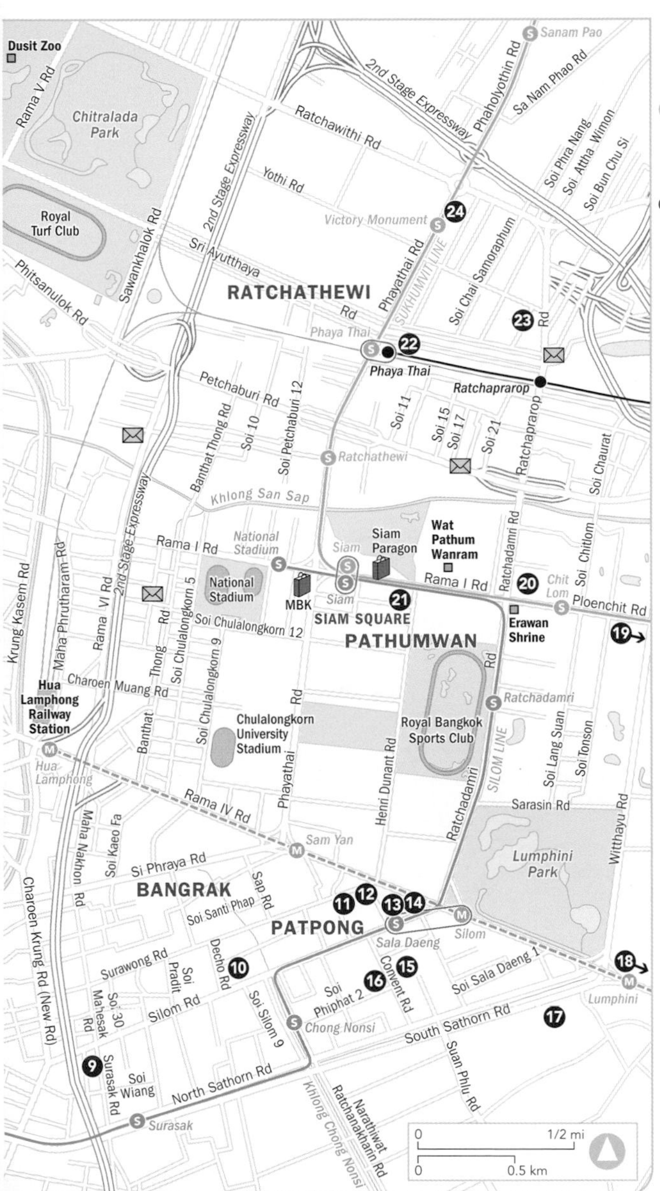
Dusit Zoo
Chitralada Park
Royal Turf Club
Rama V Rd
Sawankhalok Rd
2nd Stage Expressway
Ratchawithi Rd
Yothi Rd
Sri Ayutthaya Rd
Phitsanulok Rd
RATCHATHEWI
Victory Monument
Sanam Pao
Phaholyothin Rd
Sa Nam Phao Rd
Soi Phra Nang
Soi Attha Wimon
Soi Bun Chu Si
Phayathai Rd
SUKHUMVIT LINE
Soi Chai Samoraphum Rd
Phaya Thai
Ratchaprarop
Petchaburi Rd
Banthat Thong Rd
Soi 10
Soi Petchaburi 12
Soi 11
Soi 15
Soi 17
Soi 21
Ratchathewi
Soi Chaurat
Khlong San Sap
Rama I Rd
National Stadium
Siam
Siam Paragon
Wat Pathum Wanram
Ratchadamri Rd
Chit Lom
Soi Chitlom
Ploenchit Rd
MBK
SIAM SQUARE
PATHUMWAN
Erawan Shrine
Krung Kasem Rd
Maha Phrutharam Rd
Rama VI Rd
Soi Chulalongkorn 5
Soi Chulalongkorn 12
Soi Chulalongkorn 9
Hua Lamphong Railway Station
Charoen Muang Rd
Chulalongkorn University Stadium
Royal Bangkok Sports Club
Ratchadamri
SILOM LINE
Soi Lang Suan
Soi Tonson
Hua Lamphong
Rama IV Rd
Henri Dunant Rd
Sarasin Rd
Witthayu Rd
Lumphini Park
Maha Nakhon Rd
Soi Kaeo Fa
Sam Yan
Si Phraya Rd
BANGRAK
Sap Rd
Soi Santi Phap
PATPONG
Sala Daeng
Silom
Charoen Krung Rd (New Rd)
Surawong Rd
Soi Pradit
Decho Rd
Convent Rd
Soi Sala Daeng 1
Lumphini
Soi Phiphat 2
Soi 30
Mahesak Rd
Silom Rd
Soi Silom 9
Chong Nonsi
South Sathorn Rd
Surasak Rd
Soi Wiang
North Sathorn Rd
Suan Phlu Rd
Surasak
Khlong Chong Nonsi
Narathiwat Ratchanakharin Rd
0 1/2 mi
0 0.5 km
9
10
11
12
13
14
15
16
17
18
19
20
21
22
23
24

Sukhumvit Road Nightlife

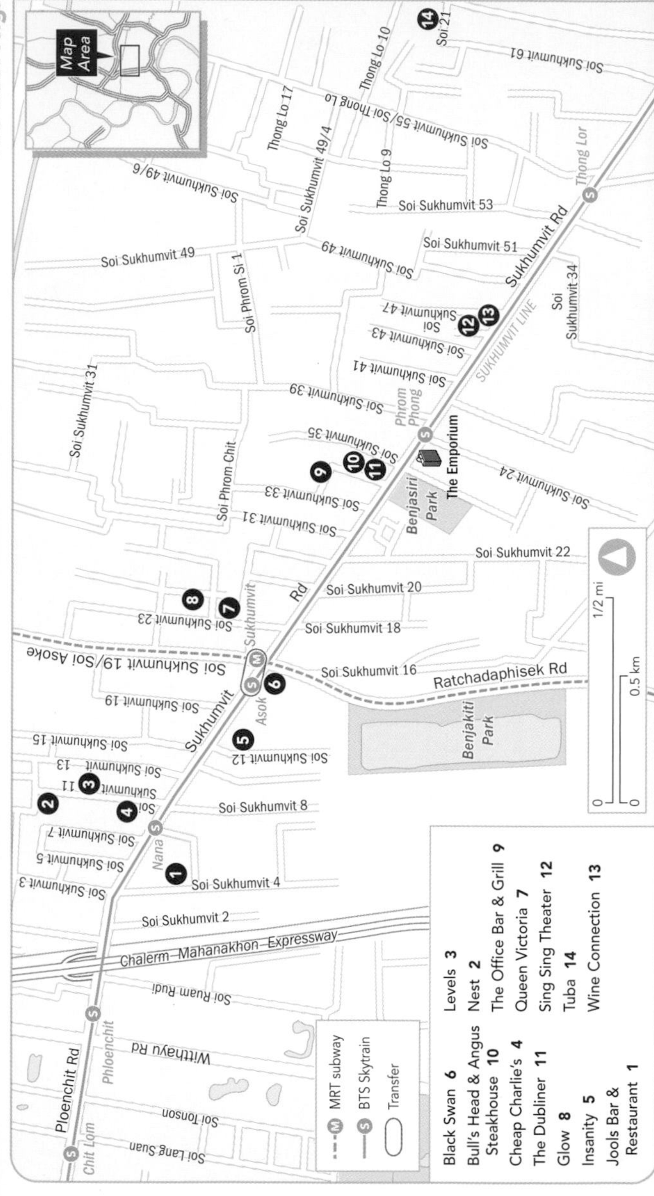

Bangkok Nightlife A to Z

Bars & Pubs

Black Swan SUKHUMVIT Recently relocated but still in the same area, this British pub is as authentic as you can get, and is your place if you're homesick for a full English breakfast, roast dinners, fish and chips, Guinness and John Smith bitter. The Black Swan is especially popular for live sports on the plasma. *Soi 19, Sukhumvit Rd.* ☎ *02 229 4542. blackswanbangkok.com. BTS SkyTrain: Asoke or MRT subway: Sukhumvit. Map p 114.*

Bull's Head & Angus Steakhouse SUKHUMVIT This is a boisterous British pub with comedy nights, quizzes, club meetings, and raucous behavior by Bangkok expats. The Bull's Head & Angus Steakhouse offers a selection of British and Irish ales and steak pies with chips. *595/10–11 Sukhumvit Rd, Soi 33.* ☎ *02 259 4444/02 261 7747. www.greatbritishpub.com. Metro: Phrom Phong. Map p 114.*

Cheap Charlie's SUKHUMVIT An institution in Bangkok! As the name suggests, Cheap Charlie's is an unpretentious watering hole—nay, wooden shack—where travelers and expats come to drink the night away. Oh, and it's cheap. *2/7 Soi 11, Sukhumvit Rd. BTS SkyTrain: Nana. Map p 114.*

Deep BANGLAMPHU For the young and reckless, this is a spot to wrap up a good night out. Deep is always busy and, oft times, sweaty. It's dark and seedy, but always full of characters and loud pounding beats. *329/1–2 Rambutri Rd.* ☎ *02 629 3360. No SkyTrain or MRT. Map p 112.*

★ **The Dubliner** SUKHUMVIT Recently relocated from Washington Square, arguably Bangkok's best Irish pub has all the usual Guinness and Kilkenny, shamrocks, and leprechauns you would expect, but what sets it apart is its playful ambience. It's like a homecoming, even if you're not Irish. Soi 33/1 Sukhumvit Road. ☎ *02 204 1841.* www.thedublinerbangkok.com. *BTS SkyTrain: Phrom Phong Map p 114.*

★ **Flann O'Brien's** SILOM Conveniently located right next to a SkyTrain station, this friendly pub is popular with expats and locals. There's a good menu of British fare and Thai favorites, imported beers, and live music most nights. *62/1-4 Silom Rd,* ☎ *02 632 7518. www.flann-obriens.com. BTS SkyTrain: Sala Daeng or MRT subway: Silom.*

★★ **Iron Fairies** THONG LOR Expats, Thai hi-so and tourists hang out in this fantasy world of a Dickensian factory-themed shophouse. It's one of the city's most creative places to enjoy food and drink. *404 Sukhumvit Soi 55 (Thong Lor) Bangkok. BTS SkyTrain: Thong Lor. www.theironfairies.com.* ☎ *02-714-8875.*

Molly Malone's BANGRAK For an Irish pub it's a bit brightly lit and feels like a franchise. Nonetheless, you get a friendly crowd in night after night and all the accouterments you would expect—Sunday lunches, happy hour (4 to 7pm daily), pool sharks, live music, and, of course, Guinness on tap. *1/5–6 Convent Rd (behind Silom Rd).* ☎ *02 266 7160. www.mollymalonesbangkok.com. BTS SkyTrain: Sala Daeng or MRT subway: Silom. Map p 112.*

★★ **Moon Bar at Vertigo** SATHORN Vertigo is the word! This sophisticated open-air bar/restaurant sits on the rooftop of the

When Is a Bar Not a Bar?

Bangkok is notorious for its nightlife; but it's not all go-go dancers and sex workers. There's everything from basement jazz clubs to sophisticated wine bars and old-fashioned pubs to high-tech nightclubs.

There's no cover charge or drinks minimum in bars (if they do ask for an entry fee, it's no doubt a girly bar). However, nightclubs often ask a cover charge, usually with one free drink included. Note that the admission fee can vary considerably and may depend on "theme nights," supply and demand, or simply how you look!

Police regulations force most bars to close at 1am, though nightclubs and bars in heavy tourist zones stay open until at least 2am. You must be 20 years old to enter a nightclub. Carry ID and note that there's no smoking inside venues.

61-storey Banyan Tree. The views are spectacular, so cocktails or champagne at sunset are a must. Dress smartly; don't go if it's raining. *The Banyan Tree, 21/100 South Sathorn Rd, Silom. ☎ 02 679 1200. www.banyantree.com. MRT subway: Lumphini. Map p 112.*

Nang Nual Riverside Pub CHINATOWN A Chinese-Thai haunt where you can bop around your table with whisky sets, snacks, and loud pop tunes. On hot nights it catches sweet breezes from the river. *Trok Krai, Mahachak Rd. ☎ 02 223 7686. No metro. Ferry: Saphan Phut (Memorial Bridge) N6. Map p 112.*

★★ **Nest** SUKHUMVIT For a private group of revelers, this is the perfect rendezvous. An elegant rooftop bar (with cover in case of

Bring a group of friends so you can take over one of the couches at Nest.

The aptly named—and quite chic—Skybar is literal a highlight of Bangkok's nightlife scene.

rain), intriguingly designed with gardens and a labyrinth of rattan beds and colorful sofas. Expect excellent service and a quiet atmosphere. *9th floor, Le Fenix, 33/33 Soi Sukhumvit 11.* ☎ *02 255 0638 9. www.nestbangkok.com. BTS SkyTrain: Nana. Map p 114.*

The Office Bar & Grill SUKHUMVIT Fans of rugby and cricket will quickly steer towards this watering-hole-cum-hostess bar with its big-screen TV, draft beer, steaks, and ribs. *Sukhumvit Rd, Soi 33.* ☎ *02 662 1936. www.theofficebkk.com. BTS SkyTrain: Phrom Phong. Map p 114.*

Phranakorn Bar BANGLAMPHU A funky, chic place to meet arty characters. It has a rooftop terrace and often hosts exhibitions. *58/2 Soi Damnoen Klang Tai.* ☎ *02 622 0282. No metro. Map p 112.*

Queen Victoria SUKHUMVIT A friendly traditional British style pub offering and extensive menu of Thai and western food, and a good choice of draught beers and ciders. The spacious bar has TVs screening sports action, and there is an outside area for dining. *Soi 23 (opposite Soi Cowboy), Sukhumvit Rd.* ☎ *02 661 7417. www.queenvicbkkcom. BTS SkyTrain: Asoke, MRT subway: Sukhumvit. Map p 114.*

Silk Bar BANGLAMPHU This cozy open-air cocktail bar is ideal for people-watching on Khao San Road. Lots of young expats and Thais turn up here on Friday and Saturday nights before heading to nightclubs. *129–131 Khao San Rd.* ☎ *02 281 9981. www.silkbars.com. No SkyTrain or MRT. Ferry: Tha Phrat Arthit. Map p 112.*

★★★ Sky Bar at Sirocco BANGRAK At first glance, the neon-lit round bar seems to be slipping off the edge of the rooftop into the Chao Phraya River, so precarious is its situation. But on a clear night, in your most stylish attire, with martini in hand and someone special on your arm, you'll feel like you're on top of the world. *63rd floor, Tower Club at lebua, 1055 Silom Rd.* ☎ *02 624 9555. www.lebua.com/the-dome. BTS SkyTrain: Saphan Taksin. Map p 112*

★ Tuba EKKAMAI This is a second-hand furniture shop morphed into a retro '70s bar with pool tables and flatscreen TVs by night. Popular with college students and groovy hipsters, Tuba is a great place to dip your toe into Thai youth culture without drowning. Try the mega cocktails! *30 Soi 21, Sukhumvit Rd, Soi 63 (Soi Ekamai). ☎ 02 711 5500. www.design-athome.com. BTS SkyTrain: Ekkamai. Map p 114.*

Vesper Cocktail Bar & Restaurant BANGRAK A trendy bar reminiscent of those from 1930s Europe, here bartenders mix, muddle, and shake great cocktails. There's also a good selection of imported ales and a Spanish and Italian-inspired menu. A very cool joint. *10/15 Convent Rd (just of Silom Rd). ☎ 02 235 2777. www.vesper-bar.co. BTS SkyTrain: Sala Daeng or MRT subway: Silom. Map p 112.*

Water Bar RATCHATHEWI A whisky bar, Thai style. This is a great place to meet tipsy locals as revelers knock back shots into the wee hours. *107/3–4 Soi Rang Nam, Phayathai Rd. ☎ 02 642 7699. BTS SkyTrain: Victory Monument. Map p 112.*

★ **Wong's Place** SATHORN If you are having a very late night and want to plant yourself somewhere dark and dingy, Wong's is the place on the east side that pulls in the most eccentric characters. Parties often go on until dawn. *27/3 Soi Sri Bumphen, Rama IV Rd, Yannawa. ☎ 02 286 1558. BTS SkyTrain: Lumphini or MRT subway: Klong Toei. Map p 112.*

Gay & Lesbian Bars & Clubs

The Balcony BANGRAK This big-fun tavern is the centerpiece of Silom Soi 4, the city's most overtly gay street. You'll always find a boy beauty contest, a cabaret show, or something sexy and outrageous going on. It has a reasonable wine list, too. *86–88 Soi 4, Silom Rd. ☎ 02 235 5891. www.balconypub.com. No cover. BTS SkyTrain: Sala Daeng or MRT subway: Silom. Map p 112.*

DJ Station BANGRAK This nightclub has three floors of grinding tunes, sofas, and all-night dancing, and is usually packed with Bangkok boys, expats, and tourists. *Soi 2, Silom Rd. ☎ 02 266 4029. www.dj-station.com. Cover 200 baht. BTS SkyTrain: Sala Daeng or MRT subway: Silom. Map p. 112.*

Bangkok is becoming known for its expert mixology.

Telephone Pub BANGRAK More intimate and less flamboyant than its neighbors on Silom Soi 4, this is a tourist-friendly rainbow bar, named for the old telephones at each table that you can use to dial someone sitting across the bar. *114/11–13 Soi 4, Silom Rd. ☎ 02 234 3279. www.telephonepub.com. No cover. BTS SkyTrain: Sala Daeng or MRT subway: Silom. Map p 112.*

The Stranger Bar SILOM A New York-styled gay bar offering premium cocktails, DJs, and good times in a modern, stylish atmosphere. The venue features a main bar, mezzanine, and a second floor with a private balcony. *114/14 Silom Soi 4. ☎ 02 632 9125. BTS SkyTrain: Sala Daeng or MRT subway: Silom.*

Live Music

★★★ Ad Here the 13th BANGLAMPHU Another "in" place I shouldn't even be telling you about. Singer Georgia fills to bursting this hole-in-the-wall tavern with her booming "blues mamma" voice. She's backed by a live band playing Monday to Saturday. There's only space inside for a handful of aficionados; make sure you're one of them! *13 Samsen Rd. ☎ 02 769 4613. No BTS SkyTrain or MRT. Map p 112.*

Bamboo Bar BANGRAK An exquisite up-market venue, with marvelous international jazz and blues bands and a play-it-again-Sam ambience. Adjoining the bar is a Cuban cigar store that acts as a smoking lounge. *Mandarin Oriental, 48 Oriental Ave. ☎ 02 659 9000, ext 7690. BTS SkyTrain Saphan Taksin. Map p 112.*

★ Brown Sugar: The Jazz Boutique PATHUMWAN After 3 decades, Bangkok's legendary jazz venue has relocated from Lumphini to Banglumphu. As well as live jazz, the 200-seater space features art exhibitions, film screenings, and more. Arrive at about 11pm for the best jazz bands and atmosphere. *469 Wanchad Junction, Phra Sumen Rd, Banglumphu. www.brownsugarbangkok.com. ☎ 02 282 0396. No SkyTrain or MRT. Map p 112.*

★ Fat Gut'z Saloon THONG LOR A vintage-type joint serving fish and chips, cocktails and straight-up blues from the live band nightly from 9pm. *1st Floor, Grass Thonglor lifestyle mall, 264 Thonglor Soi 12. ☎ 02 714 9832. Nearest BTS SkyTrain: Thonglor.*

Flann O'Briens's Irish Pub & Restaurant BANGRAK This Irish pub-cum–sports bar is best known for its British pub grub and live music, including a Thai Beatles cover band on Fridays—it's great! *62/1–4 Silom Rd. ☎ 02 632 7518. www.flann-obriens.com. BTS SkyTrain: Sala Daeng or MRT subway: Silom.*

Legions of taxis whisk partiers around the city after dark.

★★ Overtone Music Cave HUAY KWANG I heartily recommend this racy international tavern for those who crave seriously raw tunes. Check the program for rock, blues, jazz, ska, reggae, funk, or fusion nights, Wednesday to Sunday, as well as impromptu jam sessions. *29/70–72 Royal City Ave (RCA) zone D, Rama IX Rd. ☎ 02 203 0423 5 or 02 641 4283. MRT subway: Rama IX. Map p 111.*

Retro Live Cafe KLONG TOEY This large venue acts as a concert hall for raunchy local bands—usually playing Thai songs and covers of western hits. A state-of-the-art sound and light system encourages a party atmosphere for the young crowd. It also serves very spicy Thai meals. *Lakeside, Queen Sirikit National Convention Centre, 60 New Ratchadaphisek Rd. ☎ 02 203 4000. MRT subway: Klong Toey or Queen Sirikit. Map p 112.*

★ Saxophone RATCHATHEWI Everyone knows Saxophone. It's been around since 1987 and pulls in all the swingers and hipsters in town for its rocking atmosphere and jazz and blues bands. It also has an excellent dining area. *3/8 Phayathai Rd, Victory Monument. ☎ 02 246 5472. www.saxophonepub.com. BTS SkyTrain: Victory Monument.*

Tawandang German Brewery YANNAWA A big Bavarian beer hall with steins of frothy beer, German food and Thai-style entertainment—a big band banging out Thai-western hits and the odd cabaret number. *462/61 Narathiwat Rd, Rama III. ☎ 02 678 1114 6. www.tawandang.co.th. No SkyTrain or MRT. Map p 111.*

To-Sit THONBURI In recent years To-Sit bar-restaurants seem to be popping up all over the city. I go to the venue at Pier 92—it's on the west bank of the river, has a beautifully laid-out floor plan and unobtrusive acoustic music every night. It's a university student hangout and has good food, too. *115 Soi Charansantiwongse 92, Charansantiwongse Rd, Bang Phlad. ☎ 02 879 1717. No SkyTrain or MRT. Map p 111.*

Nightclubs

Concept CM² SIAM SQUARE If you like dancing to live bands—especially hip-hop and trip-hop—you'll find there's a new one every night at this tightly packed (loud) venue. *Basement, Novotel, Siam Square Soi 6, Pathumwan. ☎ 02 209 8888. www.cm2bkk.com. Cover 200 baht. BTS SkyTrain station: Siam. Map p 112.*

★ Glow SUKHUMVIT Small, intimate and sexy, Glow is popular with the less pretentious, more earthy clubber. There are lots of theme nights—check the website. *96/4–5 Soi 23, Sukhumvit Rd. ☎ 02 261 4446. www.glowbkk.com. Cover 300 baht. BTS SkyTrain station Asok or MRT subway: Sukhumvit. Map p 114.*

Insanity SUKHUMVIT A huge nightclub in the heart of downtown Sukhumvit. Daily promotions, with up to 50 percent of selected drinks keep it crowded along with loud music from a top-notch sound system, visiting international DJs and dancing girls. *234 Sukhumvit Soi 12. www.clubinsanitybangkok.com. ☎ 02 653 2923. BTS SkyTrain: Nana. Map p 114.*

Lava Club BANGLAMPHU International backpackers and funky young Thais descend into the inferno of Lava late at night to dance to trance, hip-hop, and R&B. *Basement, Bayon Building (opp. Nana Plaza), Khao San Rd.*

Bar @494 is known for its wine happy hours, which draw legions of locals and tourists.

☎ *02 281 6565. No cover. No SkyTrain or MRT. Nearest ferry: Tha Phra Arthit. Map p 112.*

Levels SUKHUMVIT After the closure of Bed Supperclub and Q Bar, Levels has revitalized the Sukhumvit club scene. The venue has an exclusive ambience and is divided into four zones: an alfresco terrace, a lounge, a VIP section, and the club. Local and guests DJs spin and control a fab lighting system. *6 Floor, Aloft Hotel, 35 Sukhumvit Soi 11 Bangkok. www.levelsclub.com.* ☎ *082-308-3246. BTS SkyTrain: Nana. Map p 114.*

★ **Sing Sing Theater** SUKHUMVIT This bar-cum-club features one of the most creative interiors in the city. There's a distinctly Chinese aesthetic, mezzanines, sunken bars, secret passages, and single table balconies. A seriously cool hangout. *Sukhumvit Soi 45.* ☎ *097 285 6888. www.facebook.com/SingSingTheater. BTS SkyTrain station: Phrom Phong. Map p 114.*

Slim HUAY KWANG Slim (also known as Siam Life in Motion) is an acquired taste, but those who go always go back. Evenings start slowly with small groups of Thais and expats huddled around tables. As the night unwinds, so do the young dudes and dudettes. Alternative rock and hip-hop are the staple musical diet. *Block B, 29/22–32 Royal Crown Ave (RCA), Rama IX Rd.* ☎ *02 203 0226. Cover varies. MRT subway: Rama IX. Map p 111.*

The Club BANGLAMPHU The biggest and most popular club on Khao San Road. Like the discos in Sukhimvit, it plays mostly electronic and house music, but entry is free. The crowd is a good mix of locals, expats, and tourists. *123 Khao San Rd, Bangkok. www.theclubkhaosan.com.* ☎ *02-629-1010. No metro. Nearest ferry: Tha Phra Arthit.*

Ztudio Live Hall HUAY KWANG The latest offering from the city's RCA party district, Ztudio Live Hall keeps revelers on the dance floor with electronic music and guest DJs. *Royal City Ave (RCA). www.facebook.com/ztudiolivehall.* ☎ *093-939-9893. MRT subway: Rama IX.*

Wine Bars

Bar@494 PATHUMWAN This popular after-work venue has and an excellent selection of food and

Vino and a view at Scarlett, which is known for its expansive wine cellar.

wine. Daily Happy Hours and a hard-to-beat-for-value Unlimited Wine Buffet from 7pm–9pm pull in the punters here. *The Grand Hyatt Erawan Bangkok, 494 Rajdamri Rd. www.bangkok.grand.hyatt.com* ☎ *02 254 1234. Nearest BTS Sky-Train: Chid Lom.*

Scarlett BANGRAK With panoramic views from the 37th floor of Pullman Hotel G, an expansive terrace, chic décor, impressive wine list, and an excellent menu of Mediterranean cuisine, Scarlett is the perfect venue for a chilled night out. *Pullman Hotel G, 188 Silom Road, Suriyawongse. www.pullmanbangkokhotelg.com.* ☎ *02 238 1991. BTS SkyTrain: Chong Nonsi. Map p 112.*

Wine Connection Deli & Bistro SUKHUMVIT Cold cuts, pastas, pizzas, cheeses, and more are served at this popular wine bar and bistro. There are several branches across the city, most with a deli counter and wine shop for take-away. Daily 10am–1am. *Branches at Silom Complex on Silom Road and Rainhill Community Mall on Sukhumvit Road. Room A116-118, G/F, K. Village, 93-95 Sukhumvit Soi 26. www.wineconnection.co.th.* ☎ *02 661 3940. Nearest BTS Skytrain Phrom Phong station or MRT subway Klong Toey. Map p 114.*

Wine Loft SUKHUMVIT Choose tasters, half, or full glasses from extensive selection of wines. There's a wine shop as well as a lounge. Also venues at Lang Suan and Sukhumvit 31. *Soi 4, Sukhumvit 55. www.wineloft.com.* ☎ *02 392 2080. BTS SkyTrain: Thong Lor.*

8 The Best Arts & Entertainment

Arts & Entertainment **Best Bets**

Best **Art Gallery**
★ 100 Tonson Gallery, *100 Soi Tonson, Ploenchit Rd (p 128)*

Best **Bicycle Tours Around Town**
★ Velothailand, *88 Soi 2, Samsen Rd (p 132)*

Best **Cinema**
House RCA, *31/8 Royal City Ave, New Petchalouri Rd (p 129)*

Best **Classical Thai Dance**
★★★ Silom Village, *Silom Rd (p 130)*

Best **Dinner Theatre**
Sala Rim Nam, *Oriental Hotel, 48 Oriental Ave (p 130)*

Best **Puppetry**
★ Joe Louis Puppet Theatre, *Asiatique (p 131)*

Best **Place to Hear 'No Way She's a Boy!'**
★ Calypso Cabaret, *Asiatique (p 130)*

Best **Place to Listen to the Bangkok Symphony Orchestra**
Thailand Cultural Centre, *Ratchadaphisek Rd (p 129)*

Best **Place to Rub Shoulders with Royalty**
Thailand Cultural Centre, *Ratchadaphisek Rd (p 129)*

Best **Siamese Masked Theatre Show**
Sala Chalermkrung Royal Theatre, *66 Charoen Krung Rd (p 132)*

Most **Spectacular Theatre Show**
★★★ Siam Niramit, *19 Tiam Ruammit Rd (p 130)*

Best **Thai Boxing Venue**
★ Lumphini Boxing Stadium, *6 Ramintra (p 131)*

Previous page: A traditional Thai dancer getting ready for her performance.

Dancers perform at the oldest cultural show in Bangkok, the Siam Nimarit.

Greater Bangkok
Arts & Entertainment

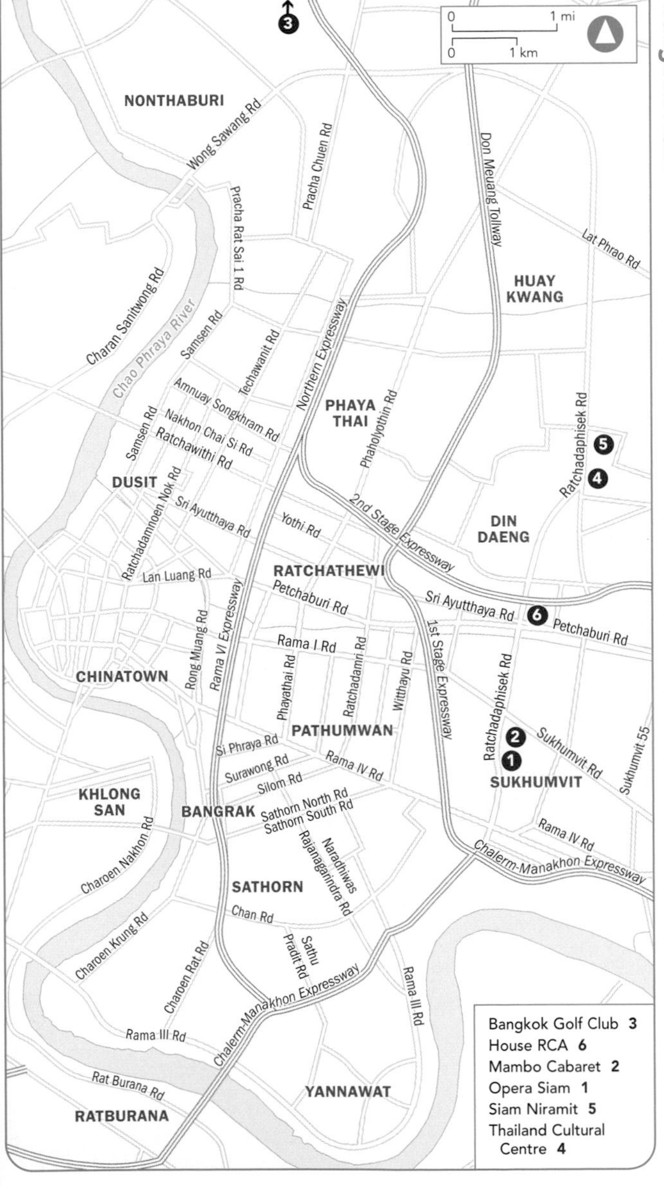

- Bangkok Golf Club **3**
- House RCA **6**
- Mambo Cabaret **2**
- Opera Siam **1**
- Siam Niramit **5**
- Thailand Cultural Centre **4**

Central Bangkok
Arts & Entertainment

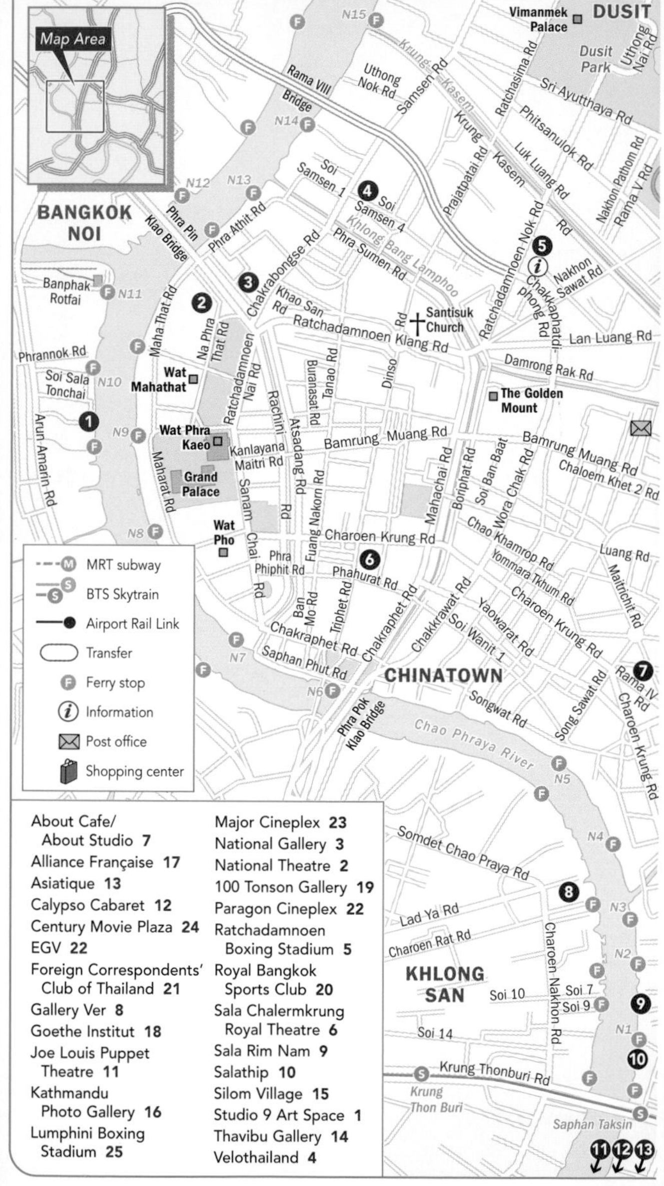

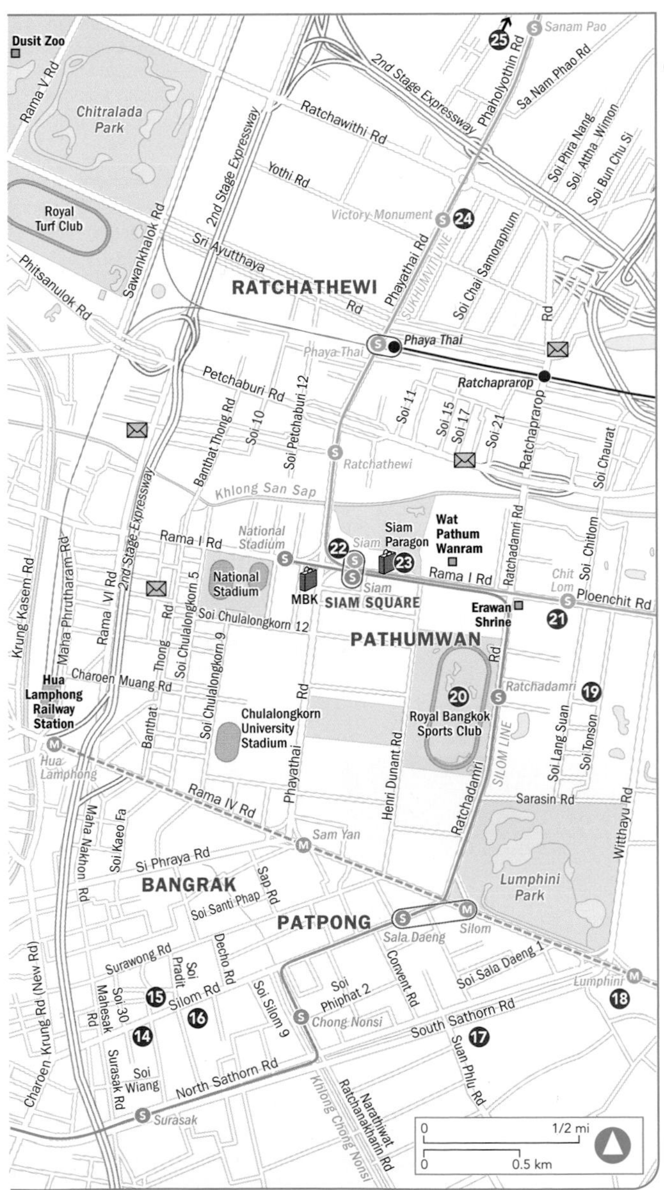
Dusit Zoo
Chitralada Park
Royal Turf Club
Rama V Rd
Sawankhalok Rd
Phitsanulok Rd
2nd Stage Expressway
Ratchawithi Rd
Yothi Rd
Sri Ayutthaya Rd
RATCHATHEWI
Phaholyothin Rd
Sanam Pao
Sa Nam Phao Rd
Soi Phra Nang
Soi Attha Wimon
Soi Bun Chu Si
Victory Monument
Phayathai Rd
SUKHUMVIT LINE
Soi Chai Samoraphum
Phaya Thai
Ratchaprarop
Ratchaprarop Rd
Petchaburi Rd
Banthat Thong Rd
Soi 10
Soi Petchaburi 12
Soi 11
Soi 15
Soi 17
Soi 21
Soi Chaurat
Ratchathewi
Khlong San Sap
Rama I Rd
National Stadium
Siam Paragon
Wat Pathum Wanram
Siam
Ratchadamri Rd
Soi Chitlom
Chit Lom
Ploenchit Rd
MBK
SIAM SQUARE
Erawan Shrine
Soi Chulalongkorn 5
Soi Chulalongkorn 12
Soi Chulalongkorn 9
PATHUMWAN
Krung Kasem Rd
Maha Phrutharam Rd
Rama VI Rd
Hua Lamphong Railway Station
Charoen Muang Rd
Chulalongkorn University Stadium
Royal Bangkok Sports Club
Ratchadamri
Soi Lang Suan
Soi Tonson
SILOM LINE
Hua Lamphong
Rama IV Rd
Henri Dunant Rd
Sarasin Rd
Witthayu Rd
Maha Nakhon Rd
Soi Kaeo Fa
Sam Yan
Si Phraya Rd
BANGRAK
Sap Rd
Soi Santi Phap
Lumphini Park
PATPONG
Sala Daeng
Silom
Surawong Rd
Soi Pradit
Decho Rd
Convent Rd
Soi Sala Daeng 1
Lumphini
Soi 30
Mahesak Rd
Silom Rd
Soi Silom 9
Soi Phiphat 2
Chong Nonsi
South Sathorn Rd
Suan Phlu Rd
Charoen Krung Rd (New Rd)
Surasak Rd
Soi Wiang
North Sathorn Rd
Surasak
Khlong Chong Nonsi
Narathiwat Ratchanakharin Rd
0
1/2 mi
0.5 km
14
15
16
17
18
19
20
21
22
23
24
25

Arts & Entertainment A to Z

Art Galleries

★ 100 Tonson Gallery PATHUMWAN This is a cool and modern private gallery. You can discover exhibitions of almost anything here—painting, sculpture, installation, photography—you name it. *100 Soi Tonson, Ploenchit Rd. ☎ 02 684 1527. www.100tonsongallery.com. Admission free. Thurs–Sun 11am–7pm: BTS SkyTrain: Chit Lom or Ratchadamri. Map p 126.*

★ About Cafe/About Studio CHINATOWN If I am ever waiting for a train, I head over to About for a coffee and an amble around the cutting-edge fine art. Call ahead to make sure it's open. *418 Maitrichit Rd. ☎ 02 639 8057. Admission free. MRT subway: Hua Lamphong. Map p 126.*

★ Gallery Ver THONBURI This gallery is owned by Thailand's best-known artist, Rirkrit Tiravanija. You'll usually find Thailand's boldest conceptual art here. *2nd Floor, 71/31–35 Klongsarn Plaza, Charoean Nakhon Rd, Klongsarn. ☎ 089 988 589. www.facebook.com/Gallery-VER. Admission free. Closed Mon & Tues. BTS SkyTrain: Krung Thonburi then taxi or ferry across from Sri Phaya pier (N3). Map p 126.*

Sights of Solitude by Chatchai at 100 Tonson Gallery.

Kathmandu Photo Gallery BANGRAK Housed in a handsome restored wooden Portuguese colonial house, this is Bangkok's only gallery devoted entirely to photography. (There's also a good Nepalese restaurant opposite.) *87 Pan Rd, off Silom Rd. ☎ 02 234 6700. www.facebook.com/kathmanduphoto.silomgallery. Admission free. Closed Mon. BTS SkyTrain: Surasak or Chong Nonsi. Map p 126.*

National Gallery RATTANAKOSIN You'll find contemporary art—including Thai cubism and surrealism—on the ground floor, and traditional Thai art upstairs at this gallery. The courtyard hosts a small art market at weekends; entry is free. *Chao Fa Rd. ☎ 02 282 2224. www.facebook.com/TheNationalGalleryBangkok. Admission 30 baht. Closed Mon & Tues. No BTS SkyTrain or MRT. Ferry: Tha Chang (N9). Map p 126.*

Thavibu Gallery BANGRAK The gallery's name is a clumsy amalgamation of Thailand, Vietnam, and Burma. Visitors will find revolving exhibitions of contemporary art by emerging artists from these three countries. *JTC Jewelry Trade Center, 4th floor, suite 433, 919/1 Silom Rd. ☎ 02 266 5454. www.thavibu.com. Admission free. Closed Mon. BTS SkyTrain: Surasak. Map p 126.*

Cinemas

Century Movie Plaza RAJATHEWI Near Victory Monument, this plaza has eight screens featuring the latest movies, plus restaurants, a shopping arcade, and a karaoke zone. *15 Phayathai Rd. ☎ 02 247 9940. www.centurythe movieplaza.com. Tickets 120–260 baht. BTS SkyTrain: Victory Monument. Map p 126.*

SF World Cinema PATHUMWAN A modern cinema complex with 10 screens that feature all the latest blockbusters and plenty of animated movies. There are a dozen other branches around the city but this is the biggest. *7th floor, 999/9, CentralWorld, Ratchadamri Rd, Pathumwan. ☎ 02 268 8888. www.sfcinemacity.com. Tickets from 120 baht. BTS SkyTrain: Chid Lom.*

House RCA HUAY KWANG The first boutique cinema in town is a refuge for lovers of arthouse/indie films. It also has Thai movies with subtitles and at least three movie festivals a year. *31/8 Royal City Ave, New Petchaburi Rd, Bangkapi. ☎ 02 641 5177 8. www.houserama.com. Tickets 100 baht. MRT subway: Petchaburi. Map p 125.*

Paragon Cineplex SIAM SQUARE This luxurious cinema in Siam Paragon shopping mall shows all the new releases from Hollywood. *5th and 6th floors, Siam Paragon, Rama I Rd, Pathumwan. ☎ 02 129 4635. www.majorcineplex.com.Tickets 140 baht. BTS SkyTrain: Siam. Map p 126.*

Quartier Cine-Art at Emquartier SUKHUMVIT Four high-end cinemas here include one with bedlike seating with a blanket and a pre-movie meal from Dean & Deluca. *4/F, Emquartier, Sukhumvit Rd. ☎ 02 261 0199. www.majorcineplex.com. Tickets 1,000 baht. BTS SkyTrain: Phrom Phong.*

Classical Music

Thailand Cultural Centre RATCHADAPHISEK Here's your chance to rub shoulders with the

Southeast Asian sculpture at the National Gallery.

city's cultured high society and listen to the 70 classical musicians of the Bangkok Symphony Orchestra. *Ratchadaphisek Rd, opp. Robinson's. ☎ 02 247 0028 or BSO: 02 255 6617 8. Ticket prices vary. MRT subway: Thailand Cultural Centre. Map p 125.*

Cultural Institutes

Alliance Française SATHORN Old French movies, language classes, a French library, a bistro, and regular art exhibitions are available here. *29 South Sathorn Rd. ☎ 02 670 4200. www.afthailande.org. BTS SkyTrain: Silom or Chong Nonsi, MRTsubway: Lumphini. Map p 126.*

Goethe Institut SATHORN The German culture center hosts German movies, language classes, art exhibitions, and musical recitals. *18/1 Soi Goethe, Sathorn Rd Soi 1. ☎ 02 108 8200. www.goethe.de/bangkok. MRT subway: Lumphini. Map p 126.*

★ Foreign Correspondents' Club Of Thailand PATUNWAN Is it a bar? An art gallery? A restaurant? In fact, the FCCT is an open clubhouse and the favored watering hole of the city's journalists, photographers, and, ahem, guidebook writers. It hosts jazz bands, exhibitions, panel discussions on current affairs, and

A group admires contemporary art at the Goethe Institute at BACC.

screenings of documentaries. *Maneeya Center, 518/5 Ploenchit Rd. ☎ 02 652 0580 1. www.fccthai.com. BTS SkyTrain: Chit Lom. Map p 126.*

Dinner Theatre

★★★ Sala Rim Nam BANGRAK A superb evening of awe-inspiring traditional Thai music and dance, complemented by a sumptuous meal at this majestic venue. *Mandarin Oriental, 48 Oriental Ave. ☎ 02 437 3080. www.mandarin-oriental.com. Tickets from 2250 baht (including dinner). BTS SkyTrain: Saphan Taksin. Map p 126.*

★ Salathip BANGRAK Romantic, intimate dining in a teak pavilion can be had here, against a backdrop of Thai classical musicians, dancers, a cultural show, and a view of the Chao Phraya River. *Shangri-La Hotel, 89 Soi Wat Suan Plu, Charoen Krung Rd. ☎ 02 236 7777. Tickets from 2000 baht. AE, DC, MC, V. Daily 6:30pm–10:30pm. BTS SkyTrain: Saphan Taksin. Map p 126.*

Siam Niramit HUAY KWANG This is the granddaddy of all cultural shows; a spectacular 80-minute performance on a gigantic stage. The show features more than 150 performers, 500 costumes, and state-of-the-art technical wizardry. A must-see experience. *Show begins at 8pm. Tickets from 1,500 baht for show or 1,850 baht for show and dinner. 19 Tiamruammit Rd, Huay Kwang (opposite the Thailand Cultural Center, shuttle service available from Exit 1 of MRT station), Bangkok. ☎ 02 649 9222. www.siamniramit.com. MRT Subway: Thailand Cultural Center. Map p 125.*

★★★ Silom Village BANGRAK Reun Thep Thai classical dance at Silom Village is a six-act show from the epic Ramakian masked dance-drama, originally performed only for the royal court. The show includes a Thai dinner. *286/1 Silom Rd. ☎ 02 635 6313. Tickets from 700 baht. BTS SkyTrain: Chong Nonsi. Map p 126.*

Ladyboy Cabaret

Calypso Cabaret RATCHATHEWI A lively transvestite cabaret with the emphasis squarely on the ladyboys themselves, from silicone-enhanced Marilyn Monroe to the gay Geisha. Part song and dance, part slapstick—it's inoffensive and good fun. *2194 Asiatique, Warehouse 3, Charoenkrung Rd. ☎ 02 688 1415. www.calypsocabaret.com. 900 baht for show only, 1500 baht with dinner. Dinner from 6:15pm for 8:30pm show, and 8:30pm dinner for 9:45pm show. BTS SkyTrain: Saphan Taksin then free ferry from the pier. Map p 126.*

Performers at the colorful Sala Rim Nam Thai cultural show.

Opera

Opera Siam SUKHUMVIT Formerly Bangkok Opera, Opera Siam stages productions at the Thailand Cultural Center. These have included *The Magic Flute* and Thai productions written by the company's founder, S.P. Somtow. *48 Soi 33, Sukhumvit Rd. ☎ 02 231-5273. www.operasiam.music-now.org. Map p 125.*

Puppet Shows

★ kids **Joe Louis Puppet Theatre** LUMPHINI There are nightly performances of the Hindu classic *Ramayana* featuring beautifullyhand-carved puppets. *Asiatique, S13, 2194 Chareon Krung Rd. ☎ 02 1084000. www.joelouistheatre.com. Tickets 400 baht Thais, 900 baht foreigners. Daily 8 & 9:15pm. BTS SkyTrain: Saphan Taksin, then free ferry from the pier. Map p 126.*

Sports Venues

Bangkok Golf Club PATHUM THANI You can rent clubs and a caddy and enjoy a day out on this finely manicured 18-hole course, known for its maze of water hazards. It's 30 minutes north of the city center by taxi. *99 Tiwanon Rd. ☎ 02 501 2828. www.golf.th.com. Tickets (non-members) 1600 baht per round. AE, DC, MC, V. No metro. Map p 125.*

★ **Lumphini Boxing Stadium** BANG KHAEN This brand new stadium has seating for 500 and great sound and lighting systems. There's also a boxing school, museum, restaurant, and café. Fights are held every Tuesday and Friday at 6pm, and on Saturdays at 2pm. Like many attractions in Thailand, there is one price for Thais and another for foreigners. *6 Ramintra, Anusavaree, Bang Khaen, Bangkok. ☎ 02 252 8765. www.muaythailumpinee.net. Nearest MRT subway Phahonyothin station, then a taxi ride. Map p 126.*

★ **Ratchadamnern Boxing Stadium** POM PRAP Muay Thai (Thai kickboxing) is the national

A ladyboy cabaret performer.

sport, and this is the country's number-one venue for this fast and brutal bloodsport. The crowd goes crazy and you can eat, drink, gamble, and scream throughout. *1 Ratchadamnern Nok Rd. ☎ 02 281 4205. www.rajadamnern.com. Tickets 1000 baht (nosebleed), 2000 baht (ringside). Nearest BTS SkyTrain: Phaya Thai then a taxi. Map p 126.*

Royal Bangkok Sports Club and Polo Club LUMPHINI The grounds include a golf course ringed by a horse-racing track and a huge clubhouse. Races are held on Sundays, every 2 weeks, plus the Chakri Cup in April, the Queen's Cup in August, and the King's Cup in December. The club includes jogging, badminton, squash, swimming, cricket, and football. *1 Henri Dunant St., Pathumwan, Bangkok. ☎ 02 652 5000. www.rbsc.org. Admission from 50 baht–500 baht. BTS SkyTrain: Ratchadamri or Siam. Map p 126.*

★ kids **Velothailand** BANGLAMPHU Velothailand offers day and evening tours around the backstreets and temples, along the riverfront, across the bridge to Thonburi and back within 4 hours. The bikes and equipment are very good quality. *88 Soi 2, Samsen Rd. ☎ 02 628 8628 or 089 201 7782. Tours from 100 baht. No credit cards. No metro. Nearest ferry: Phra Arthit (N13). Map p 126.*

Theatre

National Theatre RATTANAKOSIN If you are in Bangkok on the last Friday of the month, you can take in a Thai classical drama and masked theatre at this impressive venue. Performances are in Thai language. *Rachini Rd, Sanam Luang. ☎ 02 224 1342. No metro. Nearest ferry: Tha Chang (N9). Map p 126.*

Sala Chalermkrung Royal Theatre PAHURAT Built in 1933, this theater now hosts *khon* (Siamese masked theatre). It's an acquired taste—the music screeches somewhat—so first have a look at the video clip on the website to see if it's your cup of tea. *66 Charoen Krung Rd. ☎ 02 222 0434. www.salachalermkrung.com. Tickets 1000–1200 baht. Nearest MRT subway: Hua Lamphong. Ferry: Saphan Phut (Memorial Bridge N6). Map p 126.* ●

A Velothailand bike tour.

9 The Best **Hotels**

Hotel Best Bets

Best **Buffet Breakfast**
Grand Hyatt Erawan Bangkok $$$$$ *494 Ratchadamri Rd (p 140)*

Best **Cocktails by the Swimming Pool**
★ Anantara Bangkok Riverside Resort $$$$ *257 Charoen Nakorn Rd (p 138)*

Best **Decor**
★★ Conrad Bangkok $$$$
87 Wireless Rd (p 140)

Best **Facilities for Sports Enthusiasts**
★ Swissôtel Nai Lert Park $$$$$
2 Wireless Rd (p 146)

Best **Flashback to 19th-Century Siam**
★★★ The Eugenia $$$$
267 Sukhumvit Soi 31 (p 140)

Best **Hotel in the World!**
★★★ Mandarin Oriental $$$$$
48 Oriental Ave (p 142)

Best **Riverside Dining**
★★ The Peninsula $$$$
333 Charoen Nakorn Rd (p 143)

Best for a **Romantic Evening for Two**
★★ Ibrik Resort $$$
372 Rama III Rd (p 141)

Best **Self-Catering**
★ Siri Sathorn $$ *27 Soi Sala Daeng, 1 Silom Rd (p 145)*

Best for **Shopaholics**
Novotel Bangkok $$$$
Siam Square Soi 6 (p 143)

Best **Stopover Near Suvarnabhumi Airport**
★ Queen's Garden Resort $
85/5 Prachakorn Road, Lad Krabang Rd (p 144)

Best **Views at Sunrise**
★★ Chakrabongse Villas $$$$$
396 Maharaj Rd (p 139)

Best **Views at Sunset**
Shangri-La Hotel $$$$
89 Soi Wat Suan Plu, Charoen Krung Rd (p 145)

Best **Views of the City**
★ The Banyan Tree $$$$$
21/100 South Sathorn Rd (p 138)

The pool area of the Anantra Bangkok Riverside Resort.

Previous page: This terrace suite comes with a Jacuzzi at the Spa at the Peninsula Hotel.

Greater Bangkok Hotels

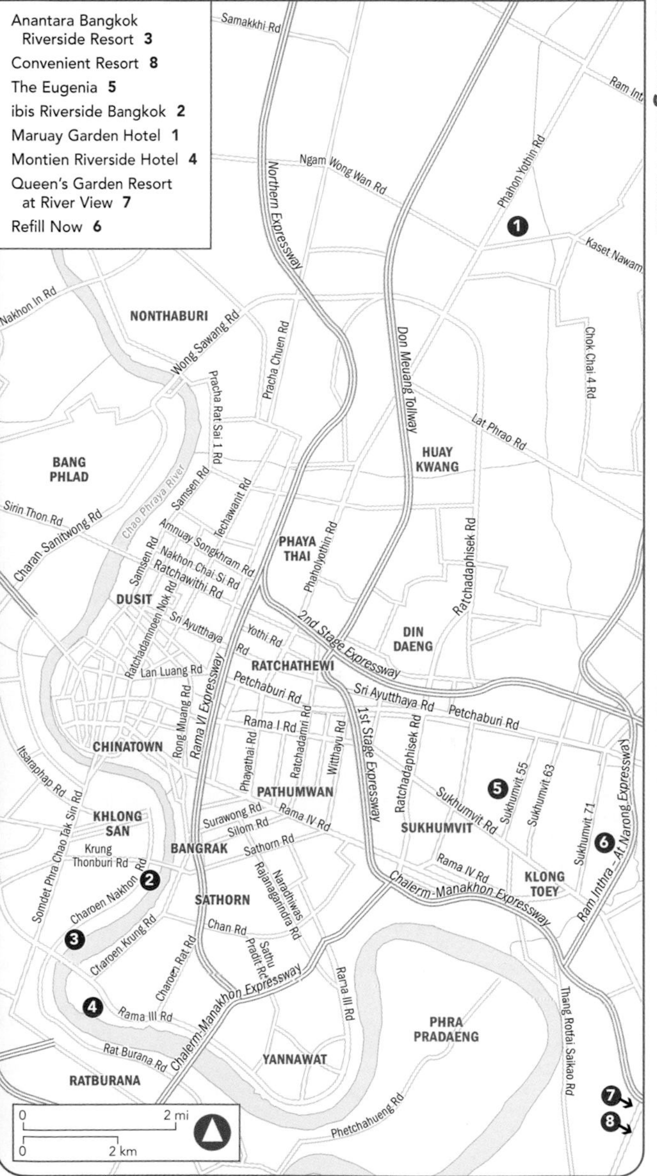

Central Bangkok Hotels

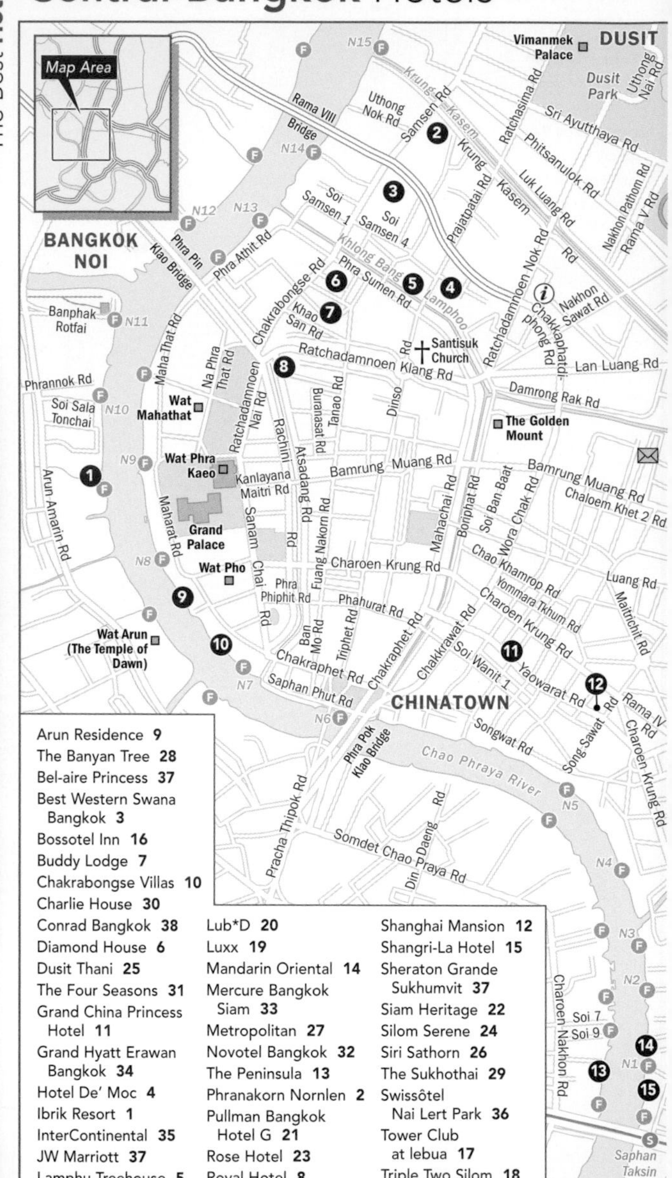

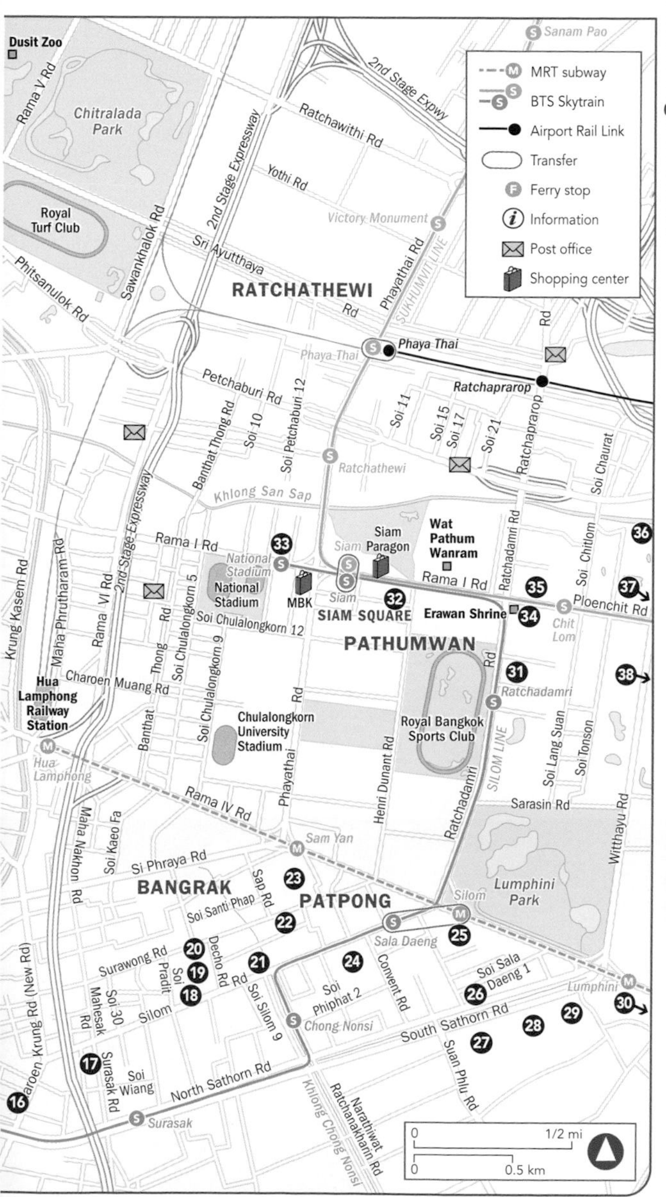
MRT subway
BTS Skytrain
Airport Rail Link
Transfer
Ferry stop
Information
Post office
Shopping center
Dusit Zoo
Chitralada Park
Royal Turf Club
RATCHATHEWI
PATHUMWAN
SIAM SQUARE
BANGRAK
PATPONG
Victory Monument
Phaya Thai
Ratchaprarop
Ratchathewi
Siam
Siam Paragon
Wat Pathum Wanram
National Stadium
MBK
Erawan Shrine
Chit Lom
Ratchadamri
Royal Bangkok Sports Club
Chulalongkorn University Stadium
Hua Lamphong Railway Station
Hua Lamphong
Sam Yan
Silom
Sala Daeng
Lumphini Park
Lumphini
Chong Nonsi
Surasak
Sanam Pao
Rama I Rd
Ploenchit Rd
Rama IV Rd
South Sathorn Rd
North Sathorn Rd
Petchaburi Rd
Khlong San Sap
Witthayu Rd
Sarasin Rd
0 1/2 mi
0 0.5 km

Bangkok Hotels A to Z

★ Anantara Bangkok Riverside Resort THONBURI Located on the west bank of the Chao Phraya River, the Anantara (formerly the Marriott) is like a tropical beach resort with its exotic pool, outdoor Jacuzzi, and open-air spa. It's for those who don't want to stay right in the big city but are happy to have access to a convenient free shuttle ferry to the SkyTrain. *257 Charoen Nakorn Rd. ☎ 02 476 0022. www.bangkok-riverside.anantara.com. 413 units. Doubles 7600–9900 baht w/breakfast. AE, DC, MC, V. Nearest BTS SkyTrain: Saphan Thaksin. Map p 135.*

★★ Anantara Siam Bangkok SUKHUMVIT This tropical paradise in the heart of the city offers spacious deluxe suites decorated with historical Thai murals. I recommend dining here even if you are staying elsewhere. *155 Ratchadamri Rd. ☎ 02 126 8866. http://.siam-bangkok.anantara.com. 353 units. Doubles 10,000–16,000 baht w/breakfast. AE, DC, MC, V. BTS SkyTrain: Ratchadamri.*

★★ Arun Residence RATTANAKOSIN Opt for this charming boutique hotel if you are spending most of your time visiting the nearby Grand Palace and the historical sites. The romantic suites have an old-world charm and command amazing views of the Temple of Dawn. *36–38 Soi Pratoo Nok Yung, Maharaj Rd. ☎ 02 221 9158. www.arunresidence.com. 7 units. Doubles 3500–5800 baht w/breakfast. AE, MC, V. No metro. Nearest ferry: Tha Tien (N8). Map p 136.*

★ The Banyan Tree SATHORN The Banyan Tree is popular with businesspeople, and renowned for its spa (see p 49) and its 61st-storey rooftop restaurant and bar (see p 136). *21/100 South Sathorn Rd. ☎ 02 679 1200. www.banyantree.com. 216 units. Doubles from 11,500 baht. AE, MC, V. SkyTrain: Sala Daeng or MRT subway: Lumpini. Map p 136.*

★ BelAire Bangkok SUKHUMVIT This is a lovely hotel set in a quiet side street near Bangkok's business and shopping districts. It has elegant, modern rooms and a

A one-bedroom suite at the Anantra Siam Bangkok.

At Chakrabongse Villas wood walls and traditional decor take visitors back to colonial-era Bangkok.

restaurant offering a spicy buffet and Thai cooking classes. *16 Sukhumvit Rd, Soi 5. ☎ 02 253 4300. www.belairebangkok.com. 160 units. Doubles 3300–4200 baht w/breakfast. MC, V, AE. Metro: Nana. Map p 136.*

Best Western Swana Bangkok PHRA NAKORN The Best Western is a little sterile, but an inexpensive option for those who find comfort in the reliability of a standard chain hotel. *322 Visuttikasat Rd. ☎ 02 282 8899. www.swanabangkok.com. 55 units. Doubles 1130–1600 baht w/ breakfast. AE, MC, V. No metro. Nearest ferry: Rama 8 Bridge (N14). Map p 136.*

★ **Bossotel Inn** BANGRAK A cozy alternative with all the mod-cons for the budget traveler. And it's not rowdy. *55/8–14 Soi Charoen Krung 42/1. ☎ 02 630 6120. www.bossotelinn.com. 81 units. Doubles 1800–2200 baht. AE, MC, V. BTS Sky-Train: Saphan Thaksin. Map p 136.*

Buddy Lodge BANGLAMPHU This is the safest and most reputable hotel on Bangkok's most infamous and wild backpacker street. It also has a swimming pool. *365 Khao San Rd. ☎ 02 629 4477. www.buddy lodge.com. 76 units. Doubles 2000–2400 baht w/breakfast. MC, V. No metro. Nearest ferry: Phra Arthit. Map p 136.*

★★ **Chakrabongse Villas** RATTANAKOSIN If someone else paid, I would live here! Formerly a royal residence, these traditional Thai-Chinese-style wooden chalets look over the Chao Phraya River towards the Temple of Dawn. It's an ideal spot for eating breakfast and reading the morning newspapers. Book well in advance. *396 Maharaj Rd, Tha Tien. ☎ 02 222 1290. www.thaivillas.com. 4 units. Doubles 13,000–23,000 baht w/ breakfast. MC, V. No metro. Nearest ferry: Tha Tien. Map p 136.*

Charlie House SATHORN Budget travelers rejoice! You don't have to get down and dirty at Khao San Road. Charlie's is cheap, cozy and friendly, and still manages to provide satellite TV, air-conditioning, and hot showers. *1034/36–37 Soi Saphan Khu, Lumphini. ☎ 02 679 8330 1. www.charliehousethailand.com. 19 units. Doubles 540 baht. MC, V. BTS SkyTrain: Sala Daeng or MRT subway: Lumphini. Map p 136.*

★★ Conrad Bangkok SUKHUMVIT A classic, centrally located hotel in the business district near Lumphini Park. The rooms are luxurious and chic with wooden decor and silk drapes. *87 Wireless Rd. ☎ 02 690 9999. www.conradhotels3.hilton.com. 391 units. Doubles 8000–9000 baht w/breakfast. AE, DC, MC, V. BTS SkyTrain: Ploen Chit. Map p 136.*

Convenient Resort LAD KRABANG Named for its close proximity to Suvarnabhumi Airport (it's just 5 minutes away); several of the comfortable, modest rooms at this hotel have countryside views. A good choice if you have an early flight out, otherwise no reason to stay here. *9–11 Lat Krabang Soi 38. ☎ 02 327 4118 21. www.convenientresort.com. 67 units. Doubles 1100 baht w/breakfast. MC, V. No metro. Map p 135.*

kids Diamond House BANGLAMPHU You'll be pleasantly surprised by the comfortable, well-fitted rooms at this budget hotel, which is located within walking distance of Khao San Road, the National Museum and Dusit Zoo. *4 Samsen Rd. ☎ 02 629 4008. www.thaidiamondhouse.com. 22 units. Doubles 1200–1400 baht. AE, MC, V. No metro. Nearest ferry: Phra Arthit. Map p 136.*

★★ Dusit Thani SILOM For me, the amphitheater-like lobby at the Dusit makes it all happen. The piano bar, the concierge, several lounges, and a cocktail bar create an atmosphere that makes this one of Thailand's favorite hotels. *946 Rama IV Rd. ☎ 02 200 9000. www.dusit.com. 517 units. Doubles from 6000 baht. AE, DC, MC, V. BTS SkyTrain: Sala Daeng or MRT subway: Silom. Map p 136.*

★★★ The Eugenia SUKHUMVIT This renovated 19th-century colonial house is a boutique hotel with a difference and houses an intricate collection of private antiques. My favorite features are the period furnishings, right down to four-poster beds and feather pillows. *267 Sukhumvit Soi 31. ☎ 02 259 9017 9. www.the-eugenia.bangkokthaihotels.com. 12 units. Doubles 5800–7200 baht w/breakfast. AE, MC, V. BTS SkyTrain: Asok or Phrom Phong or MRT subway: Sukhumvit. Map p 135.*

Grand China Princess Hotel CHINATOWN Situated at the intersection of Ratchawong and Yaowarat roads in the heart of Chinatown, this hotel offers spacious rooms and a revolving restaurant on the 25th floor. *215 Yaowarat Rd. ☎ 02 224 9977. www.grandchina.com. 155 units. Doubles 2300–2600 baht. AE, MC, V. MRT subway: Hua Lamphong. Map p 136.*

Grand Hyatt Erawan Bangkok PATHUMWAN The palatial

The plush lobby of the Dusit Thani.

Contemporary digs at the Grand Hyatt Erawan Bangkok.

entrance of white pillars and marble floors paves the way to stylish executive suites. Don't miss the buffet! *494 Ratchadamri Rd.* ☎ *02 254 1234. www.bangkok.grand.hyatt.com. 380 units. Doubles from 16000 baht w/breakfast. AE, DC, MC, V. BTS SkyTrain: Ploen Chit. Map p 136.*

kids ★ Hotel De' Moc PHRA NAKORN This is a cozy, friendly hotel has surprisingly spacious rooms and all mod-cons. It's located close to vibrant Khao San Road and is next to the expressway, so it's quick to and from Don Muang Airport. *78 Prajatpatai Rd.* ☎ *02 629 2100. www.hoteldemoc.com. 100 units. Doubles 1600–1700 baht w/breakfast. MC, V. Nearest ferry: Phra Arthit. Map p 136.*

★ ibis Riverside Bangkok THONBURI This value-for-money hotel has a great riverside location. It's just a short free shuttle ride to the SkyTrain and three stops to downtown Silom Rd. A great location for explore the sights and shopping at Asiatique. *27 Soi Charoen Nakorn, 17 Charoen Nakorn Rd.* ☎ *02 659 2888. www.ibis.com. 266 units. From 1500 baht. BTS SkyTrain: Krung Thonburi. AE, DC, MC, V. Map p 135.*

★★ Ibrik Resort THONBURI Calling itself "The Smallest Resort in the World," the Ibrik has three suites that are romantic and chic, offering lovely views across the river. Going on honeymoon? Book in advance. *372 Rama III Rd, Bangkhlo.* ☎ *086 008 5589. www.ibrikresort.com. 3 units. Doubles 3500–4000 baht w/breakfast. MC, V. No metro. Nearest ferry: Tha Tien then a ferry across the other side of the river. Map p 136.*

★★ kids Tower Club at lebua BANGRAK The lebua is easily recognizable by the gilded dome on the 64-storey tower. All suites come with kitchenettes, a washing machine, and comfortable lounges. The higher floors have spectacular views. *1055 Silom Rd.* ☎ *02 624 9999. www.lebua.com. 350 units. 1-bed suites 12,250 baht; 2-bed suites 24,500 baht w/breakfast. AE, DC, MC, V. BTS SkyTrain: Saphan Taksin. Map p 136.*

InterContinental PATHUMWAN This hotel is located in the heart of the business district. The rooms have high-speed Internet and the huge soundproof windows offer great views. *973 Ploenchit Rd.* ☎ *02 656 0444. www.intercontinental.com. 381 units. Doubles 6650–9500 baht w/breakfast. AE, DC, MC, V. BTS SkyTrain: Chit Lom. Map p 136.*

JW Marriott SUKHUMVIT Popular with businesspeople, this hotel is a beehive of activity and is located very close to the city's main business, shopping, and entertainment centers. *4 Sukhumvit Rd, Soi 2.* ☎ *02 656 7700. www.marriott.com. 442 units. Doubles 10,000–12,000 baht w/breakfast. AE, DC, MC, V. BTS SkyTrain: Ploenchit Map p 136.*

★ Lamphu Treehouse PHRA NAKORN Come here for traditional Thai-style rooms, all made from and outfitted in 100-year-old golden teak. *Soi Bann Pan Thom,*

155 Wanchat Bridge, Prajatpatai Rd. ☎ *02 282 0991 2. www.lamphutree-hotel.com. 40 units. Doubles 1200–1800 baht w/breakfast. MC, V. No metro. Nearest ferry: Phra Arthit. Map p 136.*

★ **Lub*D** BANGRAK I always find this a fun and friendly hostel, especially popular with young international travellers. It's located close to Silom Road. *4 Decho Rd, Suriyawong.* ☎ *02 635 7373. Also at Siam Square. www.lubd.com. 36 units. Doubles 1800 baht. MC, V. BTS SkyTrain: Chong Nonsi. Map p 136.*

★★ **Luxx** BANGRAK I thoroughly recommend this trendy boutique hotel with minimalist retro '70s decor. If you are here for the nightlife, it's located close to, but out of earshot of, Silom Road and Patpong. *6–11 Soi Decho, Silom Rd.* ☎ *02 635 8800. Also at Langsuan Rd.* www.staywithluxx.com.*13 units. Doubles 2800–5000 baht w/breakfast. AE, DC, MC, V. BTS SkyTrain: Chong Nonsi. Map p 136.*

The Tower Club is an eminently livable hotel, thanks to apartment-like suites. It's also a major nightlife destination.

★★★ **Mandarin Oriental** BANGRAK Like Joseph Conrad, W Somerset Maugham, Noel Coward, and many other writers of old, I would love to lay my hat at the Oriental for months at a time. It's timeless. Founded in 1876, the Oriental has long been regarded as one of the greatest hotels in the world—a testament to Thai history and a tribute to the Thai sense of personal service and harmony. *48 Oriental Ave.* ☎ *02 659 9000. www.mandarinoriental.com. 393 units. Doubles 13,000–31,500 baht w/breakfast. AE, DC, MC, V. BTS SkyTrain: Saphan Taksin. Map p 136.*

Maruay Garden Hotel CHATUCHAK This Asian-style hotel is a pleasant option if you want to stay in the north of the city, near Don Mueang Airport and Chatuchak Market, or simply want to avoid Western tourists. *1 Phaholyothin Rd, Senanikhom, Chatuchak.* ☎ *02 561 0510 47. www.maruaygardenhotel.com. 315 units. Doubles 1800 baht. AE, DC, MC, V. BTS SkyTrain: Mo Chit or MRT subway: Kamphaeng Phet. Map p 135.*

★ **Mercure Bangkok Siam** PATHUMWAN Steps from the BTS SkyTrain station and close to MBK shopping mall and Siam Square make this new hotel a top choice for shoppers. Rooms, suites and club floor options, plus free Wi-Fi, restaurant and bars, swimming pool, and fitness center. *927 Rama 1 Rd.* ☎ *02 659 2888. www.mercure.com. 189 units. From 2500 baht. BTS SkyTrain: National Stadium. AE, DC, MC, V. Map p 136.*

★ **Metropolitan** SATHORN A stylish, minimalist hotel that prides itself on health and holism with a menu of accessories and activities—such as spas, yoga, and meditation—designed to protect your body and soul. *27 South Sathorn Rd.*

Few hotels are as luxurious—or as celebrated—as the Mandarin Oriental.

☎ *02 625 3333. www.comohotels.com/metropolitanbangkok. 171 units. Doubles 10,850 baht. AE, DC, MC, V. BTS SkyTrain: Sala Daeng or MRT subway: Lumphini. Map p 136.*

Montien Riverside Hotel BANG KHO LAEM Located south of the city center, this towering hotel overlooks the Chao Phraya River and has excellent facilities and graceful service. *372 Rama III Rd.* ☎ *02 292 2999. www.montien.com. 462 units. Doubles 5500 baht. AE, DC, MC, V. BTS SkyTrain: Saphan Taksin. Map p 135.*

Novotel Bangkok SIAM SQUARE Smack in the center of Bangkok's most popular shopping district, Novotel Bangkok offers a relaxing lobby and rooms with wonderfully soft beds. Intriguingly, it hosts a raunchy nightclub in the basement. 392/44 *Siam Square Soi 6.* ☎ *02 209 8888. www.novotelbkk.com. 429 units. Doubles 6500–8500 baht w/ breakfast. AE, DC, MC, V. BTS SkyTrain: Siam. Map p 136.*

★★ **The Peninsula** THONBURI This award-winning east-meets-west hotel is five-star in every way. The marble lobby is exquisite, the service is subtle and refined, and the Asian cuisine is sumptuous. *333 Charoen Nakorn Rd.* ☎ *02 861 2888. www.peninsula.com. 370 units. Doubles 8400–10,500 baht w/*

The Nahm Restaurant sits right beside the pool at the slick Metropolitan Hotel.

breakfast. AE, DC, MC, V. BTS SkyTrain: Saphan Taksin, then free shuttle ferry across the river or Krung Thonburi and a taxi. Map p 136.

Phranakorn Nornlen POM PRAP This cozy and friendly boutique hotel is set around a relaxing garden.*46 Thewet Soi 1, Pharnakorn, Bang Khunprom, Krung Kasem.* ☎ *02 628 8188 90. www.phranakorn-nornlen.com. 23 units. Doubles 2200–2400 baht w/breakfast. MC, V. No BTS SkyTrain or MRT. Nearest ferry: Rama 8 Bridge (N14) Map p 136.*

Pullman Bangkok Hotel G BANGRAK A chic modern lifestyle hotel with sleek white rooms and suites, great city views, and cool bars and restaurants. *188 Silom Rd.* ☎ *02 238 1991.* www.pullmanbangkokhotelg.com. *469 units. Doubles from 7200 baht w/breakfast. AE, MC, V. BTS SkyTrain: Chong Nonsi. Map p 136.*

★ **Queen's Garden Resort at River View** BANG NA You'll enjoy good value at this clean and friendly bed-and-breakfast-style resort, located close to Suvarnabhumi Airport. It's ideal for an overnight stopover and a relaxing Thai massage. *85/5 Prachakorn Road, Lad Krabang Rd.* ☎ *02 329 2135. www.queensgardenresort.net. 76 units. Doubles 1200 baht. AE, DC, MC, V. No BTS SkyTrain or MRT. Map p 135.*

Refill Now KLONG TOEY This friendly budget travellers' hostel located near the Ekamai Bus Terminal, is modern, clean, and comfortable, and handy for those catching morning buses to eastern beaches. Single-sex dorms or private rooms. *191 Soi Predi Bhanomyong 42 Yak 5, Sukhumvit 71.* ☎ *02 713 2044 6. www.refillnow.co.th. 16 units. Doubles 1400 baht. MC, V. BTS SkyTrain: Phra Khanong. Map p 136.*

Rose Hotel BANGRAK Contemporary Thai décor and artworks give this stylish hotel a special ambience. Located in the heart of Silom's main shopping area. *118 Surawongse Rd, Silom.* ☎ *02 266 8268 72. www.rosehotelbkk.com. 72 units. Doubles 2000–2500 baht w/breakfast. AE, DC, MC, V. BTS SkyTrain: Silom. Map p 136.*

Shanghai Mansion CHINATOWN Enjoy an ambience of 1930s Shanghai at this bustling boutique hotel. *479–481 Yaowarat Rd.* ☎ *02 221 2121. www.shanghaimansion.com. 55 units. Doubles from 2250 baht w/breakfast. AE, MC, V. MRT subway: Hua Lamphong. Map p 136.*

The Peninsula's swank infinity pool looks like it ends in the river (it doesn't).

Though the rooms at the Pullman are a chic white, its entrance and lobby are a riot of colors.

Shangri-La Hotel BANGRAK Book a room on a higher floor to take in the spectacular views across the river. The elegant rooms are outfitted in teak with marble bathrooms. *89 Soi Wat Suan Plu, Charoen Krung Rd. ☎ 02 236 7777. www.shangri-la.com. 799 units. Doubles 7600–9900 baht w/breakfast. AE, DC, MC, V. BTS SkyTrain: Saphan Taksin. Map p 136.*

★★ Sheraton Grande Sukhumvit SUKHUMVIT The Sheraton is popular with international businesspeople and is renowned for its excellent service and top-notch facilities. An elevated walkway from the hotel lobby provides a direct link to the SkyTrain station. *250 Sukhumvit Rd. ☎ 02 649 8888. www.sheratongrandesukhumvit.com. 440 units. Doubles 8000–14,000 baht w/breakfast. AE, DC, MC, V. BTS SkyTrain: Asok or MRT subway: Sukhumvit. Map p 136.*

★ Siam Heritage BANGRAK You wouldn't imagine such a delightful boutique resort was just around the corner from the red-light zone, Patpong, but that's Thailand. Suites are furnished in either a central or northern Thai style. For a little extra, the executive suites with living rooms are excellent value. *115/1 Surawong Rd. ☎ 02 353 6166. www.thesiamheritage.com. 73 units. Doubles 2500–3250 baht w/breakfast. AE, DC, MC, V. BTS SkyTrain: Sala Daeng or MRT subway: Sam Yan. Map p 136.*

★ Silom Serene BANGRAK At these prices, I don't think you can find many cozier boutique hotels than this one. The garden is lush and shaded and a perfect spot for reading and relaxing. *7 Soi Pipat, Silom Rd Soi 3. ☎ 02 636 6599. www.silom-serene.com. 86 units. Doubles 2900–3300 baht w/breakfast. MC, V. BTS SkyTrain: Sala Daeng or Chong Nonsi. Map p 136.*

★ kids Siri Sathorn BANGRAK The spacious suites here are like Japanese-style apartments with kitchens, all mod-cons, and cozy terraces. This place has good facilities for families and those who prefer self-catering. *27 Soi Sala Daeng 1 Silom Rd. ☎ 02 266 2345. www.sirisathorn.com. 44 units. Doubles 1650–3650 baht. AE, DC, MC, V. BTS SkyTrain: Sala Daeng or MRT subway: Silom. Map p 136.*

★ The Sukhothai SATHORN If you can weave your way through the labyrinth of pathways, pagodas, shops, and archways you'll find a beautiful, tranquil, grassy courtyard in the center of this eye-catching but pricey hotel. *13/3 South Sathorn Rd. ☎ 02 344 8888. www.sukhothai.com. 210 units. Doubles*

The handsome courtyard of the Sukhothai Hotel.

12,000–19,700 baht w/breakfast. AE, DC, MC, V. BTS SkyTrain: Sala Daeng or MRT subway: Lumphini. Map p 136.

★ kids **Swissôtel Nai Lert Park** SUKHUMVIT Previously the Hilton Bangkok, but now managed by Raffles, this is a family-friendly hotel with excellent sports facilities and a pool. *2 Wireless Rd. ☎ 02 253 0123. www.swissotel.com. 338 units. Doubles 7700–13,000 baht w/breakfast. AE, DC, MC, V. BTS SkyTrain: Ploen Chit. Map p 136.*

★ **Triple Two Silom** BANGRAK The open-plan suites here are modern yet homely in a chic Japanese way. The hotel runs a free shuttle-bus service, which I think is a thoughtful touch. *222 Silom Rd. ☎ 02 627 2222. www.tripletwosilom.com. 75 units. Doubles 4800–5500 baht w/breakfast. BTS SkyTrain: Chong Nonsi. AE, DC, MC, V. Map p 136.* ●

The Sheraton's rooms may not be trendy, but they are among the most comfortable in town (especially the beds).

10 The Best Day Trips & Excursions

Kanchanaburi

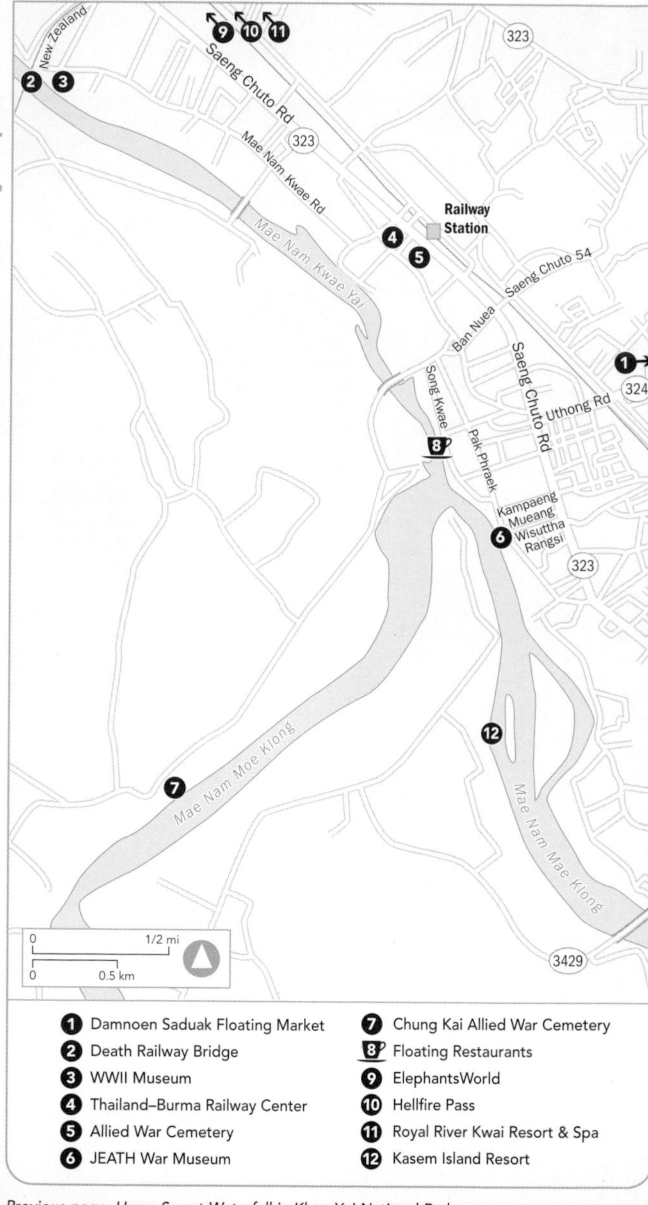

Previous page: Haew Suwat Waterfall in Khao Yai National Park.

Surrounded by limestone cliffs, rice paddies, and fields of sugarcane, Kanchanaburi feels much further than 130km from Bangkok. It's a 2-hour drive west towards Burma, though I recommend a stop at the Damnoen Saduak Floating Market on the way. The scenery en route is often breathtaking. Kanchanaburi itself is most famous as the scene of the Death Railway immortalized in the book and film *The Bridge over the River Kwai*. Many foreign visitors to Thailand make the pilgrimage to pay their respects to relatives who died as POWs here. You should rent a bicycle to see the sights, stay overnight, and take a trip on one of the floating restaurants, which transform into pulsating discotheques and karaoke cruisers every evening. **START: On Hwy 35 heading south-west, the Southern Bus Terminal or Bangkok Noi Station.**

❶ Damnoen Saduak Floating Market. You've seen the images in travel brochures and James Bond films—elderly Siamese women of yesteryear in bamboo hats, rowing their *sampan* boats full of fruit, vegetables, and chickens down the busy, narrow canals and crying out merrily to customers. Nowadays, I'm afraid, it's all mostly a mock-up for tourists, who arrive in buses every day around 9am or 10am. However, it's colorful, fun, and very photogenic. Arrive early to avoid the crowds. ⌚ *1 hr. Bang Phae-Damnoen Saduak Rd. Admission free.*

A vendor paddles up to a boat of tourists at Damnoen Saduak Floating Market.

❷ ★ Death Railway Bridge. During World War II, thousands of allied POWs and locals were forced by the Imperial Japanese Army to construct a railway to link Bangkok and Burma. The bridge over the River Kwae (not Kwai) symbolized the sacrifices made (although it is not the original bridge). The pleasant surrounding countryside is best visited by bicycle on a nice day. ⌚ *1 hr. 2km north of Kanchanaburi. Admission free.*

❸ WWII Museum. Strictly for war buffs and historians, this modest exhibition has photographs and memorabilia, but little else to spark the imagination. ⌚ *30 min. East bank, Mae Nam Kwae Rd. Admission 40 baht. Daily 8am–6pm.*

❹ Thailand–Burma Railway Center. A better museum than ❸, but still only for war buffs. Details the war and politics around the railway. Japanese visitors are advised to avoid it. ⌚ *30 min. Jaokannun Rd.* ☎ *034 512 721. www.tbrconline.com. Admission 120 baht adults, 60 baht kids. Daily 9am–5pm.*

The recreated bride over the River Kwae (Death Railway Bridge).

5 Allied War Cemetery. This is an immaculately preserved resting place for 7,000 allied soldiers who died working on the railway. *30 min. Saenchuto Rd. Admission free, donations welcome. Daily 7am–6pm.*

6 ★ JEATH War Museum. Whereas the area's other museums commemorate the deaths of allied soldiers in Kanchanaburi, the JEATH (Japan, England, Australia, Thailand, Holland) Museum depicts the lives of the POWs. Visitors can experience the bamboo huts and bunkers where POWs lived and some personal stories and belongings. It's a moving testimony to the sorrow of war. *1 hr. Wat Chaichoompon, Pak Phraek Rd. 034 511 263. Admission 50 baht. Daily 8am–5pm.*

7 Chung Kai Allied War Cemetery. This smaller graveyard is located on a scenic plain south of town. *15 min. Mae Nam Kwae Noi Rd. Admission free. Daily 7am–6pm.*

8 ★ Floating Restaurants. At night, holidaying Thais love to eat, drink, sing, be merry and bob down the river on a giant raft. The houseboats offer a good variety of spicy Thai dishes and beer. It's a great place to meet Thais, albeit mostly drunk ones. *Song Khwae Rd. Daily 6pm–11pm. $$.*

9 kids ElephantsWorld. This nonprofit organization is dedicated to caring for sick, old, disabled, abused, and rescued elephants. The sanctuary offers 1- and 2-day programs where you can help care for the elephants, prepare their food, feed, and bathe them. Pickup at your hotel at 9am. Ends at 4pm. The 2-day program includes on-site accommodation. There is also a 1- to 4-week mahout training course. *90/9 Moo 4, Ban Nong Hoi, Amphoe Mueang, Tambon Wang Dong, Kanchanaburi.*

Cleaning the tombstones at the Allied War Cemetery.

Practical Matters: Kanchanaburi

The easiest way to get to Kanchanaburi is by car. When you're on Hwy 35, drive 65 km to Samut Songkam. Turn right onto Hwy 325 and drive 16 km to Damnoen Saduek Floating Market. After visiting the market, continue along Hwy 325 and then turn left on Hwy 323 for 56 km. Trains and busses are also doable, but will be more time consuming.

A Kanchanaburii floating restaurant.

☎ *086 335 5332. http://www.elephantsworld.org. ElephantsWorld is a whole day experience. Prices from 2,500 baht.*

⑩ **Hellfire Pass Memorial Museum.** Built and maintained by the Australian government, this memorial and walking trail dedicated to the allied POWs who labored to cut a pass through the mountain is a must-do experience and one of Thailand's best museums. The self-guided audio tour is extremely moving. *To get there, take the early morning train from Kanchanaburi to Nam Tok, (a very scenic ride) then a minivan to the museum.* 🕓 *1 hr. Hwy 323, 75km north of Kanchanaburi.* ☎ *034 919605. www.hellfire-pass.commemoration.gov.au. Admission free but donations accepted. Daily 9am–4pm.*

⑪ **Royal River Kwai Resort & Spa.** This elegant resort boasts a touch of rural luxury in a romantic pastoral setting by the river. Treat yourself to a spa treatment or stay the night. *88 Moo 2, Kanchanaburi-Saiyok Rd.* ☎ *034 653 342. www.royalriverkwairesort.com. Doubles from 2450 baht w/breakfast, spa costs vary.*

⑫ **Kasem Island Resort.** As far from the big city as you can go in 1 day. Basic but tranquil cottages sit on an island on River Kwae. *44–48 Chaichumphol Rd (office on Chukkadon Rd to arrange ferry).* ☎ *0381 499 4941, or Bangkok 02 254 8871. www.kasemisland.com. Doubles from 1500 baht. No credit cards.*

Khao Yai National Park

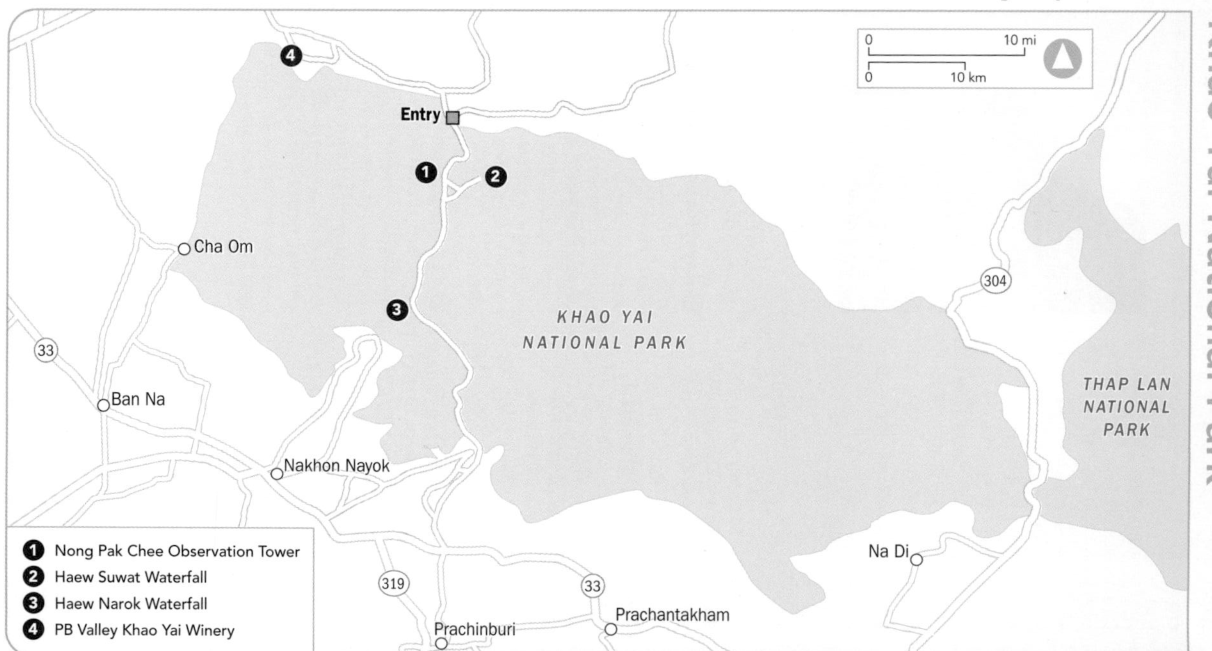

A trip to Thailand's oldest and second-largest national park is a delight. In a city such as Bangkok, where humidity and crowds can be relentless, a venture to the jungle is a breath of fresh air—quite literally. Much of the 2170-sq-km UNESCO World Heritage Site is located 400m above sea level, making it a haven for varying ecosystems, including monsoon, evergreen, and rainforest. From the top of a misty mountain, you can look over a cliff across waterfalls, grasslands, palm groves, and bamboo forests to the never-ending tropical jungle beyond. Apart from 3000 species of plants and more than 300 species of birds, you might be lucky enough to spot some rather large mammals. Walk quietly and keep your eyes peeled—they are hiding behind every tree. In the cool season (November to February) nights are sometimes very cold and you'll need warm clothes. In the rainy season (May to September) the entire forest can be swathed in a mist and cascading waterfalls seem to descend from the heavens. Waterproof clothes are essential. I recommend renting a car if you feel comfortable driving in Thailand (see p 175). **START: Mo Chit Bus Terminal or Hwy 1.**

❶ Nong Pak Chee Observation Tower. As you pass through the entrance, head to the visitor center and book your place for this round trip. Climb the wooden ladder up into the observation tower. If you linger here, your patience might indeed be rewarded with some animal sightings—you may spot elephants and deer in the mornings. ⏱ *1 hr.*

❷ Haew Suwat Waterfall. This beautiful 25m teeming waterfall is particularly impressive in the rainy season. If you walk to the bottom of

The grasslands of Khao Yai National Park.

The great pied hornbill is one of 600 birds indigenous to Thailand.

the falls you can enjoy a refreshing swim. Haew Suwat Waterfall has a claim to fame in that it is the location of the famous "jump" scene in the movie *The Beach.* *45 min.*

❸ Haew Narok Waterfall. Take a picturesque 30km journey to this lesser-visited waterfall, which is higher and has pools for bathing. At 150m, these are the tallest and most spectacular falls in Khao Yai National Park. *1 hr.*

❹ PB Valley Khao Yai Winery. The temperate climes of the park have, in recent years, sparked an interest in planting grapes. Connoisseurs will surely cringe at the taste, but the wines are getting better every year. Harvest is from the end of January to the end of March. Three tours daily at 10:30am, 1:30pm and 3:30pm. *90 min.* *036 226 415 6. www.khaoyaiwinery.com. Admission 200 baht adults, 10 baht kids. Daily 7:30am–4:30pm.*

Practical Matters: Khao Yai National Park

Outside Bangkok, of course, the driving is much easier and it is the best way to get around the park. Head out of Bangkok past Don Mueang Airport to Hwy 1. Drive north about 130km to Saraburi, then take Hwy 2 heading east. Drive 30km and turn right at Muak Lek and continue 20km to the national park entrance.

Catch a bus from Mo Chit (North and Northeastern) Bus Terminal in Bangkok to Pak Chong. Buses leave every 30 minutes from 5am to 10pm. The trip takes 3 hours, and tickets are 139 baht. Take a red pickup from Pak Chong train station to the park entrance (about 25 baht).

The other alternative is to book a tour from Bangkok. Admission 400 baht plus 50 baht per car; daily 8:30am–4:30pm).

Flora and Fauna

National parks cover 13% of Thailand's 514 000 sq km, protecting much of the country's flora and fauna. As a humid tropical country with mountains, rainforest, and an abundant coastline, Thailand has great diversity in its plant and animal life.

The mountainous north has mixed deciduous and dry dipterocarp forests and is rich in pines and bamboo. The teak forests, unfortunately, have all but disappeared. Nestled in the canopies of the southern rainforests, you'll find mangroves, rattan, ferns, banana plantations and coconut palms. Exotic flowers can be found everywhere, with orchids and birds of paradise being favorite exports.

Human migration and hunting have killed off many species of mammal, but once upon a time tigers, leopards, elephants, gaurs, tapirs, wild cattle, one-horned rhinoceroses, otters, deer, civet cats, tapirs, gibbons, macaques, bears, wild hogs, and various types of monkeys were abundant in Thailand. Today there is little in the way of wild fauna.

There are plenty of reptiles, though—from the harmless mosquito-eating geckoes to crocodiles, monitor lizards, and snakes. Venomous snakes include the banded krait, the cobra, and the viper. Nowadays, all hospitals in Thailand keep stocks of snake anti-venom, which is produced at Bangkok's snake farm (see p 45).

Excluding migratory birds, more than 600 species are indigenous to Thailand, such as hornbills, flycatchers, warblers, pitta, pheasants, egrets, herons, storks, and the supreme white-bellied sea eagle.

The seas around Thailand are home to corals, sharks, rays, barracuda, moray eels, reef fish, parrot fish, angel fish, sturgeons, and big squelchy sea cucumbers, making them some of the world's most popular diving spots.

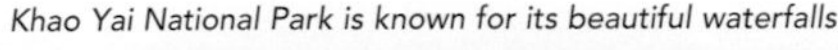

Khao Yai National Park is known for its beautiful waterfalls.

Pattaya

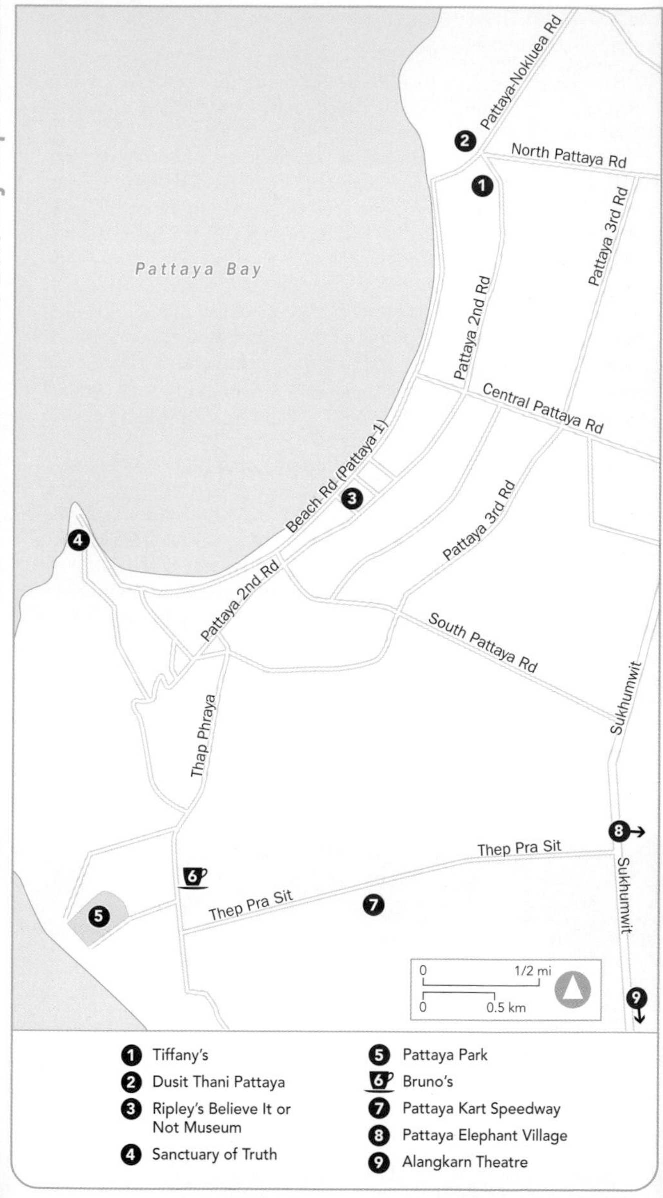

1 Tiffany's
2 Dusit Thani Pattaya
3 Ripley's Believe It or Not Museum
4 Sanctuary of Truth
5 Pattaya Park
6 Bruno's
7 Pattaya Kart Speedway
8 Pattaya Elephant Village
9 Alangkarn Theatre

Just 150km south-east of Bangkok, Pattaya is the nearest resort to the big city and is Thailand's most visited beach. It is easily accessible—many tourists jump straight off the plane, grab the next bus to Pattaya and are on the beach in no time. It has hotels, restaurants, bars, nightlife, theme parks, and everything else you could imagine of a tropical resort. However, there's no hiding from the fact that Pattaya is perhaps the most notorious resort in the world for sex tourism. Go-go bars, prostitutes, massage services, and the like are unavoidable. Those who feel uncomfortable with this should avoid Pattaya completely. Also be aware that visiting sex workers is a crime, and doing so perpetuates abuse. That said, Pattaya does have a lot to offer. In recent years a concerted effort has been made to attract families and non–sex tourists. Kitesurfers and windsurfers flock here to catch the waves, kids are kept amused by theme parks, and there are first-class entertainment venues, golf courses, restaurants, scuba diving courses, shopping malls, and much more. Or, of course, you can just laze out on the white, sandy beach on a lounger, eat seafood from passing vendors, get your hair plaited, and swim in the sea. **START: Eastern Bus Terminal, Hua Lamphong Station or Sukhumvit Road.**

1 Tiffany's. Tiffany's is a spectacular transvestite cabaret show in a palatial 1000-seat setting. The show is tasteful and very popular with tour groups. It also hosts the number-one ladyboy beauty pageant in the country. There are four shows nightly from 6:30pm. *464 Moo 9, Pattaya II Rd. ☎ 03 842 1700. www.tiffany-show.co.th. Admission 650–1000 baht.*

2 Dusit Thani Pattaya. The spacious suites with sea views here are a class above the seedy city below. The Dusit also offers a swimming pool, spa, gymnasium and a Jim Thompson silk outlet. *240/2 Pattaya Beach Rd. ☎ 03 842 5611. www.dusit.com. 457 units. Doubles from 7000 baht. AE, DC, MC, V.*

3 kids Ripley's Believe It or Not Museum. A weird and wacky

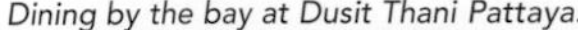

Dining by the bay at Dusit Thani Pattaya.

The elaborate, wooden Sanctuary of Truth temple.

collection of trivia, a haunted house, a simulator, a walk-through maze, and other bizarre activities that are great for a rainy day. ⏲ *2 hr. 2nd floor, Royal Garden Plaza, 218 Moo 10, Beach Rd.* ☎ *03 871 0294 8. www.ripleysthailand.com. Admission 600–1500 baht. Daily 11am–11pm.*

❹ **Sanctuary of Truth.** This 105m wooden temple stands out on the Pattaya skyline. It's quite magnificent with Hindu-inspired carvings, Buddha heads, three-headed elephants, and a thousand other carved figurines that dance in the sunset. ⏲ *1 hr. 206/2 Moo 5, Naklua Soi 12, Pattaya-Naklua Rd, Banglamung.* ☎ *03 836 7815 or 03 838 7229. www.sanctuaryoftruth.com. Admission 500 baht adults, 250 baht kids. Daily 8am–6pm.*

❺ **kids** **Pattaya Park.** Fun for all the family—a hotel, restaurant and entertainment complex in one. On offer is a water park with slides, tubes, and a swimming pool area—excellent for kids. There is a carousel, a rollercoaster, kids' rides. and a tower-shot plunge, all inside the so-called "Funny Land." On the top floor of the tower there's a nice revolving restaurant and, after lunch, you can slide back down to earth on mini ski lifts. ⏲ *4 hr. 345 Jomtien Beach.* ☎ *03 825 1201 8. www.pattayapark.com.*

6 **Bruno's.** Pattaya is wall-to-wall with fast-food joints, so let me suggest you take a taxi to Bruno's for a fantastic French meal instead. The set lunch is always excellent value for money. *306/63 Chateau Dale Plaza, Thappraya Rd, Pattaya Beach.* ☎ *03 836 4600. www.brunos-pattaya.com. AE, MC, V. Daily noon–2:30pm, 6pm–midnight. $$.*

Lovely Ladies and Ladyboys

Transvestites are accepted and ubiquitous in Thai society. No party is complete without a few of these colorful characters (known as *khatoeys* or ladyboys). While most Thais may be shy, ladyboys are usually extroverts. Many Thai celebrities and TV stars are ladyboys. In Pattaya, hundreds of *khatoeys* work as prostitutes—often to save money for operations.

Practical Matters: Pattaya

Buses leave Eastern Bus Terminal in Bangkok (adjacent to Ekamai BTS SkyTrain station) every 30 minutes from 5:20am to 11:20pm and the trip takes 2 hours; tickets are 117 baht. Alternatively, Suvarnabhumi Airport (☎ 02 134 4099) operates a minibus service direct to Pattaya leaving the airport bus terminal at 9am, noon, and 7pm daily. The trip takes 2 hours and costs 106 baht. Book via ☎ 02 246 0973, hotline 184, or www.bmta.co.th.

Another option is to catch a train from Hua Lamphong Station at 7am (but check first). The trip takes 3 hours. Book via ☎ 02 621 8701, 24-hour hotline 1690, or www.railway.co.th.

If you have a car, head to Ekkamai from Sukhumvit Road and keep driving east. The road eventually turns into Hwy 34. Follow signs for Chonburi and Pattaya. The trip should take 2 hours (traffic should ease a bit after Chonburi).

7 kids Pattaya Kart Speedway. A 1km go-kart track with good safety standards. There's also a beginner's track. Prices from 300–750 baht. *1 hr. 248/2 Thep Prasit Rd, Soi 9. ☎ 03 842 2044. www.kart.thai.li. Daily 9am–6pm.*

Performing elephants at Pattaya Elephant Village.

8 kids Pattaya Elephant Village. Here's your chance to ride an elephant and watch the beautiful beasts painting, playing sports, and bathing. Tickets include lunch, an elephant ride, rafting, and a show. *3 hr. 48/120 Moo 7, Tambon Nong Prue, Pattaya City. ☎ 03 824 9818. www.elephant-village-pattaya.com. Tickets 1200–2000 baht. Daily 10:30am–4pm.*

9 kids Alangkarn Theatre. Calling itself "The Extravaganza Show," this late-afternoon dinner theatre and show is part circus, part cabaret. A Thai meal is served at 5pm and the show begins at 6pm. It features elephants, fireworks, traditional dancing, music, theatrical renditions of Thai mythology, and much color and razzamatazz. *3 hr. Sukhumvit Rd Km 155. ☎ 03 825 6000 or 02 216 1869. www.alangkarnthailand.com. Tickets from 1100 baht. Dinner, 5pm–6pm, show, 6pm–7pm daily.*

Ayutthaya

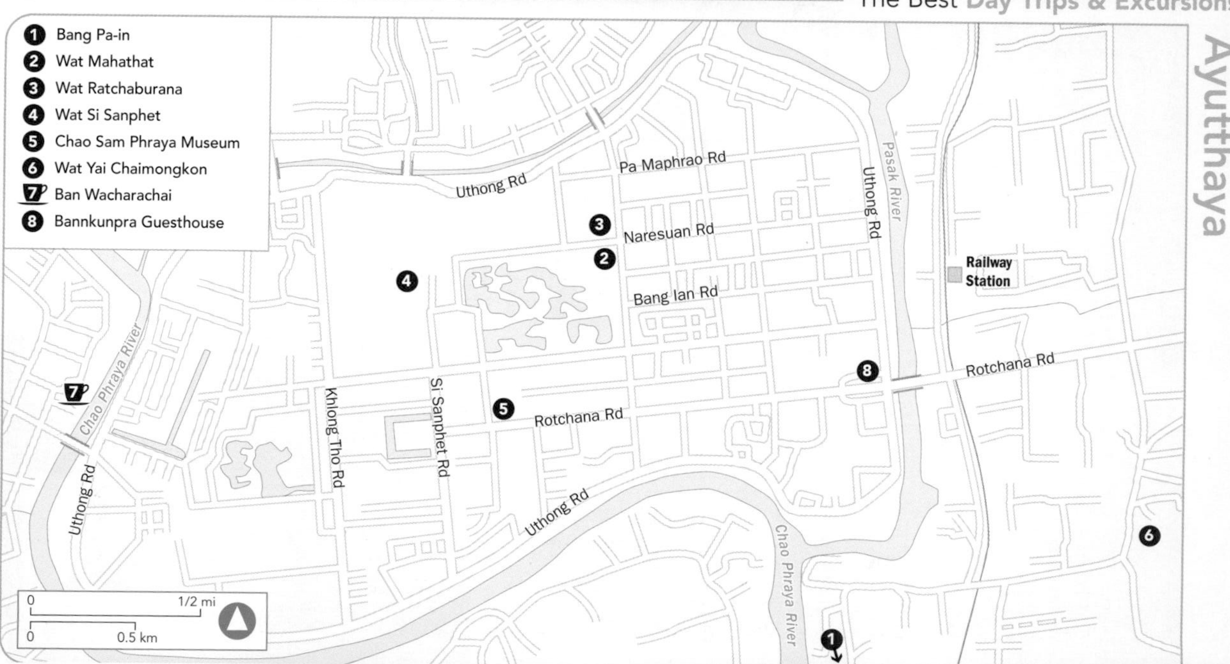
1 Bang Pa-in
2 Wat Mahathat
3 Wat Ratchaburana
4 Wat Si Sanphet
5 Chao Sam Phraya Museum
6 Wat Yai Chaimongkon
7 Ban Wacharachai
8 Bannkunpra Guesthouse
Uthong Rd
Pa Maphrao Rd
Naresuan Rd
Bang Ian Rd
Uthong Rd
Pasak River
Railway Station
Rotchana Rd
Rotchana Rd
Khlong Tho Rd
Si Sanphet Rd
Chao Phraya River
Uthong Rd
Uthong Rd
Chao Phraya River
0 1/2 mi
0 0.5 km

Once the capital of Siam and regarded as the greatest city in Asia, Ayutthaya is now a UNESCO World Heritage Site, and offers visitors the chance to reminisce back to the days when Bangkok was no more than a fort guarding the river to this divine city of 1 million people. The city was founded in 1350, and Ayutthayans were advanced and powerful, their influence felt around the region. They tidily conquered the almighty Khmer at Angkor and extended their kingdom to Burma, Laos and southern China. The glory of Ayutthaya was destroyed in 1767 by rampaging Burmese armies, who looted the Siamese capital and destroyed many of its great buildings. Most visitors arrive by train or tour bus. The best way to see the ruins of Ayutthaya, in my opinion, is to rent a bicycle and meander around at your own speed. You can rent bicycles just outside the train station for about 50 baht a day, or at any one of several stores in town. **START: Mo Chit Bus Terminal, Hua Lamphong Station or Hwy 1.**

---

❶ **Bang Pa-in.** About 53km north of Bangkok lies the former royal palace of Bang Pa-in. It sits on an island in the Chao Phraya River and is very picturesque. It was built in the 17th century, but fell into disrepair before King Mongkut revived the palace in 1872. The architecture is a real clash of Chinese, Thai, and Gothic styles. You can reach Bang Pa-in by boat from Ayutthaya (45 minutes). A dress code applies: long sleeves, no shorts, or short skirts. Bang Pa-in makes for a beautiful journey on a nice day. *🕓 2 hr. ☎ 03 526 1044/03 526 1549. www.palaces.thai.net. Admission 100 baht. Daily 8am–4pm.*

❷ **Wat Mahathat.** Like a scene from *The Jungle Book*, these ancient red temples are littered with overgrown pathways and staircases that speak of the decadent times of yore. Built in 1374, the main *pang* (stupa) is Khmer in architectural style, perhaps resembling a melting candle. The most photographed image in Ayutthaya must be the Buddha head at Wat Mahathat, which is set within the intertwining roots of a fig tree. *🕓 30 min.*

❸ **Wat Ratchaburana.** Erected by King Boromracha II in the 15th century, this hulking great temple once housed much of the city's treasure, some of which is now on display at the Chao Sam Phraya Museum ❺. Around the main stupa you can see fine carved figures of the mythical *naga* serpent and the bird-god Garuda. *🕓 15 min.*

❹ **Wat Si Sanphet.** This beautiful row of *chedis* was built in 1492 to house the ashes of some of the relatives of King Rama Thibodi II. This is probably the most photogenic area in Ayutthaya and a great chance to wander around stone Buddha images and temples in a neat grass park. *🕓 15 min.*

❺ **Chao Sam Phraya Museum.** Opened in 1961, this is where much of Ayutthaya's wealth is on display—that which wasn't pillaged or melted down by the Burmese. There are bronze and stone sculptures, terracotta pieces, wood carvings, gold jewelery, and precious stones. There is also the sculpture of a seated Buddha, which dates to the 11th or 12th century. *🕓 45 min. 108 Moo 4 Rotchana Rd. ☎ 03 524 1587. Admission 150 baht. Wed–Sun 9am–4pm.*

The exquisite Wat Yai Chaimongkon.

6 Wat Yai Chaimongkon. Even if you have cycled around enough temples and Buddhas to last a lifetime, you still have to take in the towering 60m *chedi* here. Built in 1357 by King U Thong, the site boasts a reclining Buddha and a shrine of toys. A small community of white-robed Buddhist nuns live here, mostly practicing meditation. *30 min.*

7 Ban Wacharachai. Situated next to Wat Kasat and overlooking the river, this splendid, lush restaurant is a must. It's popular day and night, and is best known for its smoked snakehead fish. It offers a few western dishes, but I highly recommend trying an assortment of central Thai specialties. *9 Moo 7 Baan Pom. ☎ 03 532 1333. Daily 10am–9pm. $$.*

8 Bannkunpra Guesthouse. This is not luxury accommodation, but rooms in this 100-year-old teak building overlooking the river are authentic and exotic. Staff are friendly and the location is good, but there are only a few en-suite rooms, so book in advance. *48 Moo 3, U Thong Rd. ☎ 03 524 1978. www.bannkunpra.com. 15 units. Doubles 600 baht.*

Practical Matters: Ayutthaya

Buses leave from Mo Chit Bus Terminal (North and Northeastern Terminal) every 20 minutes and the trip takes 1 hour; tickets start at 60 baht.

Trains to Ayutthaya leave Hua Lamphong Station roughly every 30 minutes and the trip takes 1½ hours; tickets start at 30 baht. Then walk 5 minutes to the river and take a small ferry ride across.

If you have a car, leave Bangkok via the expressway north of Don Mueang Airport, where the road becomes Hwy 1. Drive 65km to Wang Noi, then turn northwest on the 309 and drive 18km into Ayutthaya. It's a fairly boring drive—the only plus being that you can stop at Bang Pa-in (**1**).

The Savvy Traveller

Before You Go

Government Tourist Offices

Australia: 111 Empire Circuit, Yarralumla, Canberra ACT 2600 (☎ 02 6273 1149 or 02 6273 2937). **Canada**: 180 Island Park Dr, Ottawa, Ontario K1Y QA2 (☎ 613 7224444). **France**: 8 Rue Greuze, 75116 Paris (☎ 1 4704 3222 or 1 4704 6892). **Germany**: Ubierstrasse 65, 53173 Bonn (☎ 0228 355065). **Japan**: 3/146, Kami Osaki, Shinagawa-ku, Tokyo 141 (☎ 03 3441 1386). **The Netherlands**: 1 Buitenrustweg, 2517 KD. The Hague (☎ 070 345 2088 or 070 345 9703). **New Zealand**: 2 Cook Street, PO Box 17–226, Karori, Wellington (☎ 476 8618 or 476 8619). **Spain**: Calle del Segre, 29–2A, 28002 Madrid (☎ 563 2903 or 563 7959). **UK**: 29–30 Queen's Gate, London SW7 5JB (☎ 071 589 0173 or 071 589 2944). **U.S.**: 2300 Kalorama Rd NW Washington DC (☎ 202 483 7200).

The Best Time to Go

The best time to visit Bangkok is during the cool season, from November to February. This is when most tourists arrive. March to May is the hot season. The rainy season generally runs from May to October. A city of over 10 million people, Bangkok is always busy and the humidity is very high.

Festivals & Special Events

Thailand is a land of many ceremonies and festivals. Many visitors plan their trips especially to take in one or more of the annual festivals. Thais simply love their culture, their religion, and their royal family, and any festival is somehow turned into a carnival of fun with lots of eating, drinking, music, fireworks, beauty pageants, and millions of smiles.

SUMMER. The **River of Kings Festival** in January is a colorful sound-and-light show. Set on the Chao Phraya River with the Grand Palace as a backdrop, the 10-night spectacle (daily, 7pm and 9:30pm) depicts tales of ancient Siamese kings and warriors, complimented by dancers, fireworks, and fountains. You can catch a glimpse of the show free from the riverside or buy tickets to enjoy the performance from the luxury of a river cruiser or a floating stadium (☎ 02 250 5500).

Chinese New Year is a weeklong explosion of fireworks and Chinese dragons when Chinatown all but closes down in January or February. It's a good time to visit Chinatown and Chinese temples.

Makha Bucha is held at the first full moon of the third lunar month (which can be either February or March), and marks the Buddha's first sermon to his followers. It's celebrated with candlelit ceremonies in the evening at all Buddhist temples. I recommend Wat Benchamabophit (the Marble Temple; see p 39, bullet ⑩)—it's very photogenic.

AUTUMN. The windy season is between February and April in Bangkok, and every Sunday you can see children (and adults) flying—or fighting—kites at Sanam Luang. In March there are contests during the **Kite-Flying Festival.** Call the Tourism Authority of Thailand (TAT) for details on ☎ 02 250 5500.

Bangkok International Fashion Week is usually in March and is held at Siam Paragon (see p 26). The event showcases the work of Thai designers (www.thaicatwalk.com).

Previous Page: Tuk-tuks are everywhere in Bangkok.

If Carnival in Rio was ever held in a giant water park, it might be like the **Songkran Festival** (Thai New Year), a weeklong extravaganza marking the Thai New Year on April 13 to 14. The country celebrates with the "Water Festival," a free-for-all frenzy of soaking and splashing. Religious activities also take place among the chaos, notably at Sanam Luang, where the image of the Phra Buddha Sihing is carried out and ritually bathed. Ratchadamnoen Avenue and Khao San Road (see p 54, bullet ❺) are also popular drenching spots. Visitors beware—you will not be spared! Arm yourself with water guns and prepare for a bath! Carry nothing that cannot survive underwater.

The **Royal Ploughing Ceremony** is reenacted every year in May at Sanam Luang in front of the Grand Palace. This ancient event is performed to gain an auspicious start to the planting season. Sacred, white oxen symbolically plough the field, which is then sown with seeds blessed by the king. After that, farmers rush in to collect the hallowed seeds to replant in their own fields.

Visakha Bucha commemorates the date of the Buddha's birth, enlightenment, and transcendence to Nirvana; candlelit processions and sermons are held at all temples. There's a larger festival at Sanam Luang. For more information, contact TAT (☎ 02 250 5500).

Miss Tiffany Universe (www.misstiffanyuniverse.com), held in May or June, is the Thai version of Oscar Night. This televised pageant in Pattaya selects the country's most beautiful ladyboy.

WINTER. Devotees flock to temples to pray on **Asanha Bucha,** the day commemorating Buddha's first sermon after his enlightenment. The following morning, **Khao Pansa,** you can often watch young men being ordained as monks at temples as Buddhist Lent begins.

The **International Festival of Music & Dance** is a month-long festival of opera, jazz, ballet, symphony, and more, usually held at the Thailand Cultural Center on Ratchadaphisek Road in September and October (☎ 02 204 2394. www.bangkokfestivals.com).

World Film Festival of Bangkok (☎ 02 338-3618-9, www.worldfilmbkk.com) screens more than 150 movies in 10 days at SF World Cinema CentralWorld showcasing Thai, Asian, and international indie films. Usually in November.

SPRING. My favorite festival, **Loy Kratong**, is a time for reflection. Similar to making New Year's resolutions, you have the opportunity to atone for your sins of the previous year and promise to make amends and pray for good luck in the year ahead. The cleansing ritual itself involves making ***kratong***—small banana-leaf rafts decorated with flowers, incense, and candles—then going down to the banks of the river, closing your eyes, making a wish, and letting your ***kratong*** (and your worries) go away with the current. With 60 million Thai people doing likewise that night, the effect of thousands of candles floating downstream together is amazing. You can also light a Chinese lantern (a ***khom loy***) and send it floating up to the heavens. The festival takes place under the first full moon in November, and is best enjoyed beside the Chao Phraya River, and across the city at lakes and canals.

Gay Pride Week involves parties, contests, parades, and more feather boas than you can shake a stick at. It's held at Silom Rd Soi 4 and various locations around the city.

Golden Mount Fair runs over 8 days and 7 nights in November—from the 11th day of the waxing moon of the 12th lunar month to the 3rd day of the waning moon of the same month. Bangkokians worship the Buddha's relics, which are said to be enshrined in the Golden Mount (see p 53, bullet ❶). There are folk plays, art shows, market stalls and lots of food. The photographic highlight of the evening is a candlelit circumambulation of the mount on the night of the full moon.

Useful Websites

- **www.1stopbangkok.com:** General information plus suggestive tips on Bangkok's notoriously hot nightlife.
- **www.bangkok.com:** Lots of tourist information, including hotel deals, rental car discounts and entertainment.
- **www.bangkokpost.com:** The Thai capital's top English-language daily is good for local and international news, weather, and sports.
- **www.thebigchilli.com:** The website of Bangkok's top expat and lifestyle magazine. Interesting features, restaurant reviews, listings, and more.
- **www.richardbarrow.com:** The site of renowned Bangkok travel blogger, Richard Barrow. A world of information. Check out his twitter feed too @RichardBarrow.

Cellphones

You should be able to use your own mobile phone in Thailand if you arrange for international roaming before you leave home. The phone charges are usually calculated from your home country to the destination number and can be expensive, so regular users should buy a SIM card in Bangkok. Service providers include True Move (Orange), AIS, and DTAC. When buying a SIM card you will need to present passport ID to register the number.

Getting **There**

By Plane

Bangkok has one international airport, **Suvarnabhumi International Airport**, situated 35km east of the city center. **Getting to and from the airport**: Although many independent **taxi** drivers operate freely at the airport, there is a 24-hour taxi rank on level 2, outside arrivals. Metered taxis are arranged quickly and efficiently with a 50-baht charge added to the taxi fare (only when coming from the airport). The average cost of a taxi to downtown Bangkok is around 300 baht. There is also a limousine service at the airport.

The overhead Airport Rail Link has three lines, a commuter rail that makes eight stops along its 28-km route, and two express lines that take you into the city in about 15 minutes. Express trains run every 20 minutes from 6am–midnight and cost 150 baht to Makasan station and BTS SkyTrain Phayathai station. The commuter train runs every 30 minutes and costs 45 baht. The t ticket office is in the basement of the Passenger Terminal Building. For timetables and routes, visit www.bangkokairporttrain.com.

Free **shuttle buses** escort passengers to the car rental center and local bus terminal.

Public **buses** run 24 hours from the terminal to various parts of the city. The fare is 35 baht.

Avis, Hertz, Budget and several other **car rental agencies** operate 24 hours at the airport.

By Train

Trains to Bangkok arrive at **Hua Lamphong Station** from Singapore and Malaysia.

By Bus

Buses from Malaysia terminate at the **Southern Bus Terminal** (24/6 Moo 8, Bamrung Ratchachonnanee Rd, Chimpli Taling Chun; ☎ 02 894 6122 ext 5). There's no shortage of taxis and local buses heading to the city center from the front door of the terminal, but there's no metro station nearby. Buses from Cambodia and Laos pull up at the **Northern Bus Terminal** (also known as Mor Chit Terminal; Kampaengphet 2 Rd, Chatuchak; ☎ 02 537 8055). Hordes of taxis wait outside the terminal 24 hours, and there are dozens of local buses to the city center. The best option for transport is the BTS SkyTrain or MRT subway; it's 5 minutes to Chatuchak Park on the MRT line or Mo Chit BST line.

Getting **Around**

By BTS SkyTrain and MRT subway

Getting around Bangkok is easier and quicker now than it was 20 years ago, mainly due to expressways and the twin metropolitan rail lines, the overhead Bangkok Transit System (BTS) or SkyTrain, and the Mass Rapid Transit (MRT) subway network.

The network covers the main shopping, business, and nightlife centers of the city. For the Old City, you should take taxis and express boats on the river.

The **BTS** and **MRT** are the fastest ways to get around; they are clean, efficient, air-conditioned, cheap, and run daily 6am to midnight. There are two lines: the **Silom line** runs between National Stadium at the Siam shopping area to Bang Wa, across the Chao Phraya River, while the **Sukhumvit line** runs from Mo Chit to Bearing. The two lines meet at Siam station, and also interconnect at two points with the underground (MRT)—at Sala Daeng and Asok stations. Easy-to-read BTS city maps are free from any station. Fares are 15 to 70 baht. A one-day unlimited **SkyTrain Pass** costs 120 baht (ideal for tourists). For more information call ☎ 02 617 7300, BTS Hotline 02 617 6000, BTS Tourist Information Center 02 617 7340 2; www.bts.co.th.

Opened in 2004, the **MRT** is as fast, efficient, and modern as the SkyTrain. There are currently 18 MRT stations with more in the pipeline. It stretches 20km in a horseshoe shape from **Hua Lamphong** (the main train station) near Chinatown to Bang Sue in the north. Fares are 15 to 40 baht. An unlimited **1-day MRT pass** costs 120 baht; a **3-day pass** costs 230 baht; and a **30-day pass** costs 800 baht. For more information call www.bangkokmetro.co.th. ☎ 02 624 5200. Both the BTS and MRT routes are being currently being extended.

By Express Boat

My favorite way of traveling in Bangkok is by boat. It's the best way to get to famous historical attractions such as the Grand

Palace. It also affords you the opportunity to visit the canals around the city. While the **express boat** service runs south to north, ferries can be used to cross the river at various points. You can buy tickets as you get on at each port—fares are 10 to 34 baht—or invest in a **day pass** for 150 baht (can only be used outside peak hours). For more information call ☎ 02 222 5330 or 02 225 3003; hotline 02 623 6143; www.chaophrayaboat.co.th.

By Public Bus (BMTA)

Buses are a very cheap but slow way to get around Bangkok. Since destinations on most **buses** are written in Thai, the best way for visitors to figure out which bus goes where is by the bus number and its colors, which is where the BMTA bus map comes in very handy. Be aware that buses with the same number but different colors don't necessarily share the same route. Fares are collected by the bus conductor, not the driver; use coins and small notes only. Keep the small receipt because sometimes it will be checked. Fares are 7 to 10 baht. For more information call ☎ 02 246 0973; hotline 184; www.bmta.co.th.

By Taxi

Most **taxis** are new, comfortable, air-conditioned, and come in an array of bright colors. Taxis will usually find you, especially at hotels, shopping malls, and tourist attractions. As almost anywhere in the world, there are taxi drivers who will try to overcharge tourists. However, if you insist on paying by the meter you should be fine. Fares start at 35 baht for 2km, and then go up by roughly 2 baht per kilometer. Therefore a typical journey, say from Silom Road to the Grand Palace, costs 120 baht. Bangkok Taxi Radio Center can be reached on ☎ 02 880 0888 (24 hours) or dial 1661.There's a 20 baht surcharge for pick-up.

GrabTaxi is the first taxi app in Thailand designed to help passengers book a cab safely and quickly. The app is a free download available in Thai and English. All GrabTaxi drivers use the meter and provide good service. Just key in your destination on your smartphone to make a booking. The app will show available taxis in the area and the estimated fare. An extra safety measure is the "share my ride" feature that allows family and friends to receive GPS-tracked ride details and driver information. www.grabtaxi.com.

By Tuk-tuk

No visit to Bangkok is complete without a bouncing, screeching, heart-thumping ride around town in a **tuk-tuk**. Designed like mini-discotheques and driven by Formula 1 drivers, these tiny terrors are always popular with visitors. Fares start from about 30 baht, but must be agreed with the driver before setting off. Avoid taking a tuk-tuk during rush hour, because the traffic is very slow and the air is thick with fumes.

By Motorbike Taxi

Bangkok's most frightening experience is zigzagging along Sukhumvit Road at high speed on the back of a 100cc bike, but it is fast and cheap. Easily recognized by their orange vests, motorcycle chauffeurs gather at metro stations, busy junctions, tourist areas, shopping malls, and the like. Fares start from 10 baht, but must be negotiated prior to take-off.

By Car

No foreign visitor in their right mind rents a car to drive around Bangkok. It's slow, expensive, irritating, there's nowhere to park, and it's dangerous. However, if you are heading out of the city, it can be a good option if you're confident driving in reckless traffic. You will need an international driving license and your passport to rent a car. Prices start at about 1500 baht per day.

By Plane

Domestic flights are relatively cheap in Thailand. In Bangkok, Don Mueang International Airport has two terminals serving domestic and international flights by low-cost carriers, including Thai Smile, Nok Air, Thai AirAsia, Thai Lion Air, Orient Thai Airlines, and others. Suvarnabhumi International Airport is served by major international airlines, and Bangkok Airways which flies internationally as well as to local destinations such as Koh Samui, Phuket, and Chiang Mai. www.donmueangairportthai.com.

By Train

The main station is **Hua Lamphong**, situated in central Bangkok near Chinatown (Rama IV Road; ☎ 02 621 8701, 24-hour hotline 1690; www.railway.co.th). It is on the MRT subway line. Trains run daily north to Ayutthaya, Chiang Mai, Phitsanulok, Nakorn Ratchasima, Ubon Ratchathani, and Udon Thani. A line also runs south to Hua Hin, Chumpon, Suratthani, Trang, and Songkhla. Another runs southeast to Pattaya.

From **Bangkok Noi** train station in Thonburi (Rod Fai Rd/Train Rd, Sirirach, Bangkok Noi; ☎ 02 411 3102; www.railway.co.th and www.seat61.com/Thailand), trains run daily to Kanchanaburi.

Fast **Facts**

ATMS ATMs are plentiful in Bangkok and accept most western debit cards. You can use your PIN from home. You'll find 24-hour ATMs in shopping malls, at 7-Elevens, at petrol stations and on busy streets. Or just ask your taxi driver to stop at an ATM en route. They offer an excellent exchange rate usually.

BABYSITTING Asking a stranger to babysit for you is not common in Thai culture and there are no recommended agencies. The best option would be to ask your hotel staff.

BIKE RENTALS Velothailand (see p 132) rents quality bicycles and organizes cycling tours of Bangkok. There is also a list of bike rental stores at: www.yellow.co.th/YellowPages/Bangkok/bicycle-rental.

BUSINESS HOURS Banks: 8:30am to 3:30pm Monday to Friday. Some bank branches in malls such as Siam Paragon keep longer hours and open on Saturday and Sunday. Government offices: 8:30am to 4:30pm Monday to Friday. Temples: usually 8am to 6pm daily. Bars: usually 6pm to 1am daily. Pharmacies: usually 9am to 7pm Monday to Saturday.

CONSULATES & EMBASSIES
Australia: 37 Sathorn Tai Rd, Sathorn (☎ 02 344 6300). **Canada**: 15th Floor, Abdulrahim Place, 990 Rama IV Rd, Bangrak (☎ 02 636 0540). **China**: 57 Ratchadaphisek Rd, Din Daeng (☎ 02 245 7043 4). **France**: 35 Soi Rong Phasi Kao (Soi 36), Charoenkrung Rd, Bangrak (☎ 02 657 5100). **Germany**: 9 Sathorn Tai Rd, Sathorn (☎ 02 287 9000). **India**: 46 Soi Prasanmit, Sukhumvit Soi 23 (☎ 02 258 0300 5). **Japan**: 177 Witthayu Road, Lumphini,

Pathumwan (☎ 02 207 8500 or 02 696 3000). **The Netherlands**: 15 Soi Tonson, Ploenchit Rd, Lumphini, Phatumwan (☎ 02 309 5200). **New Zealand**: M Thai Tower, 14th floor, All Seasons Place, 87 Witthayu Rd, Lumphini (☎ 02 254 2530). **Spain**: Lake Ratchada Office Complex Building, 23rd floor, 193/98–99 Ratchdaphisek Rd, Klong Toey (☎ 02 661 8284 5). **U.K.**: 1031 Wireless Rd, Lumphini, Pathumwan (☎ 02 305 8333). **U.S.**: 120–122 Witthayu Rd, Pathumwan (☎ 02 251 7202 or 02 251 3552).

CURRENCY EXCHANGE Several banks and bureaus de change operate at the airport, though seldom from midnight to 6am. They accept foreign currency, major credit cards (American Express, Diners Club, MasterCard, and Visa), and travelers' checks. Rates are comparable to regular bank rates.

CUSTOMS REGULATIONS The duty-free allowance for all passengers arriving in Thailand is 200 cigarettes or 250g of cigars or smoking tobacco, and 1 liter of alcoholic spirits or wine.

DOCTORS Private hospitals (see "Hospitals") offer a full range of medical, health, and cosmetic treatments in Bangkok. Visitors are recommended to use their facilities rather than seek out private clinics, which generally cater for regular patients. Private hospitals are open 24 hours, and have English-speaking staff, doctors specializing in various fields, and on-site pharmacies.

DENTISTS In general, dentists in Bangkok are modern, of high quality, and a good value for money. Most hospitals also have a dental clinic. Teeth cleaning, whitening, crowns, and extractions can all be taken care of with little fuss. **Silom area**: Silomdental (439/4–5 Naratiwatrajnakarin Rd; ☎ 02 636 9091 7; www.silomdental.com; Monday to Saturday 10am to 8pm, Sunday 10am to 5pm). **Sukhumvit area**: Dental Design Clinic & Lab (10 Dental Design Bldg, Sukhumvit Soi 21; ☎ 02 261 9119 20; www.dentaldesignclinic-lab.com; Monday to Friday 9am to 6pm, Saturday and public holidays 9am to 5pm). **Ratchasapisek area**: International Dental Center (BIDC); 157 Ratchadapesik Rd; ☎ 02 692 4433; www.bangkokdentalcenter.com; Monday to Friday 10am to 8pm, Saturday 10am to 8pm, Sunday and public holidays 10am to 5pm.

DRINKING, SMOKING & DRUG LAWS There are no official age restrictions on buying alcohol; however, you must be 20 years of age to drink and enter a nightclub. You must be 18 to buy cigarettes. There is no smoking allowed inside public places. Most bars and restaurants provide outdoor smoking areas.

Buying, using, or selling any narcotic drug is strictly prohibited in Thailand. Penalties are severe. Bangkok was once a hippy haven, and in the 1970s and '80s many foreigners found they could smoke dope openly in certain bars and resorts. Those days are gone, and Thailand's prisons are full of foreigners who thought otherwise. Remember that foreign tourists are a natural target for police informers, con artists, and sometimes even off-duty policemen. A charming, English-speaking person may offer you marijuana or opium, but remember that they can make much more money by turning you in to the police than by selling drugs to you.

ELECTRICITY The voltage is 220 volt AC with flat two-pin plugs. You can buy an adapter for shavers, laptops, mobile phone chargers, and so on upon arrival at the airport, or at most department stores.

EMERGENCIES Dial ☎ 191 for the **police**, ☎ 1669 for **ambulance and rescue**, ☎ 199 for the **fire**

brigade and ☎ 1554 for a **medical emergency**.

GAY & LESBIAN TRAVELLERS Thailand is one of the most gay-friendly countries in the world. Few Thais will give a second thought to your sexuality, such is the openness of gay culture in the country. The only matter generally frowned upon is displays of physical affection—homosexual or otherwise—in public.

HOSPITALS **Bumrungrad International**: 33 Sukhumvit 3 (Soi Nana Nua), Wattana; ☎ 02 667 1000; www.bumrungrad.com. **Samitivej**: 133 Sukhumvit 49, Klongtan Nua Wattana; ☎ 02 711 8000; www.samitivejhospitals.com. **Bangkok Hospital**: 2 Soi Soonvijai 7, New Petchaburi Rd, Bangkapi, Huay Khwang; ☎ 02 310 3000 or 1719, heart hotline 02 375 2222; www.bangkokhospital.com.

INSURANCE Check your health insurance policy before leaving home to ensure that Thailand is covered. As a tropical country, there may be some restrictions. In the unfortunate event of an accident, medical staff in Thailand will always ask if you have insurance and will call your insurance company—whether it is in Thailand or abroad—to confirm your coverage.

INTERNET CAFES & WI-FI You can find internet cafes all over the city, especially at tourist areas and shopping malls. The average rate is about 1 baht per minute. If you have a local SIM card for your mobile phone, Wi-Fi coverage is excellent and cheap. Many cafes and hotels offer free Wi-Fi, but five-star hotels often charge a high fee.

LOST PROPERTY There are no lost property offices in Bangkok. If you are lucky, someone will hand your lost item to the police, but don't hold your breath on it. Items left behind in taxis can be traced through the main taxi depot. Ask your hotel staff to help you.

MAIL & POSTAGE Post offices are open 8:30am to 4:30pm Monday to Friday and 9am to midday Saturday. Letters to/from Europe, Australia, the U.S., and Canada usually take a week to arrive. For important documents use Express Mail Service (EMS) or registered post. You can mail postcards, letters, and packages at any post office.

Stamp costs are as follows: postcards 2 baht (within Thailand), 9 to 12 baht (international); letters up to 100 grams 3 baht (within Thailand), 24 to 80 baht to the U.K., 28 to 100 baht to the U.S., 24 to 80 baht to Australia. Registered post, DHL, EMS, and other international carriers also operate out of public post offices and private outlets. Many tourist-friendly shops and boutiques will arrange postage directly for you for a small commission. **Thailand Post**: 111 M3, Changwattana Rd, Laksi; ☎ 02 831 3131; www.thailandpost.com. **Bangrak**: Bangrak Post Office Building, Charoen Krung Rd; ☎ 02 236 9848. **Silom**: 333 Bangkok Bank head office building, Silom Rd, Bangrak; ☎ 02 231 4813 or 02 231 4888. **Ratchadamnoen**: 81 Ratchadamnoen Klang Rd, Soi Ratcha Damnoen Nua, Boworn Niwet, Pranakorn; ☎ 02 282 1811 ext 35 or 02 2825791 ext 49. **Rattanakosin**: 15–17 Na Pra Lan Rd, Grand Palace, Pra Nakorn; ☎ 02 222 3862 or 02 224 4705. **Pom Prab**: 77–79 Ratchawong Rd, Jakkawad, Sampanthawong; ☎ 02 222 1705. **Chulalongkorn University**: Pathumwan; ☎ 02 252 7404.

PASSPORTS & VISAS Visitors to Thailand receive an automatic 30-day tourist visa on arrival if they are a passport holder from most western countries, including Australia, Canada, France, Germany, the Netherlands, New Zealand, Spain, the U.K., and the U.S. Passports must be valid at least 6 months ahead of arrival. However, visitors who enter Thailand with a visa on arrival generally cannot apply for an extension. Visitors from countries such as China and India receive a 15-day tourist visa on arrival. Visitors who intend to stay longer than 30 days should organize a visa before arriving in Thailand. For more information, visit www.immigration.go.th.

PHARMACIES Most chemists will serve you if you have a prescription from home in English. Even if you don't, you should still be able to buy medicine and drugs—as long as you don't look like a hippy having a party.

POLICE Dial 191 for the police.

PUBLIC HOLIDAYS

Jan 1	New Year's Day
Feb 9	Makha Bucha Day
Apr 6	Chakri Day
Apr 13–15	Songkran (Thai New Year)
May 1	Labour Day
May 5	Coronation Day
May 8	Visakha Bucha Day
May 11	Royal Ploughing Ceremony
Jul 1	Mid-year Bank Holiday
Jul 9	Khao Phansa Day (Buddhist Lent)
Aug 12	HM The Queen's Birthday
Oct 23	Chulalongkorn Day
Dec 5	HM The King's Birthday
Dec 10	Constitution Day
Dec 31	New Year's Eve

SAFETY There are no unsafe areas as such in central Bangkok. However, there are certainly unsafe activities. Con-men currently target tourists to sell fake gems or invite home for whisky and a game of cards. The most unsafe activity in Bangkok, by far, involves spending a drunken night with a sex worker (especially ladyboy sex workers). A spiked drink can result in 30 hours of sleep, a severe headache, and the loss of everything but your socks!

SENIOR TRAVELERS Elderly people are treated with great respect in Thailand and will find themselves bowed to and "*wai*-ed" often. Many hotels and venues in popular tourist spots have wheelchair access, but it is uncommon elsewhere. The SkyTrain, for example, requires good legs for the stairways. Unfortunately, despite the high status you receive as a senior, you won't get discounts on transportation or at entertainment venues.

STAYING HEALTHY Thailand is generally a hygienic and healthy country. Of course, its tropical climate lends itself to diseases such as malaria and dengue fever, but these are 99.9% confined to jungle environments and not in urban Bangkok. The most dangerous aspect of life in this city is the heat. Beware of sunstroke and sunburn. Drink LOTS of water, but not tap water—even the locals don't drink tap water. Street food is generally safe, as is the ice and water from jugs, although many visitors to Thailand will catch a quick dose of diarrhea. If you do, stay out the heat, drink bottled water, and eat rice porridge.

TAXES There is no departure tax when leaving the country. It is included in the ticket price.

TAXIS See "Getting Around," earlier in the chapter.

TELEPHONES To make **international calls**, dial code ☎ 001, then the country code (Australia: 61, Britain: 44, France: 33, U.S. and Canada: 1, and so on). When phoning the U.K., the U.S., and much of Europe, the alternative prefix 008 offers a reduced rate and the code 009 accesses Voice-Over-Internet Protocol (VOIP). It is cheaper to call 9pm to 7am, when rates are reduced by 20% to 30%. For Bangkok **directory enquiries**, dial ☎ 13; for provincial directory enquiries, dial ☎ 1133.

For public telephone booths, you can use phone cards or 1, 5, and 10 baht coins. Calls within Bangkok cost just 1 baht per minute. Area code 02 is used for all Bangkok numbers. Calls around Thailand cost 3 baht per minute.

There are always promotions and new services are constantly competing. At the time of writing there is a 50% discount if you dial ☎ 1234 before any national number.

For international calls, the rates are usually 7 to 15 baht per minute. Dial ☎ 007, 008 or 009, before adding your country code (Australia: 61; U.K.: 44; U.S.: 1), then the number.

To avoid using handfuls of coins, you can of course buy a phone card. They are available at shopping malls, 7-Elevens, and convenience stores. Many do not have instructions in English, so you should ask the assistant to dial in your code to get connected.

TIPPING Tipping is seldom expected in local restaurants. In up-market establishments, a 10% service fee may be added to bills. Knowing that westerners like to tip, staff in international restaurants will be grateful for, say, a 100 baht tip for a dinner for two. Taxi fares should be rounded up to the nearest 5 or 10 baht, especially for meter-taxis.

TOURIST INFORMATION The **Tourism Authority of Thailand (TAT)** can be found at 1600 New Phetchaburi Rd, Makkasan, Ratchathewi. Call ☎ 02 250 5500, Monday to Friday 8am to 4:30pm; hotline ☎ 1672 daily 8am to 8pm; or visit www.tourismthailand.org.

TRAVEL AGENCIES **Window Tour Service**: 41/181 Family Town, Soi Intamara 29, Suthisarn Rd, Samsennai, Phayathai; ☎ 02 616 0964 6; www.thailandvoyage.com. **LSH Travel**: Two offices: 3/3 Thedsaban-Nimit-Nua Rd, Chatuchak; ☎ 02 630 6640 1; and inside Saphan Taksin BTS station; ☎ 02 630 6663 or 02 630 6640 1; www.journeyasia.com. **Express International Travel**: 10/12–13 Convent Rd, Silom, Bangrak; ☎ 02 235 0557 8; www.expressinter.com.

TOURIST TRAPS It goes without saying that tourists are often targets for con-men, pickpockets, and thieves, so beware! Crafty taxi drivers, tricky jewel salespeople, and other dodgy characters hang out around the main tourist spots, especially the Grand Palace, Patpong, Silom Road, Khao San Road, and Sukhumvit Road, not to mention the major hotels. Overcharging is common and is rarely considered a crime. In cases of theft, assault, or danger, call the tourist police (☎ 1155).

VACCINATIONS Visitors do not require any vaccinations to enter Thailand. Only those intending to go to remote areas should consider taking malaria pills.

Local Customs, Traditions & Taboos

There are a number of hints that will help you have a happy stay in Bangkok. Firstly, the Thai royal family is deeply revered, and disrespect toward the monarchy is not tolerated. Remember to stand for the Thai national anthem in cinemas, theatres, ceremonies, and at certain events. Showing anger or shouting is regarded as crude and will not get you what you want; remain calm and smile and doors will open. You should dress appropriately when visiting temples—don't go shirtless or in shorts, short skirts, or spaghetti-strap garments. Remove your shoes when entering a Thai home or a Buddhist temple. Do not point your foot at a person or an object, or touch a person's head with your hand.

Useful Phrases & Menu Terms

Thai language is usually very difficult for foreigners. There are 44 letters in the Thai alphabet, 26 of which are vowels. Each vowel is subject to a tone: rising, falling, high, low, or flat. There are short vowel sounds and long vowel sounds. For example, a word with a short "a" vowel may sound like "bat" with the "t" clipped. The long vowel sounds more like "baa," the noise a sheep makes. Listen to your Thai friends and imitate the words rather than concentrate on their spelling. Thais are usually very happy if you try to speak their language. *Chok dee!* (Good luck!)

Greetings & Common Phrases

Note: Using the following expressions, males should add the polite word *"khrup"* at the end, while females should say *"ka."*

Hello	(m) Sawadee khrup/(f) Sawadee ka
How are you?	Sabai dee mai?
I'm fine, thanks	Sabai dee, khob khun
Excuse me/sorry	Kor tort
What's your name?	Khun cheu arai?
My name is…	(m) Pom/(f) Chan cheu…
Nice to meet you	Yin dee tee dai roo juk
Do you speak English?	Khun pood pa-sa angrit dai mai?
I don't understand	Mai khao jai
Can you say that again, please?	Pood eek krang dai mai?
Please speak slowly	Pood cha cha
See you later	Pob kan mai
Goodbye	La gorn
Goodnight	Ratri sawat
Please	Dai prod
What?	Arai?
Where?	Tee nai?
Who?	Krai?
Why?	Tam mai?

Emergencies

Help!	Chuay duai!
Fire!	Fai mai!
Thief	Kha-moy
Call the police	Riak tam-ruat hai noi

Police station	Satani tam-ruat
I need a doctor	Tong-garn mor
I need to go to hospital	Tong pai rong payabarn

Directions

Left	Sai
Right	Kwa
In front of	Khang nar
Behind	Khang lang
Go straight	Trong pai
Turn	Leow
Stop	Yut
Where are you going?	Khun ja pai nai?
I'm going to…	Ja pai…
Where is…?	…Yoo tee nai?
How do i get to…?	…Pai yang rai?

Traveling

Bus	Rot mae
Bus station	Satani rot mae
Train	Rot fai
Railway station	Satani rot fai
Ticket	Tua
Airport	Sanarm bin
Ferry	Rua doy sarn
Express boat	Rua duan
Taxi	Taxi
Car	Rot keng
What time does it leave?	Ja ork kee mung?
What time is it arriving?	Ja ma kee mung?
How much is it?	Tao rai?

Places

Temple	Wat
Road	Tanon
Lane	Soi
Shop	Raan kay khong
Cinema	Pappayon
Bank	Tanakarn
Embassy	Sa tan toot
Museum	Pipittapan
Post office	Praisanee
Restaurant	Rarn-a-harn
Hotel	Rong raem
Market	Ta laad

At a Hotel

Do you have a vacant room?	Khun mee hong wang mai?
I'd like a room for 1 night	Tong garn pak neung keun

What is the charge per night?	Keun la tao rai?
May I see the room first?	Kor doo hong dai mai?
Key	Koon jair
Room	Hong
Single room	Hong diaw
Double room	Hong koo
Soap	Saboo
Towel	Par ched tua
Hot water	Narm ron
Cold water	Narm yen

In a Restaurant

Food	Aharn
Breakfast	Aharn chao
Lunch	Aharn tiang
Dinner	Aharn yen
Dessert	Kanom waan
Curry	Gaeng
Rice	Khao
Beer	Bia
Water	Narm plao
Spicy	Ped
Not spicy	Mai ped
Is it spicy?	Ped mai?
Salty	Kem
Sweet	Waan
Sour	Priaw
Can I see the menu please?	Kor menu dai mai?
It is very delicious	Aroi mak mak
Bill/check please	Keb ngoen duay/check bin

Health

I have a headache	(M)Pom/(f)Chan puad hua
I have a fever	Pom/chan pen khai
Sore throat	Jeb kor
Cough	Ai
Medicine	Yaa
I'm allergic to…	Pom pae…

Numbers

0	Soon
1	Neung
2	Song
3	Sarm
4	See
5	Haa
6	Hok
7	Jed
8	Paed
9	Gao

10	Sib
11	Sib-ed
12	Sib-song
13	Sib-sarm
20	Yee sib
30	Sarm sib
40	See sib
100	Neung roy
1000	Neung pan

Time

Day	Wan
Month	Duean
Year	Pee
Today	Wan-nee
Tomorrow	Prung-nee
Yesterday	Mua wan-nee
Sunday	Wan ar-tit
Monday	Wan jan
Tuesday	Wan ang karn
Wednesday	Wan put
Thursday	Wan pa-rue-had
Friday	Wan suk
Saturday	Wan sao
One minute	Neung natee
One hour	Neung cheu mung
What time is it?	Kee mung la

Phone Numbers & Websites

Airlines

AIR ASIA
☎ *02 515 9999*
www.airasia.com

AIR FRANCE
www.airfrance.com

BANGKOK AIRWAYS
☎ *02 265 8777*
www.bangkokair.com

BRITISH AIRWAYS
www.britishairways.com

CATHAY PACIFIC AIRWAYS
www.cathaypacific.com

JAPAN AIRLINES
www.jal.co.jp

NOK AIR
☎ *02 627 2000*
www.nokair.com

QANTAS
www.qantas.co.au

THAI AIRWAYS
☎ *02 356 1111*
www.thaiair.com

UNITED AIRLINES
www.united.com

Car Rental Agencies

AVIS
☎ *02 251 1131 2 or 02 255 5300 4*
www.avisthailand.com

BUDGET
☎ *02 203 9222 or 02 203 9294 5*
☎ *1 800 283 438*
www.budget.co.th

HIGHWAY CAR RENT
☎ *02 266 9393*

Credit Card Companies

AMEX
☎ *02 273 5500*

AMEX LOST CARDS
☎ *02 273 5100 or 02 273 0022*

DINERS CLUB
☎ *02 238 3660*

MASTERCARD & VISA (INCLUDING LOST CARDS)
☎ *02 256 7376*

Index

See also Accommodations and Restaurant indexes, below.

Accommodations

Restaurants

Photo **Credits**

p i, anekoho; p. i, Sarawut Chamsaeng; p. i, SantiPhotoSS; p. vii, anekoho; p. 4, Perfect Lazybones; p. 5, Settawat Udom / Shutterstock.com; p. 6, sippakorn / Shutterstock.com; p. 7, My Life Graphic; p. 10, LEE SNIDER PHOTO IMAGES / Shutterstock.com; p. 11, top, Frank Bach; p. 11, bottom, Mick Shippen; p. 12, Zzvet / Shutterstock.com; p. 13, Tooykrub / Shutterstock.com; p. 15, Aidan McRae Thomson; p. 16, top, Wojtek Chmielewski; p. 16, bottom, ostill / Shutterstock.com; p. 17, Gwoeii / Shutterstock.com; p. 19, F Rae; p. 20, MJ Prototype; p. 21, Imagincy; p. 22, Opas Chotiphantawanon / Shutterstock.com; p. 23, aaleksander; p. 25, Binder.donedat; p. 26, top, cowardlion / Shutterstock.com; p. 26, bottom, Tooykrub / Shutterstock.com; p. 27, Courtesy of Grand Hyatt Erwan Bangkok; p. 28, top, Courtesy of lebua Hotels and Resorts; p. 28, bottom, MJ Prototype; p. 29, NUTTANART KHAMLAKSANA; p. 31, somdul / Shutterstock.com; p. 32, bottom, MJ Prototype / Shutterstock.com; p. 33, Artistpix / Shutterstock.com; p. 32, top, tatui suwat; p. 34, top, ian_tan; p. 34, bottom, outcast85 / Shutterstock.com; p. 36, Pradit.Ph / Shutterstock.com; p. 37, top, Kitinut Jinapuck; p. 37, bottom, Daoqian Lin; p. 38, Prasit Rodphan; p. 39, LEE SNIDER PHOTO IMAGES / Shutterstock.com; p. 40, top, 1000 Words / Shutterstock.com; p. 40, bottom, opasso / Shutterstock.com; p. 42, think4photop / Shutterstock.com; p. 43, roroto12p / Shutterstock.com; p. 44, top, Lion1st / Shutterstock.com; p. 44, bottom, Blanscape / Shutterstock.com; p. 48, Courtesy of Peninsula Hotel Bangkok; p. 49, Courtesy of Mandarin Oriental; p. 50, top, Courtesy of Banyan Tree; p. 50, bottom, nimon; p. 51, Christian Mueller / Shutterstock.com; p. 53, lOvE lOvE; p. 54, top, puwanai / Shutterstock.com; p. 54, bottom, BsChan / Shutterstock.com; p. 55, Robert Brands; p. 57, Courtesy of Mandarian Oriental; p. 58, top, Ben Garrett; p. 58, bottom, Everything; p. 59, top, SasinT; p. 59, bottom, Andrea Schaffer; p. 60, Roger Howard; p. 61, Carlos Felipe Pardo; p. 63, Maddog99; p. 64, Blanscape / Shutterstock.com; p. 65, KoBoZaa / Shutterstock.com; p. 66, Lodimup / Shutterstock.com; p. 67, Mark Fischer; p. 68, GOLFX; p. 72, Mick Shippen; p. 73, smalljude; p. 74, top, Tooykrub / Shutterstock.com; p. 74, bottom, Mick Shippen; p. 75, Tooykrub / Shutterstock.com; p. 76, top, Mick Shippen; p. 76, bottom, Jorg Hackemann / Shutterstock.com; p. 78, top, CHAINFOTO24 / Shutterstock.com; p. 78, bottom, Mark Fischer; p. 79, Courtesy of Lotus Arts de Vivre; p. 81, Vladimir Volodin / Shutterstock.com; p. 83, Stripped Pixel / Shutterstock.com; p. 84, top, anandoart / Shutterstock.com; p. 84, bottom, Mick Shippen; p. 85, Mick Shippen; p. 88, top, sittitap; p. 88, bottom, Sombat Muycheen; p. 89, Courtesy of Grand Hyatt Erwa; p. 94, Couetesy of AnAn Lao; p. 95, Courtesy of La Appia; p. 96, top, Courtesy of Dusit Thani; p. 96, bottom, Courtesy of The Blue Elephant; p. 97, Courtesy of Tower Club at lebula; p. 98, Courtesy of Como Hotels and Resorts; p. 99, amadeustx / Shutterstock.com; p. 101, top, Courtesy of Mandarian Oriental; p. 101, bottom, Pietro Motta; p. 102, top, Courtesy of Maha Naga; p. 102, bottom, Courtesy of The Manohra; p. 103, Courtesy of May Kaidee; p. 104, Courtesy of Como Hotels and Resorts; p. 105, Courtesy of the Rembrant Hotel; p. 108, Courtesy of The Peninsula Hotel Bangkok; p. 107, Courtesy of Dusit Thani; p. 109, MJ Prototype / Shutterstock.com; p. 110, Mick Shippen; p. 116, Courtesy of Nest; p. 117, Courtesy of Tower Club at lebula; p. 118, Matt_Weibo; p. 119, Kojach; p. 121, Courtesy of Grand Hyatt; p. 122, Roderick Eime/ Accor; p. 123, Mick Shippen; p. 124, Kathy; p. 128, Chatchai Puipia/ 100 Tonson Gallery; p. 129, ben bryant / Shutterstock.com; p. 130, Goethe-Institut / Sorapong Sawawiboon; p. 131, top, Courtesy of Mandarian Oriental; p. 131, bottom, Mick Shippen; p. 132, David McKelvey; p. 133, Courtesy of Peninsula Hotel Bangkok; p. 134, Courtesy of Anatara Resort; p. 138, Courtesy of Anatara Siam Resort/ Johansen Krause; p. 139, Courtesy of Chakrabongse Villas; p. 141, top, Courtesy of Grand Hyatt Erwan Bangkok; p. 140, Courtesy of Dusit Thani; p. 142, Courtesy of Tower Club lebua; p. 143, top, Courtesy of Mandarian Oriental; p. 143, bottom, Courtesy of Como Hotels; p. 144, Courtesy of Peninsula Hotel Bangkok; p. 145, Roderick Eime; p. 146, bottom, Courtesy of Sheraton Grande Sukhumvit; p. 146, top, Courtesy of The Sukhothail; p. 147, Vasin Lee; p. 149, Preto Perola; p. 150, top, littlewormy; p. 150, bottom, Meghan Lamb; p. 151, theerathuch; p. 153, sittitap; p. 155, Vasin Lee; p. 154, kunanon; p. 157, Courtesy of Dusit Thani; p. 158, puwanai; p. 159, LEE SNIDER PHOTO IMAGES / Shutterstock.com; p. 162, Wuttichok Painichiwarapun; p. 163, TOMPOST / Shutterstock.com.